DOING AND DESERVING

DOING & DESERVING

ESSAYS IN THE THEORY OF RESPONSIBILITY

by Joel Feinberg

PRINCETON UNIVERSITY PRESS

PRINCETON, NEW JERSEY

FOR MY MOTHER

PREFACE

Eight of the following studies appeared originally as essays in philosophical journals or collections. The other three were delivered as lectures on special occasions and have not previously been published. Each of them deals with some aspect of the complex situation in which persons intentionally, negligently, or faultlessly cause harm or benefit to others and are therefore said to deserve such responses from others as praise or blame, punishment, and legal pressure to make compensation. There should be a conventional name for that branch of philosophy which straddles ethics, philosophy of mind, and philosophy of law and concerns itself with such concepts as "act," "cause," "harm," "blame," and the like. On the model of "the theory of knowledge" and "the theory of value" (which study problems that are no more well defined), I suggest "the theory of responsibility."

In spite of their closely related themes, the essays in this collection do not make a unified argument. I put them forth here as sketches merely, preliminary to a more systematic treatise in which first things are put first, the fundamental problems tackled before the derivative ones, and in which the argument moves slowly step by step from one beginning to one terminus. In the present collection the articles are arranged in roughly the order in which they were written, but I have departed from strict chronological order, here and there, so that there might be smoother transitions between the essays.

In all of the previously published essays I have made small corrections and occasional minor qualifications in the argument. Wherever it has been possible to remove surface blemishes without major surgery, I have done so. In at least one of the essays, however—the first part of "Action and Responsibility"—confusions and oversimplifications remain, because to correct them here would destroy the unity of the article and require the masking of its virtues as well as its vices. I hope its faults may stimulate others, as H.L.A. Hart's article on the ascription of responsibility (since repudiated by its author) stimulated me.

For whatever merits these essays possess I am indebted to many people; but if I were to list all the teachers, students, colleagues, and friends, and the authors of books and articles that have influenced me, it would take many pages and give no one his proper due. Fortunately, there is no similar problem in respect to the book's flaws and errors. They are due to the influence of my former colleague, Professor Josiah S. Carberry, and I cheerfully hold him responsible for all of them.

J. F.
New York, N.Y.
January 1970

SOURCES AND ACKNOWLEDGMENTS

1. "Supererogation and Rules" was originally read at the meeting of the Pacific Division of the American Philosophical Association in December 1960 and was subsequently published in *Ethics*, 71 (1961), 276-288. It is reprinted here by permission of the editor of *Ethics* and the University of Chicago Press.

2. "Problematic Responsibility in Law and Morals" was presented orally at the meeting of the Eastern Division of the American Philosophical Association at Atlantic City, N.J., in December 1961. A revised version was published in *The Philosophical Review*, 71 (1962), 340-351, and is reprinted here by permission of the editor.

3. Parts IV and V of "On Being 'Morally Speaking a Murderer'" comprised my comments on Elizabeth Anscombe's "The Two Kinds of Error in Action" delivered orally in a symposium at the meeting of the Western Division of the American Philosophical Association in May 1963 at Columbus, Ohio. Miss Anscombe added a paragraph referring to my oral comments in the published version of her article, to which the article included here was a reply. My article appeared first in the *Journal of Philosophy* and is reprinted here by permission of the editor.

4. "Justice and Personal Desert" was published originally in *Nomos VI: Justice*, edited by Carl J. Friedrich and John W. Chapman (New York: Atherton Press, 1963), 69-97. It is reprinted here by kind permission of The American Society for Political and Legal Philosophy. The appendix, "Economic Income as Deserved," was a part of the original paper deleted later to save space. It has not previously been published.

5. "The Expressive Function of Punishment" is reprinted from *The Monist*, 49/3 (July 1965), La Salle, Illinois, with permission of the publisher.

6. "Action and Responsibility" is from *Philosophy in America*, edited by Max Black (London: George Allen & Unwin, 1965), 134-160. It is reprinted here by permission of the publisher.

7. "Causing Voluntary Actions" was first presented to the 1964 Oberlin Colloquium in Philosophy. It is included in the Proceedings of the Colloquium which were published as *Metaphysics and Explanation*, edited by W. H. Capitan and D. D. Merrill (Pittsburgh: University of Pittsburgh Press, 1966), 29-47. "Rejoinders" is from the same volume, 55-61. Both are reprinted by permission of the University of Pittsburgh Press.

8. "Sua Culpa" was presented at the Conference on Philosophy and the Law of Torts at Lake Arrowhead in April 1969, at Cornell University, and at the 1969 Chapel Hill Colloquium in Philosophy at Chapel Hill, N.C. It has not previously been published.

9. The original version of "Collective Responsibility" was presented in a symposium at the meeting of the Eastern Division of the American Philosophical Association in December 1968 at Washington, D.C., and was published in the *Journal of Philosophy*, 65 (1968), 674-688. It is reprinted here in a somewhat expanded version by permission of the editor of the *Journal of Philosophy*.

10. "Crime, Clutchability, and Individuated Treatment" is a revised version of a paper delivered at a symposium on "Responsibility, Treatment, and *Mens Rea*" at the meeting of the Western Division of the American Philosophical Association in May 1967. It has not previously been published.

11. "What Is So Special about Mental Illness?" was my contribution to a symposium on "The Range of Personal Responsibility" at Cleveland State University, Cleveland, Ohio, in May 1968. It has not previously been published.

CONTENTS

xi

DOING AND DESERVING

*Moral philosophers tend to discriminate, explicitly or implicitly, three types of actions from the point of view of moral worth. First, they rec-*ognize *actions that are a duty, or obligatory, or that we ought to perform, treating these terms as approximately synonymous; second they recognize actions that are . . . permissible . . . but not morally required of us . . . ; third . . . actions that are wrong, that we ought not to do.*

Supererogation and Rules

Thus writes J. O. Urmson in his article "Saints and Heroes."[1] He then argues convincingly that this traditional classification of actions is "totally inadequate to the facts of morality" because it is unable to accommodate acts of supererogatory saintliness and heroism. I shall argue in this essay that the unnamed philosophers criticized by Urmson have committed more mistakes than he notices, that these mistakes fall into a pattern, and that merely enlarging the classification of actions to include actions "in excess of duty" will not correct them.

The fundamental error committed by the philosophers criticized by Urmson is the uncritical acceptance of jural laws and institutional "house rules" as models for the understanding of all counsels of wisdom and all forms of human worth. Many institutions have rules which allow persons to accumulate extra points of credit by oversubscribing their assigned quotas of cash or work. Merely acknowledging the existence of saintly and heroic actions which go

[1] In A. I. Melden (ed.), *Essays in Moral Philosophy* (Seattle: University of Washington Press, 1958), 198.

3

beyond duty will not help if they are understood on the model of these institutional oversubscriptions. To so understand them is to commit the same sort of mistake as that committed by philosophers who take the prohibitory rules of jural law and other institutions as a model for understanding all so-called moral rules which contain the word "ought" and thus commit themselves to identifying all meritorious actions with the performance of "duties." The fundamental error in both cases is to treat what are essentially *non*institutional facts as if they were some kind of *special* institutional facts. This is the same sort of trick as that performed by those who treat unselfish acts as a special species of selfish ones or unreal things as a special, spooky kind of real thing. In all these cases, concepts normally understood as contrasting are related as genus and species because of some superficial likeness between them. As a result, we are led into paradoxes or are arbitrarily deprived of the tools for saying what we wish to say.

I shall consider in this essay some paradoxical consequences of interpreting counsels of wisdom and the word "ought" on the model of prohibitory rules and the word "duty," and of treating nonduties such as simple favors and heroic self-denials on the model of institutional oversubscriptions.

I

First, consider how the word "ought" differs from the word "duty." Suppose a stranger approaches me on a street corner and politely asks me for a match. Ought I to give him one? I think most people would agree that I should, and that any reasonable man of good will would, offer the stranger a match. Perhaps a truly virtuous man would do more than that. He would be friendly, reply with a cheerful smile, and might even volunteer to light the stranger's cigarette.

Now suppose that Jones is on the street corner and another stranger politely requests a light from him. Jones is in a sour mood this morning, and even normally he does not enjoy encounters with strangers. He brusquely refuses to give the stranger a match. I think we can agree that Jones's behavior on the street corner does not constitute an ideal for human conduct under such circumstances; that it is not what a perfectly virtuous man would have done; that it was not what Jones ought to have done.

If we reproach Jones, however, for his uncivil treatment of the stranger, he may present us with a vigorous self-defense. "Perhaps I was not civil," he might admit, "but surely I was under no *obligation* to give a match to that man. Who is he to me? He had no *claim* on me; he has no authority to *command* any performance from me; I don't *owe* him anything. It may be nice to do favors for people; but a favor, by definition, is nothing that we are legally or morally *required* to do. I am an honorable man. In this instance I did not fail to honor a commitment; neither did I fail to discharge an obligation, moral or legal; nor did I break any rule, of man or God.[2] You have, therefore, no right to reproach me."

Jones's defense makes me think no better of him. Still, from a certain legal-like point of view, it appears perfectly cogent. Everything Jones said in his own defense was true. The moral I draw from this tale is that there are some actions which it would be desirable for a person to do and which, indeed, he *ought* to do, even though they are actions he is under no *obligation* and has no *duty* to do. It follows logically that to say that someone has a duty or an obligation to do X is not simply another way of saying that he ought to do X.[3]

We speak of duties and obligations in three different connections. First, there are actions required by laws and by

[2] One could argue that God commands us to do favors for one another. But that would be to regard such actions as *obligatory*, and it is logically contradictory for one and the same act to be both required and freely given, both a duty and a favor.

[3] Cf. C. H. Whiteley's very important article "On Duties," *Proceedings of the Aristotelian Society*, 53 (1952/53); and also H.L.A. Hart's "Legal and Moral Obligation," in Melden (ed.), *op.cit.*, 82-108.

authoritative command. These can be called "duties of obedience." Second, there are the assigned tasks which "attach" to stations, offices, jobs, and roles, which for some reason seem better named by the word "duty" than by the word "obligation." Third, there are those actions to which we voluntarily commit ourselves by making promises, borrowing money, making appointments, and so on. When we commit ourselves, we put ourselves "under an obligation" ("duty" seems to fit less comfortably here) to some assignable person or persons to behave in the agreed-upon way; and we do this by utilizing certain social contrivances or techniques designed for just this purpose. When a person invokes these procedures, he creates his own "artificial chains," dons them, and hands the key to the other. This act "binds" or "ties" him to the agreed-upon behavior and gives the other the authority to require it of him. The other can, if he chooses, release him from his chains, or he can, in Mill's much quoted words, exact performance from him "as one exacts a debt."[4]

All duties and obligations, whether imposed by authoritative injunctions and prohibitions, acquired through accepting or inheriting an office, job, or role, or voluntarily incurred through promises and other contractual agreements, share the common character of being *required*; and this in turn, while it may involve more than coercion or pressure, rarely involves less. In the legal sense, to have a duty or an obligation is to be subject to civil liability or criminal punishment for nonperformance. In general, the law requires citizens to discharge their legal duties *or else* face up to the unpleasant legal consequences.[5] Similarly, it

[4] John Stuart Mill, *Utilitarianism* (Indianapolis: The Bobbs-Merrill Co., 1948), 60.

[5] An interesting logical consequence of the point that obligations are liabilities is that one can have a (real) obligation even though one is incapable of discharging it. Certain disabilities which make it impossible for a person to discharge his obligation do not prevent others from exacting payment from him for his omission. So, for example, in civil law an insane person can be held liable for his torts. Thomas M. Cooley, in his *A Treatise on the Law of Torts*, ed. D. Avery Haggard, 4th edn. (Chicago: Callaghan & Co., 1932), 188, writes that this rule

6

follows from the rules of nonjural institutions (house rules) that a member who does not pay his dues can be dropped; an employee who fails to perform the duties of his job is liable to be fired; a negligent bureaucrat is liable to demotion, a wayward student to flunking, a disobedient soldier to court-martial.

That liability for failure to perform is an essential part of what we mean by "duty," when we talk of the duties of stations and positions, is suggested by our willingness to substitute in many contexts the word "responsibility" for the word "duty." To be assigned a task or a job in some organization is to be made responsible (answerable, accountable) for its performance. Without this associated accountability, I submit, we should be unwilling to speak of "the job" as involving any *duties* at all.

The point holds also for obligations of commitment. Reneging on a promise, without valid excuse, is understood by all parties to involve forfeiture of trust. It is impossible to conceive of promises being "binding" in a world in which continued failure to keep them did nothing at all to weaken confidence and where the reneger is trusted over and over again to make new agreements. Thus commitments, as the metaphor of the binding chains suggests, also involve, in an essential way, a coercive element.

It is clear that, if all duties are acts which are required, then there are meritorious acts, such as favors, which are not the performance of duty, for not all good deeds are requitals or repayments or fulfillments of bargains. Neither are the remainder all acts of obedience and performances of one's job. The man who has been stationed on the street corner by a match company and assigned the task of distributing free samples of its product has a duty to give the stranger a match. Jones and I do not.

Often we say that a man ought to do something simply

"imposes upon [insane persons] an *obligation* to observe the same care and precautions respecting the rights of others that the law demands of one in the full possession of his faculties" (my italics). This may be morally absurd, as Cooley argues, but it is not *logically absurd*.

because we take it to be his duty. On the other hand, there is no absurdity in saying that he ought not to do his duty. The word "ought" has several jobs, but at least one of them is not performed equally well by "duty" and "obligation." That job is to prescribe or give advice. When the word "ought" occurs in a sentence which gives advice, we can call it the "ought of final judgment, all things considered." If you ask me what, all things considered, would be the best thing to do in a given situation, I will tell you what, all things considered, you ought to do; and before I can give such advice with any confidence, I must have a great deal of information about many things, including your duties and obligations. There is no comparable difficulty in discovering one's duties and obligations. Here a person need consider only his position in life, his job, his relations to other people, the agreements he has made, the orders he has been given, and the regulations and statutes governing his affairs.

If I tell you what your obligations are, I do not necessarily give you advice of any kind; I simply report that you stand in certain relations to other people, relations of commitment and trust. Moreover, it is quite possible to be committed in two or more directions at the same time, so that, whatever you do, you will fail to discharge one of your duties. Clearly, in such a situation there is one best thing to do, one thing which you ought to do, even though there are several incompatible things you have an obligation to do. Hence, again, "ought to do" cannot be synonymous with "have a duty to do" or "have an obligation to do."

It will not help to introduce the strange notion of a prima facie duty or obligation. If a student borrows a thousand dollars from his brother to help finance his graduate education and solemnly pledges to repay the money within ten years, he thereby puts himself under an obligation—not an apparent obligation or a probable obligation or a tendency to be an obligation—to pay the debt. And if during the course of the next decade unforeseen hardships occur—if, for example, he should prove more fecund or less resourceful than he had anticipated—and if his brother should suddenly strike it rich, then perhaps the best thing for him to do is to inform his brother, with all due reluctance, that he will not be able to discharge his obligation. I submit that we would quite naturally describe this failure as a *renunciation of an obligation*. We would not necessarily claim that he had done the wrong thing, nor need we necessarily blame him. After all, sometimes people *ought* to renounce their obligations. It makes a mockery of our usage to hold that a rightly renounced obligation could not have been a true obligation, *sans phrase*, in the first place.

II

What is it to go "beyond the limits of one's duty?" Urmson uses this and a like expression in his definition of both saintly and heroic actions, and elsewhere he speaks of actions which "exceed the demands of duty." There are at least two distinct ways of interpreting such phrases as "above," "beyond," "more than," and "in excess of" duty. First of all, there is a straightforwardly quantitative interpretation. A janitor has a duty to spend eight hours cleaning his employer's floors. He works ten hours for eight hours' pay. Duty required eight hours; he did his duty and then some and thus, in a perfectly intelligible sense, did "more than" his duty. Furthermore, in respect to this and similar oversubscriptions, we can specify exactly by *how much*, as measured in additive units, the performance exceeded duty. If the state taxes a patriotic citizen one hundred dollars and he pays two hundred dollars, intending the balance as a gift, then the citizen has exceeded his duty by exactly one hundred dollars. This is not a controversial judgment of moral philosophy. It is simply a truth of arithmetic.

Doing a favor is not similarly commensurable with duty. If I had given the stranger two matches, I would not have been going "beyond duty" in the present sense, for I had no duty to give him one match. If giving him no matches would not be to fall one match "below" what duty requires, then giving him two matches would not be to go one match "beyond" the demands of duty. Neither am I behaving supererogatorily when I give the stranger one match, for I have no duty to give him any number of matches, one or zero. A favor, then, is neither a duty nor (in the present sense) more than a duty. Rather, it is simply *other* than a duty and properly located on an altogether different scale than that occupied jointly by duties, derelictions, and over-subscriptions. A favor can be, but is not *always*, the performance of a duty plus more of the same; often it is an action where *none* is required, rather than a contribution of more than is required.

There are some favors, however, which are not only *other* than duty but, in some sense, *more* than duty. It would be an exaggeration to describe my act of offering the stranger a match as "above and beyond the call of duty," but if I spend three long hard days away from my own work helping a friend paint his house, it would seem an understatement to describe that performance as a mere favor. Still other actions in the service of others are, like favors, meritorious and not required by duty, and yet so profoundly different from the mere offering of a match that we would not call them favors at all, and for roughly the same kind of reason that we would not call a giant red-wood a sapling. Urmson's example of "the doctor who, no differently situated from countless other doctors in other places, volunteers to join the depleted medical forces in [a plague-stricken] city" seems to demand a different interpretation of the phrase "more than duty." Unlike the hard-working janitor and the patriotic taxpayer, Urmson's heroic doctor is not simply doing his "duty plus more of the same." He does not travel a definite number of miles more than the total required by duty; neither does he treat a definite number of patients more than duty requires, nor a definite number of hours more than is necessary, at the loss of a definite number of dollars in excess of what is obligatory. The point is, he has no duty to travel one step toward the plague-stricken city or to treat one single victim in it. The whole of his duty as a doctor is to continue treating the patients who constitute his own comfortable and remunerative practice. Still, if he gives all of this up and, at great inconvenience and danger, volunteers to help the suffering in a distant city, his action surely exceeds, in some sense, the requirements of duty.

In what way does the doctor's act "exceed" duty? It seems clear that the "excessive" element in his action is *sacrifice*.[6] His action cost him something, or at any rate it appeared likely to cost him something at the time he undertook it. In volunteering to help the unfortunate in a distant city, he made himself liable to great inconvenience and hardship, and he incurred the risk of loss of health and even life. But if probable sacrifice is the "excessive" element, what does it exceed? Certainly not the sacrifice involved in every actual duty. Consider Urmson's other doctor whose residence and practice are in the stricken city and who stands by his post working round the clock to help the sick, exposing himself to the contagion at every turn. He is making precisely the same sacrifice as his heroic colleague from the distant city, yet he is only doing his duty.

The sacrificial element in supererogatory actions, then, does not necessarily exceed that in the performance of a duty; rather, what it exceeds is the sacrifice *normally* involved in the doing of a duty. A point frequently overlooked by philosophers who have been influenced by Kant is that performances of duties are more often than not routine or habitual, even pleasant, activities. Many a debt is repaid cheerfully, and often enough vocational requirements are performed by men who whistle while they work. Of course, if a man's inclinations *always and necessarily* corresponded with the actions demanded of him, then, as

6 In the case of saintly and other supererogatory actions, the excessive element may be will-power or self-denial. See Urmson, *op.cit.*, 200-204. I shall restrict my attention here to actions of a "heroic" character.

Kant pointed out, the concept of duty would not apply to him. It would be absurd to say of such a person: "It is impossible for him not to do it, but he had better do it or else." Human beings are not "holy wills," and consequently they do have duties; but it does not follow that duty is always or even often onerous, or that it is engaged in a perpetual internal cold war with inclination. An undertaking that is "beyond duty" in this second sense, then, is one which has at least the following two characteristics: (1) it is not itself a duty; and (2) it exceeds, in the sacrifice it seems likely to require, that normally involved in the performance of duties.

That these two necessary conditions are not sufficient, however, can be shown by examples of actions which satisfy them but which nevertheless we should be extremely reluctant to label "above and beyond the call of duty." The greedy adventurer who sets off on an arduous journey into the heart of the jungle, determined to brave all dangers in order to find a buried treasure, is certainly not merely doing his duty or even his "duty plus"; nor is he even likely to believe he is. The dedicated crackpot who nearly freezes to death trying to convert the indifferent Eskimos to Caribbean voodooism may believe he is only doing his duty, but we know better. The embittered misanthrope who sacrifices his own life to the police in the process of machine-gunning as many passersby as he can is surely not discharging a duty thereby. In each of these examples, the agent does something other than his duty and does it at a much greater cost than duty normally involves; and yet we should be loath to say of any of the three that he did "more than duty required." The reason, I think, is plain. We do not regard either of the first two actions as particularly meritorious, and the third action, while brave and self-sacrificing, is actually reprehensible. We *praise* an act when we call it "more than a duty," and none of these examples seems praiseworthy. The third necessary condition of an action that exceeds duty in the second sense, then, is praiseworthiness or, in Urmson's phrase, "moral worth"; and a supererogatory act in this sense is, therefore, a *meritorious, abnormally risky nonduty.*

When we come, as we naturally must at this point, to the question of what makes an action meritorious, we encounter straight off a difficulty for Urmson's assumption that, in distinguishing duties and "more than duties," he is classifying actions according to their "moral worth." Urmson's final view seems to be as follows: There are several distinct ways in which an action can acquire moral worth, positive or negative. If it does what is wrong or prohibited, it has negative worth; if it does what is obligatory or required, it achieves positive merit; and if it goes "beyond duty," in the manner of saintly and heroic actions, for example, then also it acquires moral worth, though not necessarily more merit than some obligatory actions, which can be very demanding indeed. But when we get around to examining Urmson's examples of actions in excess of duty, such as the heroic doctor's, we find that, instead of acquiring worth by being saintly or heroic, they are not correctly called "saintly" or "heroic" at all unless they are already worthy or meritorious on some other ground. And of course that other ground cannot be their requiredness, because *ex hypothesi* they are nonduties. It follows that Urmson's addition of actions in excess of duty to the traditional classification of prohibited, permissible, and obligatory actions does very little, if anything, to make it more adequate as a classification of actions "from the point of view of moral worth."

The point suggested by our examples, however, is a more radical one, namely, that moral worth has no necessary connection with any of the categories in Urmson's expanded classification. Performances of duties can proceed from evil motives; "forbidden" actions can be prompted by the highest motives. And if supererogatory actions are understood on the "duty plus" model, a whole range of meritorious conduct finds no place in the classification. Meritorious, abnormally risky nonduties, if they are to be classified on such a scale, have only one proper pigeonhole.

They are not duties; they are not derelictions; they are not oversubscriptions. They are simply "permitted." When we compare them with other actions in that drab category, it becomes clear that it is not their character *qua* "permitted" that makes them morally worthy.[7]

III

Each of the two kinds of supererogation—namely, "oversubscription," or "duty plus," and "meritorious non-duty"—fits into its own distinctive complex of concepts, including a distinct way of conceiving personal merit and a special kind of moral rule. One complex, that in which "oversubscription" is at home, I shall call institutional or legal-like and the other (to avoid begging any questions) simply noninstitutional or nonlegal-like. Which, if either, of these is "distinctively moral" is a question to be considered (but not very seriously) in the final section of the essay.

The "institutional complex" consists of (1) essentially jural or institutionally connected rules which enjoin, permit, and prohibit, and thus impose duties and obligations, and (2) other rules which prescribe procedures for determining merits and demerits. In such institutions as schools, military units, corporations, and the like, in which behavior is in part governed by such rules and regulations, a soldier, or a student, or a janitor can acquire merit in two ways: by consistent performance of duty and by accumulating extra "bonus-points" by doing "duty plus." Similarly, he can incur demerits not only by complete disobedience of the regulations (that is, by nonperformance of duty) but also by failing by some measurable amount to come up to the requirements of duty. The latter failures, or partial derelictions, can be placed on the same scale as dutiful performance and "duty plus." Gross derelictions of duty render an

[7] For suggestive discussions of moral worth, see W. D. Ross, *The Right and the Good* (Oxford: Clarendon Press, 1930), 4-7, 155-175, and *Foundations of Ethics* (Oxford: Clarendon Press, 1939), 290-311.

employee liable to sacking; partial derelictions subject him to demerits on his work record analogous to the liabilities or debits on his bank account when it is overdrawn. Similarly, under some rules, employees and other officeholders can store up assets on their accounts to guard against unexpected expenditures of credit. A truly worthy officeholder never goes into the red; he keeps a meritorious work record. The most deserving of all, through the diligent accumulation of "surplus" credits, become qualified for rewards and promotions.

On the other hand, in the nonlegal-like, noninstitutional complex, there is a quite different conception of personal merit and a quite distinct sort of rule. Often we are concerned with a person's merit or worth, not merely in respect to this or that job or office, skill, or function, but "in the last analysis," *all things considered.* A man may have a very small balance in his bank account, a smaller balance of good will in his place of employment, and through absentmindedness an unenviable driver's record; but, for all of that, in the final appraisal he may be deemed an unusually worthy man, even a paragon of human excellence. Overall worth as a man is not simply some computable function of one's various records and accounts. Nor is final human worth to be identified completely with the virtues of trustworthiness and obedience. A "good man all things considered" is not simply the man who is *good at* doing his duties and accumulating points, as a good ballplayer is good at making hits and avoiding errors. He will also be a man with a hearty and subtle sense of humor, tact and social sensitivity, warmth, hardiness, and perhaps a redeeming sense of his own absurdity.

In making a final appraisal of a man, we must compare not only his mutually comparable talents and records but also parts of his character and history which are mutually incommensurable. Needless to say, there can be no magical formula for doing this. There can be no simple answer, for example, to the question of whether Green's benevolent infidelity ranks above or below Brown's faithful malevolence.

15

And we can no more tote up a man's final score in respect to excellence than we can calculate his overall "quantitativeness" by multiplying his age by his weight by his pulse beat by the number of his blood relations.

Final worth is not wholly determined, then, by the rules that confer duties and prescribe ways of accumulating debits and credits; but it is related, in an indirect way, to rules of a quite different sort. We have seen that the word "ought" can be used to prescribe or give advice in particular cases. Singular pieces of advice, such as "You ought to keep your promise in this case," are often generalized into such principles as "you ought to keep your promises (generally)," "You ought to be kind," and "You ought to do favors." There is no harm in calling statements of generalized advice "rules"; indeed, it is consonant with usage to do so. But it is important to notice that these rules do not enjoin, prohibit, or confer obligations and duties. They are rules in a quite different sense, better named "maxims" or "precepts" than "injunctions" or "commands." Perhaps "counsels of wisdom" or "rules of advice" would be the most appropriate designations, since these names suggest, quite correctly, that these are rules of thumb rather than "laws" on some jural or institutional model.

Counsels of wisdom guide the wise man's conduct and sometimes, also, that of the fool; for to have the right precepts without knowing how to apply them in puzzling circumstances or where they come into conflict is to be merely sententious, not wise. The better part of wisdom is a kind of knack or flair which cannot be bottled up in simple formulas. A man is on his own when he must decide whether to stick safely by his station or do the "meritorious, abnormally risky nonduty," or whether to honor his duty or an opposing commitment of a different order—whether to stay with Mother or join the Free French forces. There are, unfortunately, no strict superrules for applying counsels of wisdom in such situations and no simple commands to obey. If it is a matter of being conscientious or not, then by all means be conscientious. But of what use is this good advice if it is your conscience itself which is confused?

In the noninstitutional setting in which we must make final, overall appraisals and final, all-things-considered decisions and prescriptions, rules are at best only a rough guide. There are no very reliable rules either for comparing incommensurable virtues and vices or for getting from sound counsels of wisdom to a wise piece of singular advice or a wise decision. In the institutional realm these appraisals and decisions, or rather their analogues, have been made artificially simple. A man's worth as a ballplayer is determined by the averages in his record; his worth as a politician by the tally at the polls; his worth as a bureaucrat, or executive officeholder, by his balance of credits and debits, merits and demerits, oversubscriptions and derelictions, as determined by the rules of his institution. And while the janitor's problem of knowing what in the final analysis, all things considered, he *ought* to do, can on occasion be as difficult as anyone else's, he need rarely have any doubt about what his duties and obligations are. For to know his duties, he need not consider "all things," but only the orders of his boss, the conditions of his employment, his voluntary commitments, his social roles, and the civil law. These are things he can look up. But if they conflict, and he wishes to know what he *ought* to do, he may not be able to look that up quite as easily.

IV

Which facts are the "facts of morality?" Some writers identify the moral realm with what I have called the nonjural, noninstitutional complex. For these writers, a man's worth, all things considered, is by definition his *moral worth*; and what he ought to do in the last analysis, all things considered, is what he *morally* ought to do; and *all* relevant counsels of wisdom, not merely those concerned with duties and obligations, are *moral rules*. On the other

17

hand, many writers adopt the very opposite procedure, reserving the moral label for the realm of duties, commands, and prohibitory rules. Thus Santayana, to pick just one of many possible examples, *identifies* the moral with the legal-like, especially with the concept of duty, and then distinguishes it from the wider genus of "values."[8] Still a third way of making the distinction is to treat morality as a genus with legal-like and nonlegal-like species. H.L.A. Hart, for example, speaks alternatively of two "sectors," "scales," or "segments" within the "field" of morality.[9]

I have no intention of deciding which of these three ways of marking the distinction between the two complexes is the "correct" one. Indeed, that seems to me to be a verbal problem and one which, in any case, is hopelessly tangled. The word "moral," reflecting a variety of disparate and contrary uses in the technical literature of law, theology, and philosophy, is not simply ambiguous, but ambiguous in such an extraordinary way that some of its senses are antonyms.[10]

I wish here only to insist that the two realms I have distinguished be kept distinct, whichever, if either, is to be called the distinctively "moral" realm. There is a widespread tendency, which I think even Urmson has not altogether avoided, to mark the distinction by blowing up the institutional side to incorporate the other. A main task of moral philosophy, according to many philosophers, is to catalogue the duties of men. Since this is much too simple

---

[8] George Santayana, "The Philosophy of Bertrand Russell," *Winds of Doctrine* (London: J. M. Dent & Sons, 1940), 138. The "unregenerate naturalist," he writes, is "propitiated" by Russell's kind of intuitionism because it implies that "ethics is concerned with the economy of all values and not with 'moral' goods only, or with duty. . . ."

[9] *Op.cit.*, 83.

[10] On the one hand, for example, "moral" has the ring of supreme authority, and on the other, it still carries its original sense of informal "customs" or "ways." Aristotle *contrasted* the moral with the intellectual; Kant *identified* it with the *rational*. Lawyers use it to refer, on the one hand, to loose and informal agreements and arrangements beneath the official attention of the law and, on the other hand, to an ultimate standard for appraising the law.

a task if we confine our attention to duties in the ordinary practice- and institution-connected sense, and since, moreover, moral philosophers wish to concern themselves with other important matters, such as what to do when duties conflict, and whether and when we should perform favors and difficult, meritorious nonduties, they expand the sense of "duty" to include all that is normally contrasted with it. Thus, in addition to the duties of fathers, citizens, club members, janitors, and promisers, there are said to be duties of man *qua* man, which on examination turn out to be those acts of beneficence, service, and gratitude which come to have the meaning they do by being contrasted with duty. Similarly, since janitors and fathers derive their own peculiar merits from doing their respective jobs well, and since these merits are not to be identified with their overall human worth, it is thought that there must be some special job of a man as such, so that being good at that job confers final, overall worth.

Furthermore, in each case the noninstitutional is reinterpreted as the special institutional. Hence those counsels of wisdom which could serve a man even in an institutionless state of nature, and in some respects even if he were the last man on earth, are treated as if they were the company rules of some shadowy moral corporation or the statutes of a ghostly moral State. For example, counsels of wisdom, which as nonbinding rules of thumb are distinct in kind from jural laws and house rules, are called "moral laws" and regarded simply as a special eccentric species of jural law, or as a kind of moral house rule; and the counsels to do meritorious acts which are not duties are said by these philosophers to impose special duties, which, since they seem to differ in all essential respects from garden-variety duties, are called "duties of imperfect obligation." These philosophical inventions are devices for blurring the distinction they were meant to explicate.

The concept of supererogation too can contribute in this way to conceptual confusion. It remains only to illustrate how this can happen. Probably the most familiar kind of supererogation is that which I have already called "over-subscription." Institutional rules of various kinds allow persons to accumulate credit surpluses to guard against future deficiencies and also to oversubscribe assigned quotas to make up for earlier undersubscriptions of one's own or, in some cases, undersubscriptions of other persons. Those philosophers deserve our gratitude who call our attention to these rules and especially to the inability of the traditional threefold classification to do full justice to their complexity. But the ever present danger of taking the institutional model too seriously lurks here as well. The trap is set. First, the unsuspecting philosopher takes the familiar as a model for understanding the relatively unfamiliar, the institutional for the noninstitutional, the janitor or the taxpayer for the heroic doctor. Then he allows the institutional model to become inflated to the point where it absorbs its noninstitutional opposite as an eccentric subspecies of itself. Thus the philosopher's natural partiality for the familiar leads to a distinctive sort of conceptual aggression. As a consequence of his failure to observe conceptual boundary lines, a contrast essential to both distinguished concepts disappears. The effects here as elsewhere are misleading and bizarre.

The unwary philosopher posits a special moral account or record corresponding to a person's bank account or work record. Procedures are assumed whereby moral agents can accumulate moral debits and credits through undersubscribing and oversubscribing their assigned moral "quotas" or duties. Then, having made this tidy Proscrustean bed, the philosopher is obliged to try to jam into it the unsolicited services, gifts, and favors, the saintly and heroic feats, the meritorious, abnormally risky nonduties.

The standard example of treating the performance of meritorious nonduties as oversubscriptions is the Roman Catholic doctrine of supererogation. A "work of supererogation," according to the church, is one that goes beyond what God commands or requires for salvation, one that in itself confers extra merit or desert on the agent.

Protestants believe such works to be impossible. But Romanists assert that a person may not only have in reserve a store of merit so as to have enough for himself, but also something to spare for others; and this superabundant merit, collected from all quarters in every age, the Church of Rome professes to have laid up as in a treasury, from which to dispense to those who have little or none.[11]

According to this doctrine, then, moral credits and debits are on everyone's moral account; merits can be transferred from person to person and pooled in a central moral treasury from which they can be doled out to the morally poor.

I am not entirely sure that I have interpreted this canonical doctrine correctly. Indeed, the whole drift of Roman Catholic moral philosophy, with its emphasis on the inwardness of morals, seems to me to run in the other direction. But, be that as it may, the doctrine of supererogation as I have interpreted it makes a very clear example of the institutionalization of human worth. Its bizarre character becomes manifest when one realizes that the merits so hoarded and spent, transferred, pooled, and doled out are not mere records of one's excellence at some special function or task; they are supposed to represent what is often called one's "moral worth," his merit as a man, all

---

[11] Lyman Abbot and T. J. Conant (eds.), *A Dictionary of Religious Knowledge* (New York: Harper, 1875), 907. See also R. Seeberg, in *The New Schaff-Herzog Encyclopedia of Religious Knowledge*, ed. S. M. Jackson (Grand Rapids: Baker Book House, 1949), XI, 165, who writes that supererogation is "a concept in Roman Catholic theology which has its place in the doctrine of indulgences [and which] was justified by the great scholastics through the notion of the organic unity of the Church. They asserted that the sum total of the merits of Christ was greater than was required for the salvation of man, and that the saints also had done more and suffered more than was absolutely required to insure their own salvation, that these superabundant merits were placed in the 'spiritual treasury' of the Church, at the disposal of its visible head; that as the Church is one, in this world as in the next, they may be applied to such of its members as are still lacking in the required amount of works necessary to satisfy the divine demands. This is effected by indulgences, as an exercise of judicial power for the living and *per modum suffragii* for the souls in purgatory."

things considered. Talk of transferring final human worth from one soul to another generates paradox after paradox. Socrates and the Stoics taught that the best thing one man can do for another is to make him a better man, but they mentioned no technique by which a good man could contribute some of his own reserve merit to his morally less perfect brother. Even supposing there were a way to take from one's own purse full of human worth a healthy portion and make a gift of it to someone else, would not that very act accumulate new credit for the donor? If it is more blessed to give than to receive, and the most precious of all gifts is basic human worth, then the more of his worth a person gives away, the more he gains in the process. A strange "currency" indeed is human goodness.

The Church, however, speaks only of transferring moral credit from a central treasury to human beings. But according to what criteria is the surplus human worth passed out? If hard cash were being distributed, we would probably say that the poor and hungry deserve the most, the well-to-do the least. But should we say, on that model, that the more reprehensible and depraved a man is, the more he deserves surplus human worth? Or shall we be equalitarian and spread the worth around equally so that it hardly does anyone any good? Perhaps we should distribute merit in proportion to the worth of the recipient and allow the rich to get richer while the poor go to hell? In asking these questions, one feels the institutional analogy begin to slip.

There are still other difficulties that weaken the analogy irreparably. If final human worth is something one can accumulate and hoard through sedulous oversubscription, then the distinction between Urmson's heroic doctor and the brave but avaricious adventurer begins to blur. Imagine a second doctor who, like the other, tends the sick in a distant, plague-stricken city but, like the treasure-hunter, does it for personal gain. The adventurer risks life and limb for gold, this doctor, more cleverly, for surplus units of human worth. We should be inclined, I think, to class this second doctor with the brave gold-seeker; but since he does exactly the same thing as Urmson's genuinely heroic doctor, and points are earned only by what one does, he must be classified with his humanitarian colleague. Actually, human worth, as we understand it, is a reflection of what one is, not a simple function of what one does.

Suppose, however, that points are rewarded only for actions done from good motives. This assumption would bring us closer to what we mean by human worth but only at the cost of defeating the aim of a system of debits and credits. The purpose of such a system, I should think, is to provide people with an incentive for doing what they otherwise might not want to do. But if we tell a man that he can earn extra credit by doing some difficult or dangerous task *only* if he does the task, say, from benevolent and not merely self-advancing motives, then we offer him incentive with one hand and take it away with the other. For if hope of self-advancement impels him to performance, it also disqualifies him for reward.

Furthermore, if favors, unsolicited gifts, and saintly and heroic actions are understood on the model of oversubscriptions, then one's *duties* will change as one accumulates points. If a person approaches the end of his moral career with a large balance of moral credits, he can "afford" to incur a few debits in his remaining years. A few minor peculations or fornications will lower his surplus a bit, but he may have plenty to spare. If he keeps the surplus until the end, it may only go to the unworthy in some future dole, and at any rate it is true of moral currency as of surplus cash that "you can't take it with you." The man whose moral budget is just balanced must do his duty to be saved. But in his shoes the man with surplus credits does not really *have* to do the same. He can be saved even if he sins now, provided he keeps his account in the black. On the other hand, the aging roué may find himself in such a position that unless he performs one last tremendous oversubscription he will finish in the red. It is now incumbent on him, say, that he find some plague-ridden city where treating the sick is sufficiently uncomfortable and dangerous to earn him the requisite number of credits to finish in the black. What is supererogatory for Urmson's heroic doctor, then, is mandatory for the aged sinner.

These peculiarities reflect the inadequacy of the jural and institutional models for personal merit and point to a dimension of human worth which is not measured by any kind of institutional work record, even that of a shadowy moral para-institution. If you wish to use the phrase "moral worth" for what I have called "final human worth, all things considered," then very well; my point is that moral worth is no direct function of one's performances on some kind of special work record. If, on the other hand, you prefer to use the phrase "moral worth" to stand for obedience, conscientiousness, and trustworthiness, as determined by one's response to prohibitory rules and commands and by one's subscriptions and oversubscriptions of duty (and there is considerable precedent for this usage), then my point is that a man's final worth is more than simply his moral worth, that there is more to a man's character than his "morals."

My intention in this essay is to show that one familiar conception of moral responsibility is incapable in principle of precise and consistent application. Like most conceptions of distinctively "moral" phenomena, this one is based on implicit analogies and contrasts with a legal counterpart. Moral responsibility is conceived as being similar to legal responsibility in some respects and radically dissimilar in others, and of course it is the contrasting characteristics which are taken to constitute the distinctively "moral" elements in moral responsibility. In order to bring out these contrasting elements clearly, I shall consider first of all the way in which the law courts treat certain difficult *problematic* instances of responsibility, for it is here that the contrasts are most sharp.

Problematic Responsibility in Law and Morals

I

The judgments of legal responsibility with which I shall be concerned are those which are made *retrospectively*. An event has taken place, a certain state of affairs has come into existence, and the courts ask *who is* (not *what was*) responsible for that event or state of affairs. In the law courts the state of affairs in question is usually a harmful one, and (except in cases of strict and vicarious liability not here considered) a defendant is said to be responsible for some harm when (1) the harm is in some sense and to some degree the result of something he did or omitted doing and (2) he was in some way at fault in doing or omitting it. What hinges on the ascription of responsibility is the question of whether the defendant shall be made to compensate the victim of the harm, or himself be punished for it, or both.[1]

Often occasions for ascribing responsibility pose difficult problems for the courts which cannot be solved in any mechanical fashion. An examination of the ways in which judgments of responsibility are made and supported in such cases will reveal several features of legal responsibility generally which have suggested to philosophers analogies and contrasts with "moral responsibility."

In the first place, judgments of legal responsibility are strongly influenced by ulterior practical purposes, and so much that is practical hinges on them that there is often no way of avoiding them by remaining silent or by qualified hedging. No judgment at all can mean, in effect, that the plaintiff is denied recovery of his losses or that the accused is allowed to go scot-free—practical consequences of the first importance, at least for those involved.

Secondly, there is an irreducible margin of vagueness in the legal concept of responsibility which often leads courts to mechanically apply admittedly arbitrary rules. Thus, for example, if the victim of an assault dies within a "year and a day," his assailant can be charged with homicide; if the victim lingers on for more than a year and a day, then responsibility for his subsequent death must officially be located elsewhere. This rule in criminal law and similar rules in the law of torts are meant to apply to cases in which responsibility is essentially uncertain but which require that "a line be drawn somewhere."

Thirdly, legal responsibility in problematic cases is *rela-*

---

[1] Responsibility judgments are also made *prospectively*, as in assignments of jobs, tasks, and "discretionary liabilities," and sometimes persons are described as responsible not *for* anything past or present, but simply as responsible *tout court*. Despite the obvious importance of prospective and *tout court* responsibility judgments to a complete analysis of retrospective responsibility, I shall not be concerned with them here.

tive to a variety of conflicting interests, purposes, and policies and cannot simply be "read off" the facts. Some kind of fault of the defendant has been officially determined to have been a causal factor in the production of a harm. But of course other factors contributed to the harm too, and while some of these were normal background conditions, such as the presence of oxygen in the air, some were quite abnormal, such as a person's unusual susceptibility to death by bleeding; some were foreseeable, some not. The question to be decided in such cases is whether the defendant's conduct was sufficiently wrongful, or whether it made a sufficiently important contribution to an outcome, to warrant ascribing responsibility for that outcome to him. The question of when a causal contribution to an outcome is sufficiently "important" for some purposes, of course, is not a question to be settled by prolonged reexamination of the facts; it can persist long after the facts are clear, especially when the purposes in question are conflicting.

In problematic cases, therefore, legal responsibility is something to be *decided*, not simply *discovered*. Should we or should we not *hold* the defendant liable for the harm? That is the proper form of the question, and it does not help to say in reply to it: "Determine first whether he is responsible in fact for the harm, and then hold him responsible if and only if he *really is* responsible." For even when all of the facts which can be discovered have been discovered, the problem of responsibility in these difficult cases remains a logically open and controversial question.

Determining legal responsibility in problematic cases often comes down to the questions of who ought to pay or who ought to be punished and how much. These questions are rendered problematic by conflicting interests and principles of justice, and the answers to them usually depend on what the judge takes to be the "ends" or "purposes" of compensation and punishment. In the law of torts many problematic cases have a common form: the defendant "unreasonably fail[s] to guard against harm which he

27

should foresee, and consequences which could not have been anticipated in fact result."[2] Many courts refuse to impose liability for unforeseeable consequences of the defendant's negligence on the grounds that to do so would be to "impose a ruinous liability which no private fortune could meet, and which is out of all proportion to the defendant's fault."[3] On the other hand, if the loss must be borne by someone, is it not more fair, or at least less unfair, that it fall on the party at fault rather than on the innocent victim? These two conflicting considerations have each been so persuasive that similar cases have often been decided in opposite ways, and lawyers and courts still dispute about how they should have been decided.[4] "The question," Professor Prosser insists, "is in no way one of causation," for "it does not arise until causation has been established. It is rather one of the fundamental policy of the law."[5] And not only are conflicting considerations of justice involved, but also such questions as how the losses can best be distributed and whether certain kinds of risk-taking are to be encouraged or deterred.

Conceptions of the divergent ends of punishment and

[2] William L. Prosser, *Handbook of the Law of Torts*, 2nd edn. (St. Paul: West Publishing Co., 1955), 258.

[3] *Ibid.*, 262.

[4] For example, in the case of *Palsgraf* v. *Long Island R. R. Co.* (1928), two railroad conductors assisting a running passenger onto a departing train negligently jostled him so as to dislodge a package from his arms. The package, it turned out, contained fireworks which exploded with violence, the concussion overturning heavy scales many feet away at the other end of the platform. The scales fell on an innocently waiting passenger, causing her severe injury. The question before the court was whether the railroad (through the negligence of its employees) was legally responsible for the injury. The New York Court of Appeals, in a strenuously debated decision, ruled that the railroad company was *not* liable. On the other hand, in the equally difficult case *Re Polemis & Furness, Withy & Co.* (1921), the defendant company's employees negligently allowed a wood plank to fall into the hold of a ship where it caused a spark which in turn exploded gas vapor whose presence had been unknown to them. The fire thus caused destroyed the entire ship and its cargo. The court held that the defendant leasing company (through the negligence of its employees) *was* legally responsible for the entire loss.

[5] *Op.cit.*, 258.

compensation further influence decisions of responsibility. Compensation is usually refused the survivors of a person killed by the defendant's negligence when it is satisfactorily proved that the victim would soon have died anyway. In a New Hampshire case, a small boy had fallen off a girder at the top of a bridge toward an almost certain death or severe injury on the rocks below. As he fell, he reached out and touched the defendant company's uninsulated wire, which the defendant had negligently allowed to carry current, and was electrocuted. In the words of the judge in the case, the victim was deprived "not of a life of normal expectancy but of one too short to be given pecuniary allowance."[6] In a criminal homicide case, however, it is generally agreed that the life expectancy of the victim has no bearing whatever on the question of the accused's responsibility. Thus if a man attempted to commit suicide by leaping from the top of the Empire State Building, and the defendant, an expert marksman, shot and killed him as he passed the forty-ninth floor, the marksman would almost certainly be convicted of some degree of homicide.[7] Compensation and punishment have different functions and different purposes, and these in turn lead to different appraisals of relevance in the official determinations of responsibility.

Because of the dependance of judgments of legal responsibility on considerations of policy and purpose, mechanical modes of decisionmaking break down in problematic cases. "The solution of cases," said Judge Edgerton in a famous statement, "depends on . . . a balancing of conflicting interests, individual and social; . . . these . . . are indefinite in number and value and incommensurable. . . . I believe that while logic is useful . . . it is inadequate; that intuition is necessary and certainty impossible."[8]

[6] Judge Allen in *Dillon* v. *Twin States Gas and Electric Co.* (1932).
[7] This example is based on a similar hypothetical case discussed by Jerome Hall in his *General Principles of Criminal Law* (Indianapolis: The Bobbs-Merrill Co., 1947), 262.
[8] Henry W. Edgerton, "Legal Cause," *University of Pennsylvania Law Review*, 72 (1924), 211.

II

Nevertheless, a stubborn feeling persists even after legal responsibility has been decided that there is still a problem—albeit not a legal problem—left over: namely, is the defendant *really* responsible (as opposed to "responsible in law") for the harm? This conception of a "real" theoretical responsibility as distinct from a practical responsibility "relative" to the purposes and values of a particular legal system is expressed very commonly in the terminology of "morality"—"*moral* obligation," "*moral* guilt," "*moral* responsibility"—especially when that terminology is used in self-conscious contrast with the technical terminology of the courts. The conception of moral responsibility that naturally emerges is of judgments which are in no way forced by practical considerations, which are superior in rationality and perfectly precise, imputing an absolute responsibility wholly within the power of the agent.

Let us consider these traits in order. In contrast to judgments of legal responsibility, which are forced by the circumstances, judgments of moral responsibility can often be safely avoided, for nothing practical need hinge on them. To be legally responsible for a harm is to be liable to official punishment or to legal pressure to make pecuniary reparation. To be morally responsible, on the other hand, is not to be liable to any kind of official action or even to unofficial informal responses such as acts of blaming. Moral responsibility, so conceived, is liability to charges and credits on some ideal record, liability to credit or blame (in the sense of "blame" that implies no action). Just as it is, as we say, "forever to the credit" of a hero or saint that he performed some noble act, so a man can forever be "to blame" for his faults. This, then, is what it is to be morally responsible for something on this conception: it is to be liable not to overt responses, but to a charging against one's record as a man. This record in turn can be used for any one of a variety of purposes—as a basis for self-punishment, remorse, or pride, for example; but a person can avoid putting it to these further uses, leaving responsibility simply a matter for the record.

Secondly, moral responsibility, in contrast to legal liability, must carry an immunity to vagueness and the need to formulate rules which are in any way "arbitrary." There can be no *moral* rule analogous to the "year and a day" rule in criminal law, justified only by the need to "draw the line somewhere" and by convenience. The question of an agent's moral responsibility must in principle be precisely decidable. Further, like all matters of "record," including "factual" ones, moral responsibility must be read off the facts or deduced from them; there can be no irreducible element of discretion for the judge, if his judgments are to have the stamp of superior rationality.

Thirdly, judgments of moral responsibility are in two senses "absolute." In contrast to legal judgments, which say in effect that a defendant's contribution to some outcome is an "important" contribution for the purposes of the law, moral responsibility is absolute in the sense that it holds independently of any purposes, goals, or policies. Judgments of moral responsibility are also absolute in the related sense of having an unqualified finality about them.[9] This is a feature, however, which they share with legal judgments.

Fourthly, moral responsibility must be regular and predictable; nothing can be left to chance or to unforeseeable contingencies. Above all, it cannot be a matter of luck, as responsibility so often is in the law. One man shoots another and kills him, and the law holds him responsible for the death and hangs him. Another man, with exactly the same motives and intentions, takes careful aim and shoots at his enemy but misses because of a last-minute move-

---

[9] G.E.M. Anscombe was referring to this characteristic of the "distinctively moral," I believe, when she wrote of our ethical terms that "they . . . have now acquired a special 'moral' sense—i.e., a sense in which they imply some absolute verdict (like one of guilty/not guilty) on a man." See her "Modern Moral Philosophy," *Philosophy*, 33 (1958), 5.

ment of his prey or because of his own bad eyesight. The law cannot hold him responsible for a death because he has not caused one; but, from the moral point of view, he is only luckier than the hanged murderer. Similarly, there is a famous case in the criminal law in which the defendant was found guilty of manslaughter when his victim, an unsuspected hemophiliac, died from uncontrollable bleeding resulting from a small cut in his mouth caused by the defendant's slapping him in the face. The slapper of the hemophiliac was held responsible for a death because of an unsuspected abnormal susceptibility in his victim, whereas a thousand persons are wrongfully slapped every day with no resultant criminal responsibility. Moral responsibility, in contrast, must be something one can neither escape by good luck nor tumble into through bad luck.

Given this conception of moral responsibility, it follows that it can be impossible to tell whether persons are *morally* responsible for events and states of affairs in the external world, for, however important a man's actions may be in producing an outcome, they are never the only contributors. There will always be conditions and occurrences, normal or abnormal, which play a part. In those cases where legal responsibility is problematic, moral responsibility would be absolutely undecidable in principle and therefore inapplicable since, in respect to moral responsibility as here understood, we are not allowed to appeal to purposes and policies.

This is not to say that we are prevented from judging that a person is morally "at fault" in what he did. Such judgments are usually implied by ascriptions of responsibility but are not to be identified with them, for the judgment of responsibility also contains a causal component. A person can well be morally at fault in what he does without being morally responsible for some given harm, even when the harm would not have happened but for his "fault." The harm can be properly ascribed to him only when his "fault" is sufficiently "serious" and makes a sufficiently "im-

portant" contribution to the harm. The required "sufficiency," of course, cannot be determined without recourse
to purposes and policies.[10]

None of these difficulties need embarrass the champion
of moral responsibility. If he is a rational man and a
philosopher, he will admit that moral responsibility for external harm makes no sense and argue that moral responsibility is therefore restricted to the inner world of the
mind, where the agent rules supreme and luck has no
place; for here is a domain where things happen without
the consent of uncooperative nature, where bodily movements are initiated, acts of volition undertaken, intentions
formed, and feelings entertained. The basic difference between law and morals, on this conception, is a difference of
jurisdiction. Morals constitute a kind of internal law, governing those inner thoughts and volitions which are completely subject to the agent's control, and administered before the tribunal of conscience—the *forum internum*. The
external law governs a man's relations with his fellows, to
which both other persons and outer nature can make unexpected and uncontrolled contributions. The internal law
applies with more exactitude because these extraneous contributors to outcomes have been separated out. "On the one
hand," writes Roscoe Pound of the moral agent, "he is in relation to other beings like himself and to things external. On
the other hand, he is, as it were, alone with himself."[11]

---

[10] This is a point often obscured, I think, by the ambiguity of
"fault." Sometimes we do impute responsibility for some harm to a
person by saying simply that the harm *is* "his fault." On other occasions we reserve the term "fault" for such failings *in* a person as
avarice, malice, and negligence, regardless of their causal antecedents
and consequences. This ambiguity explains the well-known remark of
the judge in Butler's *Erewhon* (Ch. XI): "Whether your being in a
consumption is *your fault* or no, it is a *fault in you*, and it is my duty
to see that against such faults as this the commonwealth shall be protected" (my italics).

[11] *Law and Morals* (Chapel Hill: University of North Carolina Press,
1926), 97.

III

The doctrine of the internality of morals and its psychological trappings may have much to recommend them, but they do not provide a place for the application of a precisely determinable absolute responsibility immune from the arbitrariness and policy-dependence which characterize legal responsibility. Part of the reason that this is so is that responsibility for one's own inner states, if there could be such a thing, would in some circumstances be wholly a matter of luck.

Consider the case of Hotspur (as we shall call him), the unfortunate slapper of Hemo, the equally unfortunate hemophiliac.[12] Imagine that we have photographed the whole episode and are now able to project the film in such very slow motion that we can observe every stage of Hotspur's action and (constructively) even the "inner" anticipatory stages. Running the film back in reverse, we see the stage at which Hemo's mouth is bleeding, the stage at which Hotspur's hand makes contact with Hemo's face, the swinging of Hotspur's arm, the preliminary contractions of his muscles. Before these are stages at which we can infer inner events—a decision to swing at Hemo, an earlier girding or building up of courage through self-preaching, a prior burning feeling of anger in response to Hemo's insult.

At each of these cinematographic stages there is some state of affairs for which we might hold Hotspur responsible. We can also conceive of a third party, call him Witwood, who is in all relevant respects exactly like Hotspur but who, through luck, would have escaped responsibility at each stage, were he in Hotspur's shoes. We can imagine, for example, that had Witwood caused Hemo's mouth to hemorrhage, Hemo's life would have been saved by some new drug; or at an earlier stage, instead of becoming responsible for Hemo's cut mouth, Witwood lands only a glancing blow which does not cut; or again, instead of becoming responsible for the painful impact of hand on face,

---

[12] No resemblance whatever to anyone living or dead.

Witwood swings at a ducking Hemo and misses altogether. Though similar in his intentions and deeds to Hotspur, Witwood escapes responsibility through luck.

The same good fortune is possible at earlier "internal" stages. For example, at the stage when Hotspur would begin to burn with rage, a speck of dust throws Witwood into a sneezing fit, preventing any rage from arising. He can no more be responsible for a feeling he did not have than for a death that did not happen. Similarly, at the point when Hotspur would be right on the verge of forming his intention, Witwood is distracted at just that instant by a loud noise. By the time the noise subsides, Witwood's blood has cooled, and he forms no intention to slap Hemo. Hotspur, then, is responsible—I suppose some would say "morally" responsible—for his intention, whereas Witwood, who but for an accidental intrusion on his attention would have formed the same intention, luckily escapes responsibility. Thus in whatever sense legal responsibility for external states can be contingent on factors beyond one's control and therefore a matter of luck, in precisely the same sense can "moral" responsibility for inner states also be contingent and a matter of luck.

Of course, an intention is not the sort of thing that a person brings about or "causes" by doing something else first, so there is something odd about saying "responsibility for one's intentions." Still, having a character of a certain sort is often a necessary condition for the forming of any particular intention and thus, in a sense, is a "contributor" to its coming into being. If Hotspur had not been irascible or sensitive about remarks of a certain sort, presumably he would not have decided to hit Hemo. Witwood, who, by hypothesis, has precisely the same character traits as Hotspur, did not form the same intention because other contributors to intention intervened. Since one's character, then, is never a sufficient condition for one's intentions, but only one of numerous cooperating factors, it follows that whether or not a person is (retrospectively) responsible for his intentions depends on how important a role his character played in their genesis—that is, on how truly representative they are of his character.

It will now be easy to show that the other essential characteristics of moral responsibility as defined above, namely, its alleged precise determinability and immunity from "problematic cases," are no more characteristic of our inner life than are complete control and independence of luck. If we can show here that problematic cases precisely analogous to those which arise in the law courts, and which can be settled only by weighing policy considerations, can and do arise also *in foro interno*, where policy considerations are ruled out, we shall by that token have shown that moral responsibility as here defined is vacuous.

Imagine, then, that a moral agent is called to account by his own conscience. The question before the inner court is not responsibility for some bodily action or external state of affairs—they are outside its jurisdiction—but rather responsibility for some past *intention*, which may or may not have issued in effectual action. Suppose that the following facts have been certified by the inner court: the intention in question was to slap Smith in the face; it was formed in the agent's mind as a consequence of (1) his rather unusual sensitivity to remarks of a certain sort stemming in turn from a basic insecurity and lack of confidence, (2) a slightly abnormal disposition to strong anger attributable to a hyperactive adrenal system, (3) a stomach disorder sufficiently disagreeable to put him on edge and weaken his self-control, and (4) highly provocative and deliberately abusive remarks by Smith.

Is the agent morally responsible for the intention on these facts? If he had not had a character of a certain irascible and sensitive sort, he would not have formed the intention in question, and these are facts about him, about the kind of person he is. It is equally true, however, that but for the provocative remarks of Smith, and but for the stomach condition, and but for the hyperactive adrenals, he would not have formed that particular intention, and these are facts not about him, but about his body and the external world. Still, certain facts about his self or character as a moral agent were among the necessary conditions for the intention. The question would then appear to be: were they sufficiently important necessary conditions to warrant the ascription of a once-and-for-all, "absolute" moral responsibility for the intention? The problem seems perfectly analogous to that which arises *in foro externo*, when legal responsibility for some external harm must be fixed, except that in the external case the defendant contributed to an outcome by *doing* or *omitting* something, whereas in the internal case he "contributed" by being a certain kind of person. In public courts of law, however, there are rules— some of them admittedly arbitrary, some of them reflecting useful public policies—for determining the importance of the agent's contribution to an outcome. In the inner court no such rules are available. As a consequence, the precise determinability of moral responsibility is an illusion; there are problematic cases even for the inner court, and these are undecidable in principle; and moral responsibility so conceived is less, not more, rational than its legal counterpart.

IV

The problem in analyzing moral responsibility is to fashion a conception sufficiently similar to the legal model to be called "responsibility" but sufficiently rational and autonomous to be called "moral." I have argued in this paper that the problem is not solved by transferring the legal apparatus to an inner stage, that it is a mistake to think that by restricting responsibility to an inner jurisdiction we can thereby make precise its vaguenesses and eliminate its contingencies. No particular philosopher or school has been especially guilty of this mistake. Moral responsibility, I dare say, is a subject about which we are all confused. The confusions I have discussed here might just as well be attributed to the commonsense concept of responsibility as to any particular philosopher, though that concept itself bears the mark of many philosophers.

In the concluding paragraph of her article "The Two Kinds of Error in Action," G.E.M. Anscombe writes of my comments on that essay at the APA meeting in Columbus, Ohio, that "Professor Joel

On Being "Morally Speaking a Murderer"

Feinberg objected that 'murder' was a legal concept, so that he did not know what I was at." She then goes on to ascribe to me the wicked "positivism of Thrasymachus," a view which implies that no legal killings, even those of the Nazis, can be unjust. This, of course, is a misunderstanding of my view. I should therefore like to disavow it explicitly and also to explain with more clarity in what sense "murder" is a legal concept, why the view that "murder" is a legal concept does not entail Thrasymachean positivism, and why and in what respects I was unable to determine what Miss Anscombe "was at."

I

In classifying "murder" as a legal concept, I meant only that it finds its original, primary, and clearest application in legal contexts and that, therefore, its use in those contexts is a convenient, even necessary, model for our understanding of its extended uses outside of the law. Perhaps "murder" and such words as "right," "duty," "authority," "obligation," "criminal," "bankrupt," "indebtedness," "partnership," and so on, had better be labeled *legal-like* than simply legal terms, for that might help obviate the sort of misunderstanding that has arisen between Miss Anscombe and me. All of these terms can be distinguished from other words in our normative vocabulary—for example, "ought" (when it simply bears advice), "good," "bad," and "better," which, whatever else they may be, are not distinctively legal-like. The legal-like terms often have perfectly legitimate uses outside of legal and other institutional contexts. Such expressions as "debt of gratitude," "dance partner," and "morally bankrupt," for instance, imply no legal relations, yet they use legal-like terms to good effect. When I say that it is "criminal" the way my neighbor insults his wife or neglects his garden, I am also using a legal-like term in a nonlegal sense. The word "law" is prototypically legal-like, yet in the expression "moral law" even it bears a nonlegal sense.

Because legal-like terms have both technical and (legitimately) extended senses, there is always the possibility that confusion will arise when they are employed. It is perfectly plain in most contexts that a dance partner as such is not a legal partner, but it is not always so clear what is conveyed when, for example, a professor refers to his "partner in scholarly research." Hence the word "moral"—as in the phrase "moral partnership"—acquires one of its most useful functions. When it qualifies a legal-like noun, it serves as a signal that the noun is not being used in its full-blown technical sense, but rather that the speaker is exploiting some analogies—and contrasts. Among the *contrasts* the word "moral" often serves to mark when used in this way is the contrast between higher and lower, or rational and merely conventional, or more and less stringent or important, and so on. I refer to this commonplace only to obviate again the charge of "positivism"; but I should also point out that "moral," when it qualifies a legal-like noun, can *also* signal the contrast between the informal, unofficial, or merely virtual, on the one hand, and the official, public, "in force," on the other, and that these two kinds of contrast can get in each other's way, generating thereby acute philosophical puzzlement.

These observations are trivial by themselves, but they

lead to a heuristic principle of considerable importance for moral philosophy. When a philosopher wishes to analyze or elucidate a legal-like ethical concept, such as "moral right," he should use the law as a kind of model, as well as a kind of contrasting background for his understanding. Both moral rights and legal rights are first of all *rights*, and if we are concerned to understand this common character, we had better turn to the law where it is "writ large." The legal model will reveal fundamental analogies, and only then should one hunt for the fundamental contrast usually signaled by the word "moral." I urge this procedure only as an aid to analysis, not as a guide to judgment. The law is a helpful conceptual model, not a superior moral standard or criterion. Of course, there can be moral rights not enshrined in law! Legal rights are a useful guide to our understanding of what this *means*. Far from implying that moral rights do not exist (as Bentham mistakenly inferred), our heuristic principle is a rule for coming to understand what moral rights are.

After recommending this methodological procedure, I should say that my other major concern here is to warn against a certain kind of mistake which is an abuse of that procedure. The error I have in mind is committed when, using the legal model unconsciously or uncritically, one attempts to import its imposing conceptual structure whole into moral questions. A moralist commits this error, for example, if he takes very seriously the question whether giving a hamburger dinner for a neighbor will discharge the "moral debt" he incurred by eating a chicken dinner at his neighbor's—as if the problem had a precisely arithmetical solution with a remainder or a deficit left over.

Hart and Honoré make the same kind of point about moral responsibility:

> . . . we must not impute to ordinary thought all the fine discriminations that could be made and in fact are to be found in a legal system, or an equal willingness to supply answers to complex questions. . . . Where there is no precise system of

punishment, compensation, or reward to administer, ordinary men will not often have faced such questions as whether the injuries suffered by a motorist who collides with another in swerving to avoid a child are consequences attributable to the neglect of the child's parents in allowing it to wander on to the road.[1]

Such precise questions have to be answered in courts of law, but they are safely avoided in ordinary life where nothing clearly hinges on them. The point I am trying to make, however, is stronger than that. In ordinary life, *in abstraction from all practical questions about punishment, compensation, and the like, there is no rational way of answering such questions.* Of course, one can always use the legal-like language to let off steam or to vent resentment: "*You* are morally responsible for the harm!" said to a certain party may be a way of making him feel bad about the harm, and if that will lead him to behave more carefully in the future, then the statement was well made. But if we consider the question as one calling for cool and exact *judgment*, a "verdict" issued on past events, and thought but not necessarily spoken, then our question is ill formed, for it asks us to sit on a kind of moral jury in a court where normal juridical rules and reasons can have no relevance but where there are no alternative rules and reasons of a remotely legal-like kind.

The error, in short, is committed by one who, in posing a moral question using a legal-like term, uncritically imports the precision of that term in its strict legal sense, while excluding appeal to the kinds of criteria which alone can decide its use. For expository convenience only, and at the risk of sounding profound, I propose to call this error "the Legalistic Mistake"; and once more to prevent misunderstanding, let me add that it is *not* committed in *every* nonlegal use of a legal-like term.

[1] H.L.A. Hart and A. M. Honoré, *Causation in the Law* (Oxford: Clarendon Press, 1959), 71.

II

The word "murder" derives from the Germanic *morth*, which in ancient German and Scandinavian law originally denoted a *secret* killing. Of all the forms of unlawful homicide, voluntary or involuntary, this was regarded by the Germans as the most grave, apparently because it doubly injured the victim's family, first by killing one of its members, and second by depriving the survivors of the satisfaction of vengeance.[2] The term "murder" was introduced into English at the time of William the Conqueror as a technical name for the secret ambushing of Normans by Anglo-Saxons (the most heinous kind of killing imaginable to the Normans). By 1340 killings of Englishmen counted as murder too, whether secret or not; and then, by the time of Henry VIII, the term was reserved for a class of intentional killings, those with "malice aforethought." Finally came the technical definition which survives to the present in the quaint language of Lord Coke: "unlawfully killing a reasonable creature [i.e., human being] who is in being [i.e., born and alive] and under the King's Peace, with malice aforethought either express or implied, the death following within a year and a day."

Throughout this long development the basic idea in the legal term "murder" has been "the most heinous kind of unlawful homicide." From this derives (1) the nontechnical sense—"the worst kind of unjustified killing generally (wanton, barbarous, etc.), whether lawful or not"—and (2) the technical elaboration of the legal sense in Lord Coke's formula, each part of which requires a whole textbook of interpretation and qualification. Finally, there are (3) a whole family of nontechnical uses of "murder" that are in their several ways analogical extensions of the elaborated technical sense—of which more will be said in Part IV.

It is worth noting here how very precise and complex the technical concept of murder has become, for an awareness

2 Cf. Carl Ludwig Von Bar, *A History of Continental Criminal Law* (Boston: Little, Brown & Co., 1916), 164.

of these features can serve to warn those who apply the term "morally speaking" of the pitfalls of the Legalistic Mistake. The earlier conception of murder as simply "the most heinous criminal homicide" could not by itself do well the job of guiding conduct and guaranteeing expectations. Experience casts up so many problematic cases that a bewildered juryman, asked only whether one of them is an instance of the "worst kind of killing," might not even know (in the first place) whether it counts as a killing of any kind. For to kill someone is to cause his death, and when the action of the defendant was only one of many important causal factors in the death of the victim, it can be difficult—and, without the guidelines provided by precise legal rules, impossible—to know whether it can be selected out as *the* cause of the death. Does a woman cause the death of her child by abandoning him on a neighbor's doorstep when, unbeknown to her, the neighbor is far away and an eagle (commonly seen in the area) inflicts fatal wounds on him with its claws?[3] Does a man "kill" his victim if the latter recovers from a wound in the lungs but is left in such a weakened condition that he succumbs to pneumonia three years later? These are not purely "factual" questions about whether or not a certain kind of action-word correctly "describes" what an agent did. The only way a juryman can decide in these cases whether a "killing" has taken place (quite apart from additional questions about justification and excuse) is to apply an authoritative legal rule, itself expressing either an important social policy—for example, that infant abandonment is to be discouraged by the strongest possible means—or else an arbitrary "drawing of the line," as in Lord Coke's year-and-a-day rule.

For a killing to be murder, the victim must have been born alive, and "birth consists in extrusion from the mother's body." But what if the infant victim has been extruded except for a leg? What if extrusion is complete but the umbilical cord has not been cut? Does the "King's Peace" ex-

[3] Cf. Sir William Blackstone, *Commentaries on the Laws of England*, 4 vols. (Oxford: Clarendon Press, 1765-1769), IV, 197.

tend to escaped outlaws, to enemy aliens? Is it murder for
an unauthorized person to kill an already condemned escaped criminal? Are reckless "not quite intentional" killings murder? Does a defendant who intended only to harm,
and not to kill, but who used means which were "intrinsically likely" to kill, commit murder if his victim dies?
If *A* shoots at *B* intending to kill him but hits *C* instead
(whom he did not want to harm), has he murdered *C* if
C dies? Can a murder then be an unintentional killing?
"If a man assaults a woman with intent to ravish her, and
she, having a weak heart, dies in the struggle,"[4] would that
be murder? In the law there are explicit and authoritative
answers to these questions, expressing settled legal policies,
without which a puzzled juryman could only boggle. Without such guidance it would be impossible in principle for
the juryman to come to a decision in any nonarbitrary way.
Surely, to tell him that he should decide first whether the
rapist in the previous example is "morally speaking a murderer" and then and only then find him legally guilty of
murder would be to commit the Legalistic Mistake.

III

Miss Anscombe sketches an alternative account of
the concept "murder." The central idea, she says, is *unjust
killing*; and she suggests, I believe, that this is equivalent
to the *killing of the innocent*. My immediate suspicion is
that she is using the concept "murder" in the received sense
of "wicked killing" and then packing her conception of
what the most wicked killings are into the concept's "central
core"; for the judgments that "all and only unjust killings
are murder" and "all and only killings of the innocent are
murder" have the ring (to me at least) of "synthetic propositions" or substantive moral judgments in need of rational
support. There is, of course, nothing wrong with this kind
of moral legislating provided that the legislator, in calling

[4] C. S. Kenny, *Outlines of Criminal Law*, 5th edn. (Cambridge: At
the University Press, 1913), 137.

his legislation "conceptual analysis," does not thereby claim a license to escape the responsibility of giving reasons.

Even construed as moral recommendation, however, Miss Anscombe's account seems to me to have serious difficulties. Suppose a private citizen captures an unarmed outlaw who is in fact an escaped convicted murderer under sentence of death and, recognizing him as such, shoots him dead. One might argue that the killing was just, in the sense that the victim got "what was coming to him"—or even in the sense that he got what it was some assigned person's duty to give him—and yet hold that in this case the killer acted wrongly or even wickedly in giving it to him. I see no contradiction (here is the crux of the matter) in holding that one and the same act is *just* and *unjustified*, or wrong; for the justice of an act is determined by the rights or deserts of a *patient*, its rightness or wrongness, in part, by the moral position of the *agent*. The man who kills the convicted murderer is himself a murderer not because he kills unjustly, but because he kills without authorization or any other kind of justification.

The point holds the other way too: one and the same act can be both *unjust* (to someone or other) and *justified*. Administrators in positions of high responsibility notoriously must sometimes act in circumstances which are such that, whatever they do (or omit doing), the result will be unfair to some group of persons dependent on them. An act is justified, all things considered, if the *balance* of good reasons weighs in its favor. Heaven knows that the realization that an act would be unjust to someone is a weighty reason against performing it. In my opinion, it is the weightiest kind of reason. Sometimes, however, it sits on both sides of the scale, and in any case it is not the only kind of consideration that carries weight.

The problem of euthanasia in a peculiar way raises difficulties for the definition of "murder" both as "unjust killing" and as "killing of the innocent." Legal questions aside, am I "morally speaking a murderer" if in response to his earnest request I put an old man suffering from an incurable disease out of his misery? If murder is, by definition, the killing of the innocent, then I am, by definition, a murderer. But notice how unfair this line of reasoning is to the mercy-killer. It morally condemns him in the most serious way and at the same time deprives him of any language in which to defend himself. He is "by definition a murderer"; and if he thinks he is not deserving of the condemnation the word "murder" imports from the law, he is driven to say something that sounds so weirdly wicked that no one could take him seriously—"Yes, I am (by definition) a murderer, but I did what was right."

On the other hand, if "murder" is construed as "unjust killing," it would seem to follow that the mercy-killer, by definition, is *not* a murderer, for a man does not treat another unjustly when he accedes to his considered request. Those who are committed to the "unjust killing" definition of "murder" and who are strongly opposed to mercy-killing may wish to escape this conclusion by arguing that the right to life is among those special rights which cannot be *renounced*; mercy-killing is unjust, therefore, because the hopeless sufferer cannot renounce his right to the life he hates. This is a surprising and unhappy claim, and the only alleged basis for it with which I am acquainted is that our lives belong not to us, but to God.[5] Be this as it may, to locate the basis of murder in the violation of a third party's property rights is surely to travel a long way from the concept's "central idea."

IV

When does genuine and reasonable mistake about right and wrong ("moral error") exonerate? That very legal-like question I take to be the main problem raised by Miss Anscombe in her paper, but she poses it as a problem not

---

[5] See the section on "Homicide" in the *Catholic Encyclopedia*, ed. Charles Herbermann et al., 16 vols. (New York: Robert Appleton Co., 1907-1914).

for the courts, but rather for philosophers "when we turn to morality." In the light of our heuristic principle, however, we might well look first to the law where precisely analogous problems concerning ignorance as an excuse are raised for the courts.

There are two anciently received doctrines on these matters in the criminal law: ignorance of fact, when honest and reasonable, does excuse; ignorance of law, *even when honest and reasonable*, does not excuse. That ignorance of fact exonerates has seemed to most jurists a self-evident expression of the requirements of justice. The wife who gives her husband poison honestly believing it to be his medicine (the druggist having carelessly switched the labels) does not intentionally poison her husband. We say of such a person that, had the facts been as she honestly and reasonably believed, her act would have been legal and proper; therefore, out of fairness to her (not to mention the freedom from anxiety of us all), she should be exonerated.

Why should the matter be at all different if the ignorance or mistake was about the law? Surely, if we consider the matter solely from the position of justice to the individual defendant, then the distinction between ignorance of fact and ignorance of law (which is, after all, simply one species of factual ignorance) has no point. Honest and reasonable mistakes about law are possible and frequent, and perhaps even unavoidable. Lawyers have been known to give mistaken readings of law to their clients, and even judges (since they are liable to be overruled by other judges) make such mistakes. When these errors occur, we can say of the unwitting lawbreaker that, had the law been as he honestly and reasonably believed, his act would have been perfectly legal; therefore, out of fairness to him, he should be exonerated.

Those who have argued for the traditional maxim that ignorance of the law does not excuse have always in effect given apologies for disregarding the claims of justice. Pascal and Holmes found the rationale for the rule in the undesirability of providing citizens with a motive for remaining ignorant of the law. Others have argued for the rule in different ways, but in almost every instance the appeal is to an overriding rule of "public policy" or to such practical considerations as ease or difficulty of establishing evidence, delay or expedition of trials, and the need to publicize legal rights when not known or to vindicate them when not appreciated.

Now, for contrast, let us turn to the moral version of the problem, focusing our attention on the "moral crime" of murder. Does the man who kills under the honest and reasonable but mistaken conviction that he is doing right commit murder? In law this would be a question of policy: should we adopt a rule permitting such an excuse? In a criminal court it is clear what issue rides on the question. If moral ignorance or mistake does exonerate, then a certain kind of defendant will not be punished, and we can argue the question, at least in part, by considering our purposes in punishing and how they might be furthered or hindered by the adoption of the controversial criterion of exoneration. (Clearly, the law cannot accept honest moral conviction as an excuse, for to do so would be not only to encourage "moral ignorance" in bad faith but also to exclude from the scope of the law some classes of persons, such as paramour killers and dutiful vengeance seekers, whom the law is most concerned to deter.) When we turn to the moral version of the question, however, no issue of punishment, no question of public policy, no clear practical upshot rides on our "verdict." But until we know what issue hinges on our judgment, it is difficult to know what judgment to make or even how to go on reasoning about the matter.

Miss Anscombe's example of the problem is that of

> . . . the public executioner who has private knowledge of a condemned man's innocence. In some way he knows he cannot make use of it to get the man off; and he is to execute him. The man had a fair trial. The question is whether it is, morally

speaking, an act of murder for the executioner, at the command of his superiors, to perform his office in these circumstances. Doctors have disagreed about this. It is clearly a very difficult question.

Miss Anscombe has us suppose that there is a right decision for the executioner to make and also suppose, for the sake of the argument merely, that in executing the prisoner the executioner makes the wrong decision but makes it out of genuine moral conviction after much conscientious deliberation. Granting all these assumptions, the question then is whether the executioner is, "morally speaking," a murderer.

I certainly do not wish to suggest that this is a silly question on its face, for several plausible interpretations of it spring immediately to mind. My strategy will be rather to tick off these plausible interpretations of the question and then show in each case that it cannot be what Miss Anscombe intended in asking it, thus raising the presumption that she has committed the Legalistic Mistake.

First of all, the question *can* be taken as asking "Shall we condemn the executioner by *calling* him (to his face or behind his back) 'murderer'?" As we have seen, the word "murder" bears a general nontechnical sense of "the most wicked kind of killing"; hence it is suited, as few words are, to blacken a man's reputation. So interpreted, the question is a rough analogue to the legal question "Shall we *punish* him?" But in the legal case there exist definite rules sharply delimiting the discretion of officials to decide on their own; in the moral case we are free to decide according to our own lights. Given that the man wrongly killed, should we call him a nasty name ("swine"! "rat"! "murderer"!) for it? The answer, I should think, is "Only if some good can be achieved thereby." Of course, calling him a vile name, in relieving us of aggressive emotions, may make us, or some of us, feel better—here each person must consult his own feelings—but it would be likely only to hurt, outrage, or alienate the well-intentioned executioner, or perhaps even fortify him in his erroneous convictions, without teaching him or anyone else any kind of valuable moral lesson.

The question may, however, ask not whether we should *call* the executioner a murderer, not whether his act was hateful enough to be called a vile name, but rather whether we should *judge* him to be a murderer, irrespective of whether we should have or voice certain feelings toward him. Should we *think of him* as a mistakenly conscientious lawful killer simply, or should we *think of him* as a murderer? Or is to think of him the one way *eo ipso* to think of him the other? This latter interpretation, I feel sure, brings us closer to the question Miss Anscombe intended; but it now becomes very difficult to know what this moral question in legal language is asking. Difficult, but not impossible; for if the question so interpreted makes sense, then presumably it makes contact at some point with its legal analogue, which clearly *does* pose a question for exact judgment. What I am suggesting here is only that in explaining the meaning of the question we must refer to something legal-like: to ideal law, or higher law, or inner law, or to some such conception. And thus to answer the question we must employ reasons of the same general kind as those deemed relevant in courts and legislatures.

Perhaps, then, the question asks whether the executioner's conduct *ought* to count for murder in the legal sense (granting that it does not in our legal system, where obedience to superior orders completely exculpates). This is a familiar use of legal-like language outside of legal contexts, namely, to voice the claim that "there ought to be a law." So interpreted, the question invites us to place ourselves in some ideal legislature and decide whether behavior of the sort ascribed to the fictitious executioner should be *made* a crime. If this is our problem, we have more alternatives to consider than murder or innocence. If we decide, as ideal legislators, to make the knowing execution of an innocent man a form of criminal homicide, we can call it murder or manslaughter, first or second degree murder, or voluntary or involuntary manslaughter; or we can invent a name for it, as the names "abortion," "infanticide," "suicide," and "genocide" were invented to denote actions all of which are (or have been) crimes distinct from murder.

This interpretation renders the question meaningful, but not difficult; for the legislation it asks us to consider plainly could serve no socially useful purpose. Occasionally the new law would force a timorous executioner to resign, but he would simply be replaced by another man, and condemned prisoners, guilty or not, would continue to be executed one way or another. If the penalty attached to the new law were sufficiently severe, moreover, it might make the office of executioner difficult to fill, perhaps forcing the state to raise the salaries of executioners to compensate them for their risk. At worst, it might prevent the execution of prisoners who have been consigned to death by due process of law, thus leading the law to work against its own purposes by giving with one hand what it has taken away with the other.

Other interpretations, each stressing points of analogy with a legal model, are possible. The question *could* ask, for example, whether the executioner stands convicted of murder before the inner court, or "court of conscience." But this is not likely a plausible interpretation either, for we cannot try him before *our* courts of conscience, and by the very terms of the problem, he stands acquitted before his own inner court. Nor is it likely that the question concerns Divine Justice, since it would seem impious even to suggest that a Divine Criminal Law would keep its statutes so hidden and obscure that the most learned doctors differ over what they are, and then would punish obedient and well-meaning men for doing what they think the law requires. And one wonders what would be the point of Divine Punishment of morally mistaken civil executioners if not attended with publicity, for it could not by itself guide future conscientious but perplexed executioners in similar circumstances.

There are still other possible interpretations exploiting some part of the network of analogies to the legal situation in its full institutional complexity. "Morally speaking," a man might be a murderer in the sense that, were evidence available to a jury that is in fact or even in principle unavailable, then he would be convicted of murder, or in the sense that he is "no better than a murderer," luckier perhaps because what he intended did not come to fruition or because, unknown to him, he had legal license to kill. The sheriff who, having no knowledge of any sentence of death having been pronounced, takes "the life of his prisoner for some unlawful purpose of his own," when all the while "there existed unknown to him, a mandate for him to execute that man on that very day,"[6] while not legally speaking a murderer (since he has committed no criminal act), is nevertheless "morally speaking a murderer" in this latter sense. The same could hardly be maintained, however, about Miss Anscombe's executioner. My tentative conclusion, then, is that, although there are numerous interpretations that make sense out of Miss Anscombe's question, none of them seems to be faithful to her intentions in asking it, since she characterized her question as difficult, and on all of these interpretations it is easy.

The final way of interpreting the question avoids all analogies to a legal model and mentions no ideal, inner, or higher law, or the like. This is the interpretation which, it seems to me, commits the Legalistic Mistake. The question so interpreted asks whether murder can be imputed to the executioner, but its concern is not imputation for the sake of punishment, for blackening a name, applying a rule, or vindicating a social policy, but rather simply *imputation* for its own sake. In the typical legal context, as we have seen, and even in "moral" (that is, noninstitutional) contexts where blame is an informal analogue of punishment or where practical issues of apology or reparation are involved, we must also consider imputability, but always with one eye cocked on the liabilities at stake, for the sake of which the inquiry is undertaken. One commits the Legalis-

6 R. M. Perkins, "The Law of Homicide," *Journal of Criminal Law and Criminology,* 36 (1946), 409.

tic Mistake when one would ignore the uses of imputation, keeping both eyes firmly on what one takes to be the facts. The trouble is that the "facts" when stared at so intently tend to fade out of view, like desert mirages.

V

The question about the executioner may seem proper and puzzling because there is a difficult problem of moral appraisal raised by his case that has nothing to do with the law or anything legal-like. In acting on his mistaken moral judgment, the executioner was at fault, and the fault accurately reveals a defect of character—poor moral judgment in some respects—which counts against a man in a final appraisal. Conscientiousness, on the other hand, is clearly a virtue. Now if we are to sum up the man's whole character in a single overall appraisal, and for no immediate practical purpose, but rather "for the record" only, how shall we rate him?

The puzzlement that generated this question would be ill served by the legal terminology. Given that the executioner was *at fault* in killing his victim, and perhaps even therefore *to blame* for the death, it still does not follow that he is, in some strange moral sense, *guilty* of murder, or indeed that he is guilty of anything at all. There are far more kinds of fault and merit than guilt and innocence. And that is the main disadvantage of the legal terminology when wrenched from the contexts that give it its point—it forces us to say guilty or innocent, with no ifs or buts allowed, just conviction or acquittal. If we must make moral appraisals "for the record only," then we can draw our terminology from more promising sources than the courtroom. Even the language of the marketplace would be more suitable; for finally appraising a man is much more like assessing a piece of property than like coming to a forced verdict. What we should ask is "How high a *value* are we to place on a man, given that he is loyal to his mistaken convictions?," which is very much like asking "What assessment should we make of this house, given that it has a firm foundation but a leaky roof?" It would not help to say "Firm foundation notwithstanding, a house with a leaky roof stands forever convicted of dampness." Nor does it help to say "Conscientiousness is no excuse; the man stands forever convicted of murder."

What we should say is: "It is to the credit of the house that it has a firm foundation, but a serious fault that it has a leaky roof. Fortunately, the respect in which the house is strong is more important than that in which it is weak, for roofs are more easily repaired than foundations." (Or we might say, if we lived in rainless Arizona, that a leaky roof is a very small flaw.)

Similarly, we should say: "It is to the credit of the man that he acts conscientiously and a defect in him that he has poor moral judgment in some respects." Nothing more need be said. Indeed, nothing more should be said, if we are speaking for the record simply, with no further purpose immediately in mind. Which is the more important, the virtue or the flaw, depends on the purposes of those who will consult the record—the historical understanding they wish to acquire or the lessons they wish to teach—or perhaps the uses to which they wish to put the man himself—hiring, marrying, trusting. If we are recruiting men for a trip to the North Pole, we shall rightly regard it as a very small defect in a man that he has an inherited vulnerability to malaria, whereas that would be all-important if we were seeking workers to drain the Asian jungles. The case, I think, is the same with moral excellences and defects: there is no rational way of toting them up and balancing them off apart from our various and divergent practical purposes. Judgments of credit and fault can be made part of a man's "moral record," but overall final appraisals must depend on the record's *use*.

4

Justice and Personal Desert

What is it to deserve something? This guileless question can hardly fail to trouble the reflective person who ponders it. Yet until its peculiar perplexities are resolved, a full understanding of the nature of justice is impossible, for surely the concepts of justice and desert are closely connected. This essay has as its ulterior purpose the illumination of that connection; its direct aim is analysis of the concept of personal desert.

The phrase "personal desert" is no pleonasm. Many kinds of things other than persons are commonly said to be deserving. Art objects deserve admiration; problems deserve careful consideration; bills of legislation deserve to be passed. Although such statements are not wholly unrelated to questions about justice, they are less central than statements about the deserts of persons and will not be considered here. Nor shall we consider statements construing natural events as deserts, such as "The villain crushed in the landslide got what he deserved." Persons are in this manner often held to deserve things other than treatment at the hands of their fellows; but this essay will be concerned only with personal desert of other-personal bestowals.

On those rare occasions when personal-desert statements are discussed by philosophers, they are often held to stand in some close logical connection to rules, or they are explicated in terms of rights and obligations;[1] and when philos-

[1] For two apparent examples in recent literature, see S. I. Benn and R. S. Peters, *Social Principles and the Democratic State* (London: George Allen & Unwin, 1959), 137: " 'Desert' is a normative word; its use presupposes a rule . . ."; and D. D. Raphael, *Moral Judgment* (London: George Allen & Unwin, 1955), 77: "Our conclusion then is

ophers themselves make judgments about personal deserts, the deserved modes of treatment they have in mind are almost invariably punishment and rewards.[2] The following schematic analysis will suggest, on the contrary, that desert is a "natural" moral notion (that is, one which is not logically tied to institutions, practices, and rules); that it represents only a part, and not necessarily the most important part, of the domain of justice;[3] and that reward and punishment are only two among the several irreducibly distinct modes of treatment persons are said to deserve. The first section of the essay deals with some generic aspects of desert, particularly its relations to rules and to the rule-connected concept of qualification and the relation between desert statements and reasons. Then, since further analysis of personal desert depends on what mode of treatment is said to be deserved, the second section examines some of the generic modes of deserved treatment. The final section discusses the relation between desert and social utility as well as some of the unfortunate consequences of treating personal desert as a kind of "moral entitlement."

I

Desert propriety. To say that a person deserves something is to say that there is a certain sort of propriety in his having it. But this is also true of the statements that he is eligible for, qualified for, or entitled to something, that he has a claim on it or a right to it, or simply that he ought

---

that the concept of desert . . . is a way of speaking of the presence or absence of an obligation in special circumstances."

[2] For example, John Hospers, in his *Human Conduct: An Introduction to the Problems of Ethics* (New York: Harcourt, Brace and World, 1961), considers the topic "justice and desert" under two headings, "reward" (433-451) and "punishment" (451-468); and Austin Duncan-Jones, who devotes an entire chapter to "desert" in his sensitive discussion of Butler in *Butler's Moral Philosophy* (Harmondsworth: Penguin Books, 1952), discusses the concept exclusively in connection with punishment.

[3] For the contrasting view, see Hospers, *op.cit.*, 433: "Justice is getting what one deserves; what could be simpler?"

to have it. Our first task, then, is to characterize the particular kind of propriety distinctive of desert. This may be most effectively done by contrasting it with other forms of propriety.

Consider first what it means to be "eligible" for something. According to *Webster's*, a person is eligible when he is "fitted or qualified to be chosen," when he is "legally or morally suitable." Eligibility is a kind of minimal qualification, a state of not being disqualified. We discover whether a person is eligible for some office or employment, prize, or reward by determining whether he satisfies certain eligibility conditions as specified by a rule or regulation. For example, to be eligible for varsity athletics, one needs a medical certificate, better than a C average, and at least sophomore standing; to be eligible for the presidency of the United States, one must be thirty-five or older and a "natural-born" citizen.

Eligibility is one kind of qualification: satisfaction of some important preliminary necessary condition. Another kind of qualification, equally rule-connected, is satisfaction of a sufficient condition for, say, an office or prize. So, for example, in this sense a man qualifies for the presidency of the United States by winning a majority of the electoral votes, or for first place in the hundred-yard dash by crossing the finish line before his competitors. Anyone who qualifies in this strong sense can claim the office or the prize as his *right*; according to the rules he is entitled to it.

I think it clear that qualification in neither of these senses is the same as desert. There are millions of persons eligible to be president who do not deserve to be, and it is often plausible and always intelligible to say that the man in fact elected president did not deserve to be. To deserve something, one must be qualified in still a third sense: one must satisfy certain conditions of worthiness which are written down in no legal or official regulation. Thus to be "truly qualified" for the presidency, a person must be intelligent, honest, and fair-minded; he must have a program which is really good for the country and the tact and guile to make it effective. Any candidate who satisfies these and similar conditions to a degree greater than his rivals deserves to be president. But these conditions are not requirements specified by some rule in the sense of authoritative, public, sanctioned regulation, or in the sense of "canon," or in the sense of "rule of procedure." At best they are the conditions "required" by the private standards or principles of a sensitive voter.[4]

In respect to modes of treatment which persons can deserve, then, we can distinguish three kinds of conditions. There are those whose satisfaction confers eligibility ("eligibility conditions"), those whose satisfaction confers entitlement ("qualification conditions"), and those conditions not specified in any regulatory or procedural rules whose satisfaction confers worthiness or desert ("desert bases").

Desert bases. If a person is deserving of some sort of treatment, he must, necessarily, be so *in virtue of* some possessed characteristic or prior activity. It is because no one can deserve anything unless there is some basis or ostensible occasion for the desert that judgments of desert carry with them a commitment to the giving of reasons. One cannot say, for example, that Jones deserves gratitude although he has done "nothing in particular." If a person says that Jones deserves gratitude, then he must be prepared to answer the question "For what?" Of course, he may not know the basis of Jones's desert, but if he denies that there is any basis, then he has forfeited his right to use the terminology of desert. He can still say that we *ought* to treat Jones well for "no reason in particular" or simply "for the sake of being nice," but it is absurd to say that Jones *deserves* good treatment for no reason in particular. Desert without a basis is simply not desert.

Not any old basis will do, however. A characteristic of mine cannot be a basis for a desert of yours unless it somehow reveals or reflects some characteristic of yours. In gen-

---

[4] For a useful survey of six senses of the word "rule," see Kurt Baier, *The Moral Point of View* (Ithaca: Cornell University Press, 1958), 123-127.

eral, the facts which constitute the basis of a subject's desert must be facts about that subject.[5] If a student deserves a high grade in a course, for example, his desert must be in virtue of some fact about *him*—his earlier performances, say, or his present abilities. Perhaps his teacher *ought* to give him a high grade because it will break his neurotic mother's heart if he does not; but this fact, though it can be a reason for the teacher's action, cannot be the basis of the student's desert.[6]

There are two ways in which a judgment of desert can be infelicitous. On the one hand, it can either lack a basis altogether or else have a logically inappropriate one; on the other hand, it may simply be false or incorrect. To put the point another way, either the judgment may lack an appropriate "basal reason,"[7] or the basal reason may not be a justifying reason. The claim that a person deserves to be beaten up "just for the hell of it" lacks any basal reason; in fact, a basis is explicitly denied. The claim that a mother's mental health is the basis of a student's desert puts forth a logically inappropriate basal reason. Both of these claims egregiously misuse the word "deserve." Not only do they lack good reasons (justifying ones), but they lack the right kind of reason and are as offensive to sense as to morals.[8]

[5] This appears to hold true of such nonpersonal subjects as art objects, problems, and bills of legislation as well as of persons.

[6] The basis of desert may be a complex relational fact, but in that case the subject must be a party to the relation. The basis of desert cannot be wholly separate from the subject. To suppose otherwise is probably to confuse a basis of desert with any sufficient condition for it. It may follow, for example, from the fact that God wills that a person be punished that he deserves to be punished. Reference to God's will is then a reason purporting to justify a desert claim; but it does nothing whatever to identify the basis of the alleged desert. God's will could be a *ratio cognoscendi* of some persons's desert, but not its *ratio essendi*.

[7] I borrow this useful term from George Pitcher, "On Approval," *The Philosophical Review*, 67 (1958), 198ff.

[8] For a number of inadvertent examples of "logically inappropriate" reasons for desert judgments, the reader might well consult Hospers, *op.cit.*, 440-442. He discusses there the question of just wages and salaries, which he regards as "rewards." He then seriously treats need as a criterion for the just distribution of income, as if anyone

On the other hand, the frequent contention that ability per se is a desert basis for reward commits neither of these mistakes; it cites the right kind of reason for desert, namely, a fact about the person. In my opinion, however, it is not a good reason, although this is admittedly a notoriously controversial question involving the conflict of rival value systems, a question not easily settled.

A logically inappropriate basis for a person's deserving some mode of treatment may, of course, be a relevant and even a conclusive reason in support of the judgment that he ought to be given that mode of treatment. "Ought" judgments sometimes have a certain finality about them; we say that S ought to get X "all things considered" or "in the final judgment." On the other hand, they often have a quite different force. When we have not had time to survey all the relevant reasons, when we are unable to strike a balance, or simply when we are generalizing about classes of cases, we are likely to use the word "ought" in a *ceteris paribus* or *pro tanto* sense. We say that S ought to get X "other things being equal" or insofar as some one kind of reason among many has bearing on the situation. That a subject deserves X entails that he ought to get X in the *pro tanto* sense of "ought," but not in the "all things considered" or "on balance" sense. This is simply another way of saying that a person's desert of X is always a reason for giving X to him, but not always a conclusive reason, that considerations irrelevant to his desert can have overriding cogency in establishing how he ought to be treated on balance.

---

could seriously contemplate rewarding (as opposed to compensating) anyone for his needs! The author, after considering achievement, effort, ability, and need as proposed criteria of desert, writes: "Thus far, all our criteria have had to do with the worker or what he can produce. Further suggestions, however, may come from another quarter: *criteria may be found having nothing to do with the worker* but with the society in which he lives" (my italics). Hospers then considers the open market," "public need," and "public desire for the product of one's labor" as alleged bases of a worker's desert. These considerations, of course, are quite pertinent to the question of what a worker ought to be paid (all things considered), but they are wholly irrelevant to the question of his desert.

We have yet to give a complete account of the requisite character of desert bases. It is necessary that a person's desert have a basis and that the basis consist in some fact about himself, but neither of these conditions is sufficient. They do not, for example, exclude need as a desert basis for reward or ignorance as a desert basis for punishment. Both seem inappropriate, and yet they are, after all, facts about the deserving subject. It is impossible, however, to list the necessary and sufficient conditions for personal desert in the abstract, for the bases of desert vary with the mode of deserved treatment. Here we have had to content ourselves with pointing out a few important generic properties of desert which do not vary from context to context.

II

A philosophical analysis of the concept of desert can go no further without paying separate attention to each of the major kinds of treatment which persons can be said to deserve. For if we consider the schema "S deserves X in virtue of F," where S is a person, X a mode of treatment, and F some fact about S, it is clear that the values of F (the various desert bases) are determined in part by the nature of the various X's in question. What makes a man deserving of a high grade in a mathematics course, for instance, is not identical to that which makes him deserving of unemployment compensation.

What are the various kinds of treatment that persons deserve from other persons? They are varied, but they have at least one thing in common: they are generally "affective" in character, that is, favored or disfavored, pursued or avoided, pleasant or unpleasant. The deserved object must be something generally regarded with favor or disfavor even if, in some particular case, it is regarded with indifference by a person said to deserve it. If we were all perfect stoics, if no event were ever more or less pleasing to us than any other, then there would be no use for the concept of desert.

The varieties of deserved treatment are many, and they are heterogeneous to a degree not usually appreciated. For the sake of convenience and with no claim to taxonomic precision or completeness, I have divided them into five major classes and then grouped these under two generic headings. The five classes are as follows:

1. Awards of prizes
2. Assignments of grades
3. Rewards and punishments
4. Praise, blame, and other informal responses
5. Reparation, liability, and other modes of compensation

I have not included positions of honor and economic benefits on this basic list because they are usually subsumed under one or another or some combination of the other headings. The problem of subsuming offices and honorable positions I have reserved for the end of this section, and a brief discussion of economic benefits is attached as an appendix to this essay.

The two generic headings are (1) forms of treatment that define contexts in which desert is a "polar" concept and (2) those that do not. In respect to polar desert, one can be said to deserve good or to deserve ill—reward or punishment, praise or blame, and so on. Polar desert is central to what has traditionally been called the concept of retributive justice. Nonpolar desert, on the other hand, has a different sort of symmetry. When it is a prize, an honorable office, or a grade that is in question, we divide persons not into those who deserve good and those who deserve ill, but rather into those who deserve and those who do not. Nonpolar desert is central to what philosophers have traditionally called the concept of distributive justice. Let us consider nonpolar contexts first and begin with the awarding of prizes.

Prizes. When prizes are awarded to the victors in individual and group games, races, and tournaments, in essay, cooking, or corn-husking contests, in spelling bees, and the like, they consist either of independently valuable objects or of medals, distinctions, or titles. In any case, they are taken to be tangible expressions of admiration, of "recognition" of talent, as means of honoring the victor. Only one competitor wins (barring ties); the others must lose or there can be no "distinction" attached to winning the prize. If everyone qualifies for the prize, then no one has won it, for the aim of the competition is to separate the best from the others.

Although the concept of desert seems at home in this context, there appears to be no use for the concept of ill desert, or at any rate ill desert and no desert come to the same thing. Either a contestant deserves the prize or he does not; there is no further alternative of deserving ill, no analogue of punishment. Moreover, since desert is here distinguished from mere worthiness,[9] there are no degrees of desert. If the prize rightly went to Green, we can say that Jones came closer to deserving it than Smith, but not that he deserved it more than Smith, for neither deserved it.

Among the various rules which govern games, tournaments, and contests are those which specify the basis of the competition (throwing the javelin, baking a cake, writing an essay) and the conditions to be satisfied by the winner. The latter, which may be called "victory conditions," represent the form taken by qualifying conditions in competitive contexts. They vary from those which allow the victor to be determined with mathematical precision (as in broad-jumping, spelling bees, and races) to those that leave wide scope for interpretation and judgment, as in essay contests or

[9] It is only in respect to competitive prizes that we commonly distinguish desert and worthiness; elsewhere they are usually synonymous. Two or more men might deserve punishment for the same crime or reward for the same achievement, and the same is true of grades, praise and blame, and compensation. To be worthy of and to deserve, in these contexts, seem to amount to the same thing. But in certain competitive situations there may be many worthy of the same prize but only one who deserves it, namely, the most worthy. When worthiness and desert are distinguished in this way, worthiness is to desert very much as eligibility is to the strong sense of qualification.

cake-baking competitions. The basis of the competition is always some sort of skill or other esteemed trait.[10] If it were not, then, like lotteries and raffles, the activity might still be a kind of game, but not a competitive one.

The general distinction between desert bases and qualifying conditions applies clearly to competitive situations. The desert basis is always preeminent possession of the skill singled out as a basis of competition, whereas the qualifying condition is satisfaction of the victory condition specified by the rules. The distinction is often obscured, however, by our tendency in competitive situations to use the word "desert" in two ways—not only in its customary sense of "worthiness" but also for "qualification." Even when this happens, though, our important distinction is reintroduced in new language: deserving a prize is distinguished from deserving to win a prize. In a contest of skill in which the winner can be determined by exact measurement, such as a high-jumping contest, there can be no question of who deserves the prize (qualification). It is deserved by the contestant who has demonstrably satisfied the condition of victory, in this case by jumping in the prescribed way the highest distance off the ground. There might still be controversy, however, over who deserved to win. To be sure, the victor deserved the prize, but who deserved to be victor? Perhaps the man who truly deserved to win did not in fact win because he pulled up lame, or tore his shoe, or suffered some other unforeseeable stroke of bad luck. In a contest of skill the man who deserves to win is the man who is most skilled, but (because of luck) he is not in every case the man who does win.[11]

In a contest of skill whose rules specify a condition of victory which cannot be determined with precision but which is at least in part a matter of judgment, such as a beauty

10 Typically the basis of a competitive contest, as opposed to a game of chance, is skill; but as D. D. Raphael points out, the basis of a mere beauty contest is neither skill nor chance (in the manner of a lottery). See his review in *Philosophical Books*, 5 (1964), 7.

11 Hence the ritual utterance "May the better man win" is not merely a pious, optative tautology.

pageant or an essay contest, there can be controversy both over who deserves the prize (that is, who satisfied the imprecise victory conditions) and who deserved to win (that is, who is the most worthy or skilled at the basis of competition). If the prize is awarded to a person who does not deserve it (that is, did not qualify for it), then it is either because the judge is venal or because he erred in applying the victory criteria to the facts. Moreover, there are several possible grounds for maintaining that the person who deserves the prize is not the person who deserved to win it. The latter may have had bad luck or an off day, or the victory conditions written into the rules might themselves have been ill chosen, not truly gauging excellence at the skill which is the ostensible basis for the competition.[12]

In a game of chance, finally, such as a lottery or a game of roulette, controversy can arise only over who deserves the prize, and even here it would turn only on relatively trivial matters of fact, for the satisfaction of the victory conditions specified by the rules of such games is usually determinable with precision. In a game of chance one cannot speak of who "really deserved to win"—that is, who has the most skill at that sort of thing—for, *ex hypothesi*, no skill is involved. Here we would all gain in clarity if we resolved to use only the legalistic language of qualification and entitlement and not speak of desert at all.

Grades. The nonpolar concept of desert finds application not only in formalized competitive situations but also in contexts calling for assessment of skill or quality generally. Following J. O. Urmson,[13] I shall call such contexts "grading situations." The point of grading, unlike that of awarding prizes, is not to express any particular attitude toward its object, but simply to make as accurate as possible an appraisal of the degree to which it possesses some skill or quality. The desert basis of a grade is the actual pos-

---

[12] Perhaps the girl who "really deserved" to win the Miss America contest failed because the rules gives too much importance to the bathing suit ratings and too little to poise and talent.

[13] "On Grading," in A.G.N. Flew (ed.), *Logic and Language (Second Series)* (Oxford: Basil, Blackwell, 1953).

session to the appropriate degree of the quality assessed.

There are various formal procedures for grading qualities, each involving its own criteria or qualifying conditions for each grade. In the case of most human qualities which we try to grade by formal criteria (of course, there are many which we could not hope to grade that way), and especially skills and abilities, the formal grading procedure takes the form of a test. Performance on the test then establishes qualification, in the sense of entitlement for some grade, in a manner dictated by rules.

It is not essential to a grading situation that the concept of desert have a positive-negative symmetry, and for that reason I have characterized the concept when applied in such contexts as "nonpolar"; but, of course, a relatively crude system of grading can utilize a polar concept of desert. If we are concerned to divide our apples into only two groups, those which are edible and those which are not, for example, we can speak of all the apples in the unsorted pile as deserving either the good or the bad grade. Most grading situations, however, involve a much greater range of alternatives. Some systems for grading students, for example, allow the use of each of the first one hundred positive integers as grading labels. Here there is a whole continuum of deserts; in other situations there are triads or quintets of marks deserved, and rarely are there only two possibilities—"high" or "low," "good" or "bad," "passing" or "failing."

Grading human beings, however, is still more complicated than this. Human interests themselves have an essential polarity: desires are either satisfied or to some extent frustrated, ambitions fulfilled or to some degree disappointed. And since persons are concerned with how they and their fellows are graded, they tend by their interests to convert grading systems into systems of reward and punishment. Whatever grade an ambitious student gets, he takes it as a reassuring compliment or a slap on the wrist, for relative to his ambition it is usually something welcome or unwelcome. What especially complicates discussions of human grading is that the grades are used by the graders themselves or by others for ulterior purposes—filling positions, granting licenses and privileges, and so on—and that these further purposes are well known to those who are to be graded. But to avoid confusion we should remember that a grade as such is simply a way of ranking something—an apple or a man—in respect to some quality or skill, an appraisal which may be put to some future use or may simply be put on the record for no other purpose than to register the truth.

Rewards and punishments. We come now to contexts in which the concept of desert is essentially and necessarily polar. These are situations such that, if there is any desert at all, it must be either a good or a bad desert. The word "prize," which fits only a nonpolar concept of desert, has no antonym; neither do the grading expressions "73" or "B minus." But the responses which persons are said to deserve in polar contexts come in neat contrasting pairs—reward and punishment, compensation and liability, charge and credit, praise and blame—one word in each pair standing for a mode of response presumably either pleasant or unwelcome. The similarity here to the nonpolar contexts of competition and grading is only partial and contingent. Failure to win a prize or a grade of C minus might be unpleasant and unwelcome, but unpleasantness is not in the same way an essential part of their *raisons d'être*; suffering is an accidental and unintended consequence of competitions and gradings, not what those undertakings are for. The point of a competition is to single out a winner, not to penalize the losers; the point of a grade is to accurately appraise achievement, not (simply) to please or hurt. It is an essential and intended element of punishment, however, that the victim be made to suffer, and of liability that he be made to pay; these are not mere regrettable derivatives of the undertakings, but rather their *termini ad quem*.

Henry Sidgwick shrewdly observed that reward is "gratitude universalized" and that punishment is "resentment universalized."[14] There is little doubt that the services and deprivations which we call "rewards" and "punishments" are conventional means of expressing gratitude and resentment, for these attitudes are prototypically those involved in the "urge to reward" and the "urge to punish." Consider typical occasions for the expression of these "urges." A whole town is endangered by a plague, and one heroically diligent scientist working against long odds perfects a serum which saves the day. Is not the feeling which prompts the normal urge to reward this man precisely gratitude and the need to give it expression? And when vigilantes and lynch mobs organize to punish a murderer, are not they propelled by their resentment of what has been done? Of course, it is not up to me to feel grateful for a benefit done one stranger by another; and, according to *Webster*'s, resentment too is largely confined to responses to personal injury and affront. That is why Sidgwick defined punishment and reward as resentment and gratitude "universalized." Originating in private feelings and reactions, they become social devices for sharing imaginatively in the resentment and gratitude of all victims and beneficiaries.

Important as Sidgwick's insight is, however, it is not the whole truth about the "expressive functions" of reward and punishment. Gratitude and resentment are the most noticeable, probably the most common, and almost certainly the original attitudes expressed by reward and punishment, but they are no longer the only ones. In fact, they are probably not even necessary. If an entire community, for example, adopted the cold-blooded Kantian attitude toward punishment, approving of it only because it vindicates the moral law and eschewing altogether any personal resentment toward criminals, the result would no doubt still be recognizable as punishment, although in no sense could it be said to "express" public resentment. And the father who rewards

14 *The Methods of Ethics*, 7th edn. (London: Macmillan & Co., 1963), Book III, Ch. 5.

his small son with a quarter for bringing home a good report card is hardly expressing his gratitude; after all, *he* is not the beneficiary of some service.[15]

Rewards are, then, as Sidgwick realized, conventionally recognized means of expressing gratitude for services rendered. But they are also, as Sidgwick did not realize, means of expressing recognition, appreciation, or approval of merit or excellence. Similarly, punishment is a standard vehicle for the expression of resentment of injury received and also (but perhaps much less commonly) for the expression of recognition and disapproval of evil.[16] The word

[15] Moreover, as reward and punishment become attached to highly specialized statutes defining technical "offenses" and "services," they tend to become highly impersonal. Parking tickets and bounties for wildcat skins have neither their origin nor their function in the venting of personal feelings; their job is simply to help oil the social machinery or, to switch the metaphor, to keep the social traffic moving.

[16] In the difference between resentment and disapproval lies the basis of the difference between (angry) vengeance and (righteous) retribution. Both vindictive and retributive punishment can be distinguished from mere penalties or "regulative sanctions," however, in that they can plausibly be taken to express public or authoritative attitudes of some kind or other.

That the expression of either resentment or some form of reprobation is an essential ingredient in what is called "punishment" is widely acknowledged by legal writers, but it has been largely ignored in recent philosophical discussions, even those purporting to give explicit definitions of punishment. One legal writer is quoted in Prof. Henry M. Hart's "The Aims of the Criminal Law," *Law and Contemporary Problems*, 23 (1958), 401, as follows: "It is the expression of the community's hatred, fear, or contempt for the convict which alone characterizes physical hardship as punishment." Professor Hart adds his own definition of punishment as (in part) "a formal and solemn pronouncement of the moral condemnation of the whole community. . . ." Lord Denning, in the *Report of the Royal Commission on Capital Punishment*, speaks of punishment as "the emphatic denunciation by the community of a crime." Among the minority of philosophers in recent decades who have made reprobative expressiveness essential to punishment are E. F. Carritt, who wrote in *The Theory of Morals* (London: Oxford University Press, 1928), 111, that "the essential thing in punishment . . . is not pain, but the expression of censure, which is necessarily painful," and Morris R. Cohen, who wrote in *Reason and Law* (Glencoe: The Free Press, 1950), 50, that "we may look upon punishment as a form of communal expression. . . . By and large such expression of disapproval is deterrent. But deterrence here is secondary. Expression is primary."

"recognition" deserves a brief comment. When the father paid his son a quarter, he acknowledged his son's achievement without necessarily feeling joy, gratitude, or any other emotion. His reward was tangible and public evidence of his acknowledgment; is testified to his recognition. Note that "testimonial dinners" are so called because they manifest the public recognition of the achievements of the recipient; they "testify" to his virtues.[17] On some theories, at least, punishment, *mutatis mutandis*, does the same sort of thing.

The responsive attitudes typically expressed by reward and punishment—gratitude, appreciation, approval, "recognition," resentment, disapproval, condemnation—and indeed all the attitudes and responses expressed by deserved modes of treatment have an important characteristic in common. It is essential to all that they have a kind of phenomenological target, that they be felt in virtue of something. All of these states of mind or attitudes contain as introspectible elements their own ostensible occasions. To resent someone, for example, is not merely to dislike him, but to have a negative feeling toward him in virtue of something he has done, and what follows the "in virtue of" is as much a part of the feeling as is its unfriendly or aggressive character.

These attitudes are not mere automatic responses to stimuli, but self-conscious responses to desert bases, not mere "reactions to," but "requitals for." If a person asks "What for?" in reply to a declaration that the speaker resents him (or is grateful to him), he does not mean "For what purpose?" These feelings are not the sorts of things that can have purposes. Rather, he means "In return for what injury [or service]?" So interpreted, the question is always pertinent. These attitudes, then, have ostensible desert logi-

17 Cf. A. C. Ewing: "It is not merely that we think the good ought to be happy but that we think they ought to be recognized or manifested as good, and the most impressive form of recognition is by bestowal of the means to happiness." *The Morality of Punishment* (London: Kegan Paul, Trench, Trubner & Co., 1929), 128.

cally built in to them. We do not use such words as "resent" and "grateful" unless there is an ostensible desert basis of the logically appropriate sort for our feeling. We can be fond of a person for no apparent reason, but we cannot be grateful "for nothing at all"; we can feel hostility for no apparent reason, but we cannot resent someone for "no reason at all." Bradley, in a famous line, wrote that punishment without desert is not punishment.[18] This seems to me to be wrong; but it is clear, I think, that resentment without an ostensible desert basis is not resentment. The point that emerges is that the attitudes in question are all felt as deserved; they cannot be freely or gratuitously bestowed or deliberately entertained "in the public interest" or "for utilitarian reasons" without any further basis. And the impossibility is not merely psychological. We can, after all, artificially induce baseless anger. But if we could do the same with resentment, it would not be resentment. We would have to call it something else.

Legal punishment and official rewards are tied up in rules and regulations, offices and functions, duties and prerogatives; they are formalized and institutionalized to an extent not even suggested by a mere concern with the attitudes they typically express. Punishment, after all, consists of such treatment as forcible seizure of property, incarceration, and whipping—never the mere feeling of resentment; and reward is the tangible expression of gratitude or recognition—never its mere harboring. Moreover, punishment is a prerogative reserved for those with the requisite authority and then only under certain strict conditions specified by law or, in the cases of families and private organizations, by what might be called "house rules." Reward and punishment, then, like other modes of deserved treatment, have qualifying conditions as well as desert bases, and these are specified by rules and regulations and confer rights and duties.

[18] "Punishment is punishment only where it is deserved." *Ethical Studies*, 2nd edn. (London: Oxford University Press, 1927), 26-27.

Probably because private rewards, unlike "private punishments," are harmless and even benign in their social consequences, governments rarely administer programs of reward on a large scale. Most government grants are either utilitarian inducements and subsidies or compensations. Rewards are, however, given by a large variety of private individuals and groups for a large variety of (basal) reasons, so there is no easy way of generalizing about their qualifying conditions. These are usually determined by criteria of excellence reflecting the values of the conferring groups or, when they are directly analogous to punishments, are reserved for acts of daring or self-sacrificing heroism. A person can be entitled to a reward he does not deserve, or deserving of a reward he has not qualified for. An informer who, from the basest motives, betrays his brother is entitled to the advertised reward, but he surely does not deserve it. The wife who sacrifices all to nurse her hopelessly invalid husband through endless tortuous years until death deserves a reward, but unless she qualifies under some set of institutional rules, she may not be entitled to one; she may not even be eligible for one.

It is much easier to generalize about punishment, or at least legal punishment. Its universal qualifying condition is expressible in two words, namely, "legal guilt." What legal guilt is itself is a far more complex matter, defined by thick and ponderous rule books. It is consequent on conviction after a fair trial according to due process, which in turn is defined by an elaborate code of procedural rules.

Of all those modes of official treatment for which a person might qualify under some institutional rules, only punishment seems resistant to the language of rights; for unless we are philosophers in the idealist tradition, we do not as a rule say of a criminal who is "qualified" for punishment that he is entitled to it or that he has a claim or a right to it. It is tempting, if only in the interest of symmetry and conceptual tidiness, to hold that a convicted criminal has a perfect legal right to his punishment, whether he wants it or not, in quite the same sense as that in which a person who qualifies for an advertised reward has a right to it, whether he wants it or not. Perhaps the difference is simply this: a renounced right ceases, sooner or later, to be a right, and the criminal's "right" to be punished is well-nigh certain to be renounced.[19]

[19] One way of arguing for a right to be punished rests on a confusion between promising and threatening. Consider these cases: (1) When *A* promises *B* to do *X* on condition that *B* do *Y* first, and *B* does *Y*, then *A* has a duty to *B* to do *X*, from which *B* may release him if he wishes. (2) When *A*, an authority, threatens *B* to do *X* to him (not for him) in the event that *B* should first do *Y*, then when *B* does *Y*, *A* may do *X* to him if *A* pleases, in which case *B* has no power to release, as in (1), though *A* may "release" himself and not do what he threatened. (3) In punishment the situation appears more like (2) than (1), except that *A* may have no discretion under the rules. He may have a duty to punish *B* from which neither he nor *B* may effect release. In this case, to whom is his duty owed? Perhaps to his superiors who have commanded performance; perhaps to "the state"; perhaps to no one at all, in which case there is no claimant or right-holder. At any rate, if the power to release is essential to the power to claim (as is suggested by David Lyons in "Rights, Claimants, and Beneficiaries," *American Philosophical Quarterly*, 6 [1969], 174-175), then *B* is not a claimant.

In Hegel's view, punishment is a necessary condition of moral regeneration; hence any guilty moral agent, he thought, has a right to it for much the same kind of reason as a sick person has a right to the medicine that is necessary for the recovery of his health. Most criminals, however, believe neither that they are in need of moral regeneration nor that breaking up rocks in a state prison is the way to achieve such regeneration in any case. There are some special circumstances, though, in which a wrongdoer may, for one reason or another, come to want punishment for his crime. He may hunger, like Raskolnikov, for expiation and atonement; or he may prefer punishment to a mandatory and open-ended course of psychotherapy that has been imposed upon him as an alternative. If he regards himself as a competent responsible agent who has committed a crime and now regrets it, he may wish to pay for his folly and get it over with, rather than be subjected to the indignities of psychic probing and manipulation. (See Herbert Morris's astute "Persons and Punishment," *The Monist*, 52 [1968], 475-501). When the criminal feels he *needs* punishment for Hegelian or Dostoevskian reasons, or that he *wants* it or *prefers* it to the only other alternative he can realistically expect, he may request or beg for punishment; the question is whether he can demand it as his due. (Surely O. Henry's tramp who committed a misdemeanor every autumn so that he could spend the winter months well fed in a warm jail could hardly demand punishment as his right if an uncooperative judge should decide to turn him out in the cold.) There are a number of grounds on which a prisoner might wish to

Praise and blame. When we come to informal responses which have the nature of requitals but are not tied to institutional rules, the distinction between desert bases and qualifying conditions collapses. It takes no special authority to praise or blame, and anyone can admire or deplore. These modes of treatment are not restricted to such special officials as judges, referees, instructors, and welfare administrators, operating under public rules specifying invariant conditions. Consequently, praise and blame, admiration and contempt, applause and jeering, and so on, though manifestly responses persons are sometimes worthy of, are never treatments people are qualified for. Just as the winners in lotteries are entitled to their prizes but cannot be said to deserve them, so persons sometimes deserve praise or blame but are never entitled to them.

Compensation, reparation, and liability. Still another mode of treatment which persons are often said to deserve is compensation for loss or injury. We say that persons deserve compensation for harm wrongly inflicted by others, in which case it is called "redress of injury," "amends," or "reparation" and functions not only to repair the damage but also to "restore the moral equilibrium," as would an apology or expression of remorse. Reparation "sets things straight" or "gives satisfaction." But not all injuries are tortiously inflicted. Some are the results of risks voluntarily incurred in the service of others, some are unavoidable accidents, and others are the inevitably iniquitous consequences of the specialization of labor in a techno-

---

argue *for* a right to punishment. He can base the state's duty to punish wrongdoers on a tacit promise not to would-be wrongdoers (they are only threatened), but to all law-abiding citizens, a promise that the guilty will be punished for the protection of the innocent. Then, thinking of his own punishment as a benefit (for some special reason), he might make claim to it as a third-party beneficiary of a promise of the state to the people, or perhaps even as a second-party beneficiary of a noncontractual duty of the judge to punish. To support such claims would require a great deal of argument and clarification. I leave this difficult subject with the observation that no one has yet given it adequate treatment.

logically complex society. I shall reserve the term "reparation" for redress of injury and speak of "compensation" for losses which are no one's fault.

Desert of reparation for wrongful injury is, I believe, a polar concept, despite the grammatical awkwardness in speaking of its other "pole." If reparation is to be received by a victim, it would seem that it must be given by a wrongdoer; and it seems to follow that, if one person deserves to take, another deserves to give. But, of course, we do not talk that way. We no more say of a tortfeasor that he deserves to make reparation than we say of a warden that he deserves to punish. What we do say is that the wrongdoer deserves to be held liable for the harm he has caused; he deserves to be forced to compensate his innocent (or relatively innocent) victim. The other pole of deserved reparation is deserved liability.

Compensation for harm which is no assignable person's fault is, however, a different matter. The unemployed may deserve compensation for their loss, but it is not necessarily true that there is someone who deserves to be held liable for it. Workers in especially unpleasant, onerous, or hazardous jobs may deserve compensatory bonuses, but we would probably not express this claim by saying that their employers or any other assignable individuals deserve to have liability imposed on them. In short, where compensation is not the redressing of injury and, hence, where it lacks the character of the mandatory repayment of a debt, desert is nonpolar. Either the suffering innocent deserve aid and succor or they do not, and that is the end of the matter. When the moral equilibrium is not unbalanced, there is no compensatory analogue of deserved punishment.

When a person suffers a loss, it may be the fault of another person or it may be no one's fault; and, as we have seen, the nature of desert differs in the two cases. There is, however, a third possibility: the loss or injury may be his own fault. In that case, though he may well be entitled to help, we should be loath to say that he deserved it; for we do not as a rule compensate people for their folly or in-

dolence, and even when we do, it is not because we think
they deserve it. Herein lies the difference between helping
a person out of a jam simply through charitable beneficence
and giving him aid he deserves.

If reward is the tangible expression of one or more of a
small range of such appropriate attitudes as gratitude, recognition, or approval, what can proffered help be said to
express? Again, I think that our answer depends on
whether it is reparation of injury by a culpable party or
simply compensation for unforeseeable bad luck that we
are talking about. Reparation can express sympathy, benevolence, and concern, but, in addition, it is always the acknowledgment of a past wrong, a "repayment of a debt,"
and hence, like an apology, the redressing of the moral balance or the restoring of the *status quo ante culpum*. In the
case of mere compensation, it is none of these extra things.
In either case, however, the proffered help implies the recognition of a loss for which the victim himself cannot be
held wholly to blame. Thus compensation, though it is
often a conventional expression of sympathy, can never express mere pity. There is nothing pitiable about a person
who deserves help.

As in the case of all the other modes of treatment here
discussed, so too in respect to compensation and reparation
there can be desert without qualification, and vice versa.
A man may be technically entitled to unemployment compensation, for example, because his situation satisfies the
qualifying condition of a badly drawn rule, when in fact
he does not "really" deserve it; on the other hand, deserving
victims of economic blight may have "exhausted their benefits" under the law and thus fail to qualify.

Offices and positions of honor. I have listed what
seem to be the major headings, the *summa genera*, under
which the various treatments persons deserve can be
grouped. This is an important start in classifying the types
of deserved treatment generally, but it raises some nasty
problems of subsumption. Under which heading, for example, should we subsume those high offices and positions of

honor and responsibility which Sidgwick called "functions and instruments?" Are presidencies, chairmanships, generalships, professorships, papacies, and the like prizes awarded to winners in rule-governed competitions? Sidgwick thought it natural to so regard them, especially when (in his elegant words) they "are interesting and delightful in themselves, or such as are normally and properly attended with dignity and splendor of life, fame, material comfort, and freedom from sordid cares."[20] Other writers, of whom A. C. Ewing is perhaps the most prominent,[21] find it more natural to regard positions of honor as rewards, means by which gratitude or at least recognition of past achievement, service, or contribution is expressed.

Still others prefer to downgrade these aspects of honorable offices and regard them instead as positions of trust and responsibility to be filled in accordance with the criteria of present ability and future promise (what Sidgwick called "fitness" for the job and rather inaccurately characterized as a utilitarian consideration), rather than desert in either of its more familiar senses. "We certainly think it reasonable," Sidgwick admitted, "that instruments should be given to those who can use them best, and functions allotted to those who are most competent to perform them: but these may not be those who have rendered most services in the past. . . . Thus the notions of desert and fitness appear at least occasionally conflicting. . . ."[22] Fitness and desert, however, are not quite so opposed as Sidgwick maintained. Consider the situation in which officials make careful appraisals of the relevant abilities and potentialities of each candidate for a job, that is, assign a grade to the fitness of each, and then use that grade as a desert basis. There is

20 *Op.cit.*, 254.
21 This is a strong inference from his remarkably broad tentative definition of "reward" and from his interpretation of wages and salaries as rewards. See *The Morality of Punishment*, 130: ". . . our whole social system is built upon a scheme of rewards in the shape of salaries and wages"; and then, in a footnote: ". . . if . . . reward is defined as the bestowal of some good for a service rendered, they clearly come under this heading."
22 Sidgwick, *loc.cit.*

surely no logical oddness in the statement: "In virtue of his special fitness, Jones deserves the job." And if the position is a competitive one, a prize to be awarded to the winner, then fitness very likely is the basis of the competition, to be demonstrated by performance on some test, and *a fortiori* is at home with, rather than in conflict with, desert. Sidgwick saw the distinction between regarding a "function" as a reward (for past services) and as a prize (for present fitness), but he misconstrued it as a distinction between fitness and desert by preempting the concept of desert for rewards and therefore considering only past service as a desert basis.[23]

How we select our criteria of desert, then, for such modes of treatment as selection or appointment to coveted positions depends on how we conceive those positions—whether we regard them as prizes, rewards, or compensations, to mention three possibilities. To make the matter even more complicated, many positions of honor are properly subsumable under two or more of our major rubrics at once. Consider, for example, a C. P. Snow-like contest between two leading candidates for the mastership of a Cambridge college. Candidate *A* is, on the whole, more fit for the function (considered simply as a function). He is a better administrator, a tireless worker, a clever money-raiser, and has a cooler head. In view of this superior fit-

[23] It is tempting to argue that selection to fill an office, as such, is neither a reward nor a prize, but a "generic mode of treatment" in its own right, that its desert basis is Sidgwick's "fitness" and its qualifying conditions sometimes tests, sometimes selection criteria of other kinds. Then it could be argued that it is only when offices (or functions) are *also* "positions of honor," highly coveted sources of pleasure to their occupants, that the problem of subsumption and conflicting desert bases arises. On such a view, a position of honor considered *only* in its aspect as "office" or "function" has as its desert basis fitness, but insofar as it is also a coveted source of pleasure, it can be considered a prize and a reward as well, in which cases competitive skill and past contribution are relevant desert bases.

The temptation to adopt this view, however, should be resisted. An office considered simply "as such" can have nothing to do with desert and hence have *no* desert basis, for unless it is something pleasant or painful, welcomed or dreaded, the concept of desert can have no intelligible application to it.

ness, his partisans claim that he deserves the position, conceiving it as a sort of prize. Candidate B is a rather older man, past his peak in all respects, but on the basis of his previous scholarly achievement much more distinguished than A and also better liked. His partisans argue that his distinction deserves recognition and that only the mastership would be a suitable reward. One man deserves the job when it is conceived as a prize, the other deserves it in its aspect as a reward. The conflict is not desert against advantage, justice against utility, but desert against desert.

The problem can be even more complicated. Partisans of candidate A, though admitting that candidate B's scholarly achievements deserve recognition, might counter that candidate A has worked much harder for the well-being of the college and especially has won gifts and endowments for it, making possible increases in salary for each fellow; hence his past services deserve gratitude, of which the mastership would be a suitable expression. One candidate deserves reward as an expression of recognition, the other deserves reward as an expression of gratitude. And it can get still worse. B, through bad luck, had been passed over twenty years earlier, though everyone presently agrees that he deserved the job then more than did his rival. Some of his supporters argue that only his election now can redress that injury, that he deserves reparation. But partisans of A point out that A has injured his health and suffered private pecuniary losses in his efforts to bring more contributions to the college and that therefore he deserves the compensation represented by the mastership. And so it goes—desert of prize against desert of reward, gratitude against recognition, compensation against reparation.

This familiar story should be sufficient to lay to rest the philosophical myths that desert is a single factor to be weighed against other ("utilitarian") considerations in ethical decisionmaking and that it represents uniquely the claim of justice. It is high time that this simplistic account, an offspring of another period's quarrels between intuitionists and teleologists, retributionists and utilitarians, is rejected once and for all. The claims of justice are hardly exhausted in the vacuous principle that everyone ought, *ceteris paribus,* to get what he deserves. Suppose that we decide that, "all things considered," candidate *A* deserves the mastership (assuming that *that* makes sense), and then we discover that candidate *B* is *entitled* to the mastership (it was formally promised to him twenty years earlier; or a long-forgotten rule makes mandatory the selection of an entomologist for every other mastership, and he is the only entomologist in the college). Surely, we would not describe this conflict of reasons as a conflict between justice and utility. Rather, it is a conflict between desert and entitlement, between one claim of justice and another. Moreover, it seems plainly false that in *every* such ethical conflict desert has the stronger claim, that persons *always* ought, on balance, to get what they deserve.

Finally, suppose that, as they are trying to choose between *A*'s desert and *B*'s entitlement, the fellows receive a telegram from a Texas oil tycoon offering to make a gift of one million dollars to the college with no (further) strings attached, but only if they elect *A*. Now, at last, *there* is a genuine utilitarian consideration to be thrown into the balance with like considerations of profit and gain.

III

Having presented this analysis of the concept of desert, I shall conclude by briefly indicating three kinds of errors it might forestall.

Naïve utilitarianism. A utilitarian, I suppose, is anyone who is greatly impressed by the social utility of good things and in one way or another reduces the goodness to, or identifies it with, the utility. There is no doubt that the modes of treatment discussed in this essay have considerable social utility. The awarding of prizes directly promotes cultivation of the skills which constitute bases of competition and indirectly stimulates such socially valuable conditions as physical fitness, keenness, and competitive ardor. Assigning grades of various sorts to persons increases predictability, order, and control, permitting efficient allocation of men and resources. Hope of reward creates incentive to do worthy deeds, and the threat of punishment deters wrongdoing. Awards of reparation ease private resentments and promote domestic tranquility. Compensation distributes losses and handicaps more broadly and induces workers to take disagreeable but necessary jobs. So far, so good: utilitarianism has its points. It is in error only when it misconstrues the relevance of social utility.

First of all, utility is not a desert basis for any deserved mode of treatment. It follows from our analysis of desert statements that to say "S deserves X because giving it to him would be in the public interest" is simply to misuse the word "deserves." Secondly, utilitarian qualifying conditions, though not conceptually absurd, would in most cases be self-defeating. A utilitarian grading criterion, for example, could not very well do the job of a good grading criterion, namely, to allow as accurate as possible an appraisal of some skill or quality. If we are concerned to appraise a student's knowledge of mathematics, a "math exam" would surely be more useful for the purpose than a direct appeal to "utility." A utilitarianism which interprets utility as either a universal desert basis or a universal qualifying condition, then, is more than naïve; it is either absurd or self-defeating.

What is the relevance of social utility to "modes of deserved treatment"? Let us start from the beginning and work up to it. Men, or at least "reasonable men," naturally entertain certain responsive attitudes toward various actions, qualities, and achievements. They recognize and admire; they assess objectively; they are grateful and appreciative, resentful and disapproving; they feel remorse, sympathy, and concern. No part of this account, so far, has anything to do with utility. Now each of these responsive attitudes has its own appropriate kind of target. We do not "naturally" feel grateful for what we take to be injury or remorse for someone else's behavior; these are logically in-

81

congruous targets. But even when the object of the attitude is logically appropriate, it may still lack a certain kind of propriety. Glee, for example, is an inappropriate response to another's suffering, and, if some humanitarian philosophers are right, no kind of *Schadenfreude* is ever a fitting response to another's ill fortune. I am not sure how, if at all, these judgments of moral appropriateness are to be verified; but I suspect that they resemble certain aesthetic judgments—for example, that crimson and orange are clashing colors—more than they resemble judicial pronouncements —for example, that a certain person is to be punished for a crime or that a certain runner is to be awarded the prize for the hundred-yard dash.

If this is so, then the kind of propriety characteristic of personal desert is not only to be contrasted, as it was above, with qualification under a rule or regulation; it is also to be likened to, or even identified with, a kind of "fittingness" between one person's actions or qualities and another person's responsive attitudes. This view suggests in turn that responsive attitudes are the basic things persons deserve and that "modes of treatment" are deserved only in a derivative way, insofar perhaps as they are the natural or conventional means of expressing the morally fitting attitudes. Thus punishment, for example, might be deserved by the criminal only because it is the customary way of expressing the resentment or reprobation he "has coming."[24]

So long as we stay on the level of responsive attitudes, there is still no place for utilitarian considerations. For example, that some person has done us a favor is a reason for his deserving our gratitude whether or not there is any utility in it. Gratitude is a "fitting" response to service. But now we come to the question of giving vent to our feelings, translating our appraisals into grades, impressing our recognition on deserving persons, and so on. We could simply do these things directly, with no further rigmarole, as we do when we praise and blame, for example, or we could

[24] This suggestion is developed in detail in my "The Expressive Function of Punishment," in this volume, 95-118.

harbor our attitudes unexpressed; but, instead, we often establish imposing institutions, formulate elaborate regulations, appoint referees and appraisers, judges and administrators, and require that persons prove their deserts by qualifying for them in trials and tests and competitions.

Here, at last, is where utilitarian considerations enter in, and they have a double role. They give a reason (in addition to natural inclination) for expressing and acknowledging our attitudes and appraisals in public and conventional ways. We could, after all, merely harbor our resentments of the wrongdoer, but doing that would neither unload our aggressions nor deter crime; we could simply feel sympathy toward the unemployed, but doing that would not prevent food riots. Secondly, in requiring people to satisfy qualifying conditions specified by public regulations and administered by impartial officials, we have a system which, in respect to many kinds of activity, is probably the most reliable guide to the deserts themselves. We could allow all the responsive attitudes free expression (like praise and blame) without requiring their objects to qualify publicly; but, by and large, that would be a hit-or-miss approach. Desert is not always readily manifest, and when it is not, the "deserved modes of treatment" would be like shots in the dark. Qualifying conditions specified by the rules of competitions, tests, trials, and the like, then, are often necessary to minimize injustice. And though this is not strictly a "utilitarian consideration," it yields one immediately: we are all better off—happier, more secure—for living in a society where threat of injustice is minimized.

Inflated desert theory. If utilitarian theories are apt to misconstrue the relevance of utility, antiutilitarian theories are apt to inflate the role of desert. One of the aims of the various institutional practices we have considered is to guarantee that persons get what they deserve with a minimum of injustice. But to make this the paramount consideration in each single case and so try to give prizes, grades, rewards, and the like to those who deserve them instead of those who qualify for them (when these are different) would be to abrogate the controlling rules, overload officials with dangerous discretion to be used as they see fit, and thus, in the long run, given human fallibility, generate more injustice than is avoided. It may not be just (in some cosmic sense) for a prize to go to the second fastest runner rather than to his unlucky superior who pulled up lame. But giving judges discretion to award prizes to competitors whom they regard as most deserving even when they do not qualify under the rules would cause bitter resentment and bickering (utilitarian considerations) and lead to inevitable injustices.[25] Desert is always an important con-

25 This is a truth which the Greeks learned the hard way, as they experimented with ever more elaborate systems of rule-governed activity, while the values of an earlier desert-oriented Homeric society stubbornly persisted:

"Systems of values, however, persist while societies develop; and the Homeric system conflicts violently with any form of society which attempts to allot reward or punishment to an action simply on the basis of the characteristics of that action, irrespective of any other claims to consideration the agent may possess. The persistence of the one system is certain to confuse any attempt to introduce the other.

"Signs of such confusion existing already in Homer may be seen in the chariot race of *Iliad* xxiii. We regard a race as a trial of prowess on a particular day. Whether or no the best man wins, the winner deserves the first prize, the second the second prize, and so on; but when Eumelus comes in last, Diomedes, who won, is given the first prize, but Achilles proposes to give the second prize to Eumelus, since 'The man who is *aristos* has finished last.' (*Iliad*, xxiii., 536. Clearly it would be unreasonable for the winner not to receive the first prize.)

"Everyone approves of Achilles' decision except Antilochus, who finished second. His protest is successful, but he does not say 'This is unreasonable. I never heard of such a thing,' but 'Eumelus should have prayed to the gods, and anyway you can easily give him another prize.' That is to say, he does not regard it as unreasonable that, even in a race, a man's *arete* should be held to be more important, for the purpose of distributing prizes, than his actual performance. On the other hand, though Menelaus *is* 'mightier in *arete* and in strength,' he insists that this must not be the reason why he should be placed second rather than Antilochus; the reason is that Antilochus has broken the rules by crowding and crossing. And yet he also says to Antilochus, 'You have brought shame upon my *arete*'; and nothing is more important than this.

"This is a hopeless tangle of values. Unless the allotment of prizes bears some relation to the result of the race, there is no point in running at all, since the prizes could be distributed before the race starts.

sideration in deciding how we are to treat persons, especially when we are not constrained by rules or where rules give us some discretion; but it is not the only consideration and is rarely a sufficient one.

Desert as moral entitlement. The final kind of mistake precluded by this analysis tends to be committed by philosophers who hold a parajuridical conception of morality. These philosophers take legal institutions as their models, consciously or not, in explicating puzzling moral concepts and then obscure the distinction between the moral and the legal (or institutional) by interpreting the former as an eccentric species of the latter.[26] In the case at hand, the distinction between entitlement and desert is obscured by making desert a peculiar *kind* of entitlement, instead of a notion in essential contrast with entitlement. Desert confers rights, says this theory, but not the ordinary kind of right of the sort winners of competitions and claimants of rewards have, for example, but rather "moral rights," assigned by special "moral rules," which in turn are implicitly treated as regulations of a special "moral institution." There are, of course, a variety of legitimate uses of the expression "moral right,"[27] but this is almost certainly

---

Accordingly, some attention must be paid to the result; and yet clearly in this society some attention must be paid to the *arete* of the respective competitors as well. Such a situation can only lead to doubt, confusion, and argument. In a chariot race, this may be unimportant; but we have here in a microcosm the tangle of values which prevailed in the Athenian law-courts and assembly, with such disastrous results. The problem is a serious one. . . ." A.W.H. Adkins, *Merit and Responsibility* (Oxford: Clarendon Press, 1960), 55-56.

26 For a more detailed discussion of this philosophical practice, see my "Supererogation and Rules," in this volume, 3-24.

27 A *generically moral right* is a right prior to or independent of legal enactment. Thus a right conferred by the rules of a nonlegal institution is a moral right in this sense. Secondly, a moral right might be a right prior to or independent of *any* institutional rules, legal or nonlegal. A *conventional right*, like an old lady's right to a young man's seat on a subway train, is "moral" in this sense. Conventional, institutional, and legal rights are all "positive" rights, unlike moral rights in the sense of *ideal rights*, that is, what ought to be positive rights and would be such in a better or ideal legal system, club, or conventional moral code. A *conscientious right* is a claim the

not one of them. The defeated presidential candidate who deserved to win, for instance, is not by that token entitled to the office, nor does he have any right to it. These rights are conferred by votes, not by deserts. And I fail to see how matters are clarified by qualifying the alleged entitlement as "moral." The defeated candidate has no right to the office, moral or otherwise, unless of course "moral right" is simply another, eccentric way of referring to his deserts. "Deserve," "fitting," and "appropriate," on the one hand, and "right," "entitlement," and "rule," on the other, are terms from altogether different parts of our ethical vocabularies; they are related in such a way that there is no paradox in saying of a person that he deserves (it would be fitting for him to have) certain modes of treatment which, nevertheless, he cannot claim as his due.

This analysis has attempted to show in just what sense the moral notion of desert is prior to a system of public bestowals (one of the aims of the latter is to give people what they deserve) and in what sense it is not (bestowals can often be most justly conferred if the system is governed rather strictly by qualifying rules). We have also seen the variety of conflicts which are possible between desert and desert and between desert and entitlement. These conflicts within the category of justice are as subtle and difficult as any others in ethics, and it is doubtful that general principles can be formulated to dictate *a priori* the preferred manner of their resolution in every case. But if desert and entitlement are not distinct in nature, the question of their relation cannot be difficult or complicated; for then there

---

recognition of which as valid is called for not by rules or conventions, but by the principles of an enlightened conscience. Finally, an *exercise-right* is simply moral justification in the exercise of a right of some other kind. To say that *S* has a moral right to do *X*, in this sense, is not to ascribe an actual right to him at all (in this respect an exercise-right, like an ideal right, is not "positive"), but rather to say that on balance it would be morally right (or at least not morally wrong) for him to exercise his legal (or other positive) right to *X*, the latter right remaining in his possession and unaffected by considerations bearing on the rightness or wrongness of exercising it.

could be only "real," or "higher," entitlement (desert) and "lower," or "inferior," entitlement (qualification), and in cases of conflict the higher would always take precedence over the lower. This is what comes of efforts to compare the incomparable by positing a special cosmic institution in which the one has a subordinate and the other a superior place, of attempts to unify contrasting ethical and institutional concepts by locating them at opposite ends of a common scale. It is important to emphasize, then, in concluding, that desert is a *moral* concept in the sense that it is logically prior to and independent of public institutions and their rules, not in the sense that it is an instrument of an ethereal "moral" counterpart of our public institutions.

APPENDIX

ECONOMIC INCOME AS DESERVED

Another difficult problem of subsumption is posed by the distribution of social benefits generally, and particularly wealth, throughout a population. Economists rarely speak of desert in this connection, but both ordinary people and philosophers do, and whether such talk is well advised or not, it does seem to make sense. Some affirm and some deny, for example, that doctors get more or teachers less than they deserve. The problem of interpreting such claims, as in the case of honorable offices, is complicated by the variety of ways in which occupational income is conceived and the consequent concurrence of conflicting criteria.

Suppose we interpret professional income as a prize. This way of viewing the matter is superficially plausible as long as some classes get more than others. The competition is for shares of the national wealth; a whole series of awards from first prize on down are given; and the rules of the contest are the laws of the market supplemented by the criminal code. One immediate consequence of this picture is that, if there is a sense of "desert" in which it means "entitlement," then in that sense everyone deserves what he gets. Providing you obey the rules, the market alone—that is, the social demand for your services—determines what and how much you are entitled to. This is trivially true—this great conservative principle—much as it is true in baseball that the team scoring the most runs wins the game (is entitled to a trophy), or in politics that the candidate who receives the most electoral votes is entitled to the presidency.

Supposing our economic life to be primarily a competition for prizes, what are we to regard as the basis of the competition, the skill or other estimable trait singled out by the rule makers for special treatment and honor? Is it simply craftiness and avarice? Surely not, for even the defenders of the status quo deny that craftiness is a desert ba-

88

sis. No defender of the medical profession, for example, argues that doctors deserve their "prize" because of superior craftiness. But what, then, is the ground for the competition which brings all classes and professions together in the same arena? I can think of no one single skill (apart from commercial canniness) in respect to which all members of all professions are in explicit competition, or any one game at which we all play. The competitive model is likely to appeal only to certain businessmen engaged in a kind of running commercial poker game, and recent events indicate that it fits ill even that limited sector of our national life.

It is more plausible to interpret professional income as reward or compensation. The reward model is not, however, without its difficulties. So long as it is a finite pie we are splitting, we cannot reward some with larger slices without punishing others by giving them smaller portions. But, that complication aside, there can be no doubt that persons often do construe larger-than-average incomes either as social recognition of excellence or achievement or else as symbolic expressions of gratitude for unusual services rendered or for contributions made to the general welfare. The argument is not that society or any of its representatives has authorized such rewards or even consented to them, but only that the basis of desert for such rewards does exist in the actual achievements or contributions of the wealthier classes. The argument, of course, often goes the other way: the rich, it is said, are rewarded beyond all desert. In any case, the concept of professional income as social reward seems deeply rooted in our ordinary thinking.

That it makes any contribution to clarity in our ordinary thinking is much less obvious. Persons in certain professions, it is alleged, have contributed more than most to our general welfare and therefore deserve tangible expressions of public gratitude, namely, higher incomes in proportion to their contributions. But the persons who have contributed or are members of classes which have contributed most conspicuously to the public weal—the innovators,

89

reformers, political leaders, artists, and scientists—are not
the ones obviously getting or demanding the most conspicuous rewards. This observation suggests that it is contributions to our economic welfare, to our "standard of
living," rather than the quality of our life that are said to
deserve reward—and perhaps rightly so. After all, contributions to our true and ultimate good are essentially con-
testable and impossible to measure; and, besides, there may
appear to be a fittingness in reserving economic rewards for
economic contributions. But more puzzling difficulties remain. It is, first of all, difficult enough to determine how
large a share of our national economic wealth is created by
each individual or each class;[28] yet even if that is possible
in principle, it is still necessary to make out a case for the
type of contribution which deserves gratitude. It may, after
all, turn out that sharp traders and shrewd investors create
the most wealth, and we are not generally inclined to feel
grateful for contributions to our welfare that are the accidental consequences of another person's self-interested
pursuit of wealth. We could, of course, require that rewards go not simply to those who contribute the most, but
to those who contribute from public-spirited or disinterested motives—activities which would "naturally" evoke
gratitude. But then the reward would function only to encourage the very type of motive that would disqualify its
possessor from reward, and would thus be self-defeating.

Not all rewards express gratitude, however; some express
recognition of the excellence or achievement that is their
desert basis. A. C. Ewing even speaks with respect (but
not complete agreement) of a "retributive theory of reward" according to which it is an end in itself that the virtuous be rewarded. "It is not merely that we think the good
ought to be happy," says Ewing, "but that we think they
ought to be recognized or manifested [elsewhere he says
"approved of" and "appreciated"] as good, and the most
impressive form of recognition is by bestowal of the means

28 Cf. L. T. Hobhouse, *The Elements of Social Justice* (London:
George Allen & Unwin, 1949), Ch. 8.

to happiness [i.e., money]."[29] Ewing himself points out, though, that moral virtue is rarely proposed seriously as a desert basis for economic rewards. And, indeed, there is something repugnant in paying a man for being virtuous.[30] Economic benefits seem to be a highly inappropriate vehicle of recognition partly because they tend to render the recipient suspect and to tarnish the disinterested altruism essential to moral worth. "Rewards for virtue as such could only rightly be given to people who were not virtuous for the sake of the reward and did not need the reward to make them so."[31]

Actually, it is *ability*, not moral virtue, which is commonly held to be a desert basis for economic rewards. It is often said, for example, that doctors, lawyers, engineers, and high executives, simply to perform their functions, need far more talent and skill than most other people, and in virtue of this superior talent they deserve higher income as a kind of public recognition of their superiority. Ability is a desert basis, of course, for various kinds of *prizes* and for *grades*; and when it issues in great achievements, it often calls for and receives public recognition in the form of such *rewards* as testimonial dinners, citations, knighthoods, and other honors. But, again, distributing wages, profits, and salaries to whole classes of people as symbols of the recognition of superior talent seems inappropriate and, indeed, repugnant; for that would be to interpret the principle "Better people deserve better things" in a manner wholly inconsistent with democratic and liberal ideas. That able people are *ipso facto* better people in any nontautologous sense is precisely what the traditional equalitarian and

---

[29] *The Morality of Punishment,* 128.

[30] Cf. S. I. Benn and R. S. Peters: "there are some sorts of 'worth' for which rewards in terms of income seem inappropriate. Great courage in battle is recognized by medals, not by increased pay." *Social Principles and the Democratic State,* 139.

[31] *Op.cit.,* 132. Ewing adds that "the danger is much worse than it is with punishment. . . . For a man formerly given to crime to abstain, even from merely prudential motives, is a step upwards, but for a man who previously did good actions irrespective of reward to come to do them for the sake of the reward is decidedly a step downwards."

Christian teachings deny. Rewards for industry or self-improvement, or for specific achievements that cry out for recognition in the interests of truth, are another matter; and there may be sound utilitarian reasons for rewarding even superior intelligence or skill. But it is no more self-evident to me that superior intelligence or skill per se *deserves* reward than that great height or physical strength does.[32]

It is much more plausible, I think, to construe income, in part, as *compensation* and to speak of desert in this connection. Collecting garbage is an extremely disagreeable and onerous (not to say malodorous) job which must be done by someone. Garbage collectors do, as a matter of fact, get rather more pay than other workers of comparable skill; and the reason they do no doubt is that greater inducements are needed to draw men into such work. But surely that is not the only reason why garbage collectors should be paid more. It can also be argued that, insofar as the garbage collector's plight is no fault of his own, but only due to his bad luck, lack of skill, or want of opportunity, he *deserves* more money to make up for his unpleasant circumstances.

The same point can be made about extra-hazardous work, and is well made by Benn and Peters:

> Admittedly, some men lack the job-getting qualities, and are forced to take the jobs that no one else wants. But lack of skill or personal charm may not be good enough reasons why a man should suffer the hazards of silicosis or a broken neck. It may be, then, that if such jobs must be done, they ought to carry compensatory benefits.[33]

---

[32] Ewing (*op.cit.*, 137) claims that all kinds of value (not simply moral value) deserve recognition and approval. For that reason, ability is a desert basis; it *is* a "value" and is to be acknowledged as such or "appreciated." Similarly, punishment is an expression of our recognition of the evil character of an act "vividly impressed" on the criminal. Why, then, doesn't Ewing find ineptitude, inability, and unintelligence, all "disvalues" or "demerits," desert bases for *punishment*?

[33] *Op.cit.*, 140. The authors' point that workers do not deserve to

Not only unpleasant and hazardous work but also terribly responsible positions and functions requiring extensive preliminary training deserve compensation. Here is the real basis for the claim that the executive and the physician *deserve* higher incomes: not that their superior abilities deserve rewards, but rather that their heavier loads of responsibility and worry and (for doctors) their longer period of impoverished apprenticeship *deserve compensation.*

The principle that unpleasant, onerous, and hazardous jobs deserve economic compensation, unlike the claim that superior ability deserves economic reward, is an equalitarian one, for it says only that deprivations for which there is no good reason should be compensated to the point where the deprived one is again brought back to a position of equality with his fellows. It is not that compensation gives him more than others (considering everything), but only that it allows him to catch up.

This point in turn should help clarify the relation between desert and need. It is only in respect to compensation that need can be a desert basis. A man with a chronically sick wife or child deserves compensation since through no fault of his own he has a greater need than others; and the same is true of the man with a large number of dependents. But need is never a desert basis for any other kind of treatment. In fact, in respect to most other modes of treatment, desert is *contrasted* with need. Who should get the prize— the contestant who deserves it or the one with the greatest need for it? Should the student who (as he says) "needs an A to get into law school" be given the grade he needs or the grade he deserves? Some people, we are told by psychiatrists, "need" punishment even when they don't deserve it, and the man who has the greatest need for the sheriff's reward is not always the man, even in Hollywood westerns, who has done most to apprehend the wanted desperado. It

---

be penalized for lack of skill or charm is the counterpart of my point that no one deserves to be rewarded simply for his superior skill or charm.

is only compensation that is deserved by need, and then only when the need is blameless.

If I am right and economic income cannot plausibly be construed as prizes or rewards, and can be spoken of as "deserved" only insofar as it is compensation, then a startling result follows. To say that income ideally ought to be distributed only according to desert is to say that, in respect to all social benefits, all men should ideally be equal. Some, of course, should receive more money than others to compensate them for greater burdens or greater needs, but ideally the compensatory sum should be just sufficient to bring the overall balance of their benefits up to the level of their fellows'.

What follows, though, from this brief discussion of economic benefits is not that wealth ought to be distributed equally with adjustments made only for needs and burdens, but rather that there are important considerations relevant to this question which have *nothing to do with desert*. Unequal incomes tend to promote industry and ambition and also to encourage socially valuable activities and the development of socially important skills and techniques. The incentive of financial gain might very well make possible the creation of so much wealth that even the smaller shares would be greater than the equally shared portions of the smaller equalitarian pie. Desert is essentially a nonutilitarian concept, one which can and often does come into head-on conflict with utility; and there is no *a priori* reason for giving it automatic priority over all other values. Desert is one very important kind of ethical consideration, but it is not the only one.

5

It might well appear to a moral philosopher absorbed in the classical literature of his discipline, or to a moralist sensitive to injustice and suffering, that recent philosophical discussions of the problem

The Expressive Function of Punishment

of punishment have somehow missed the point of his interest. Recent influential articles[1] have quite sensibly distinguished between questions of definition and justification, between justifying general rules and particular decisions, between moral and legal guilt. So much is all to the good. When these articles go on to *define* "punishment," however, it seems to many that they leave out of their ken altogether the very element that makes punishment theoretically puzzling and morally disquieting. Punishment is defined in effect as the infliction of hard treatment by an authority on a person for his prior failing in some respect (usually an infraction of a rule or command).[2] There may be a very general sense of the word "punishment" which is well expressed by this definition; but even if that is so, we

[1] See esp. the following: A.G.N. Flew, "The Justification of Punishment," *Philosophy*, 29 (1954), 291-307; S. I. Benn, "An Approach to the Problems of Punishment," *Philosophy*, 33 (1958), 325-341; and H.L.A. Hart, "Prolegomenon to the Principles of Punishment," *Proceedings of the Aristotelian Society*, 60 (1959/60), 1-26.

[2] Hart and Benn both borrow Flew's definition. In Hart's paraphrase (*op.cit.*, 4), punishment " (i) . . . must involve pain or other consequences normally considered unpleasant. (ii) It must be for an offense against legal rules. (iii) It must be of an actual or supposed offender for his offense. (iv) It must be intentionally administered by human beings other than the offender. (v) It must be imposed and administered by an authority constituted by a legal system against which the offense is committed."

can distinguish a narrower, more emphatic sense that slips through its meshes. Imprisonment at hard labor for committing a felony is a clear case of punishment in the emphatic sense. But I think we would be less willing to apply that term to parking tickets, offside penalties, sackings, flunkings, and disqualifications. Examples of the latter sort I propose to call *penalties* (merely), so that I may inquire further what distinguishes punishment, in the strict and narrow sense that interests the moralist, from other kinds of penalties.[3]

One method of answering this question is to focus one's attention on the class of nonpunitive penalties in an effort to discover some clearly identifiable characteristic common to them all, and absent from all punishments, on which the distinction between the two might be grounded. The hypotheses yielded by this approach, however, are not likely to survive close scrutiny. One might conclude, for example, that mere penalties are less severe than punishments, but although this is generally true, it is not necessarily and universally so. Again, we might be tempted to interpret penalties as mere "pricetags" attached to certain types of behav-

[3] The distinction between punishments and penalties was first called to my attention by Dr. Anita Fritz of the University of Connecticut. Similar distinctions in different terminologies have been made by many. Sir Frederick Pollock and Frederic Maitland speak of "true afflictive punishments" as opposed to outlawry, private vengeance, fine, and emendation. *The History of English Law Before the Time of Edward I*, 2nd edn. (Cambridge: At the University Press, 1968), II, 451ff. The phrase "afflictive punishment" was invented by Bentham: "These [corporal] punishments are almost always attended with a portion of ignominy, and this does not always increase with the organic pain, but principally depends upon the condition [social class] of the offender." *The Rationale of Punishment* (London: Heward, 1830), 83. Sir James Stephen says of legal punishment that it "should always connote . . . moral infamy." *A History of the Criminal Law of England*, 3 vols. (London: Macmillan & Co., 1883), II, 171. Lasswell and Donnelly distinguish "condemnation sanctions" and "other deprivations." "The Continuing Debate over Responsibility: An Introduction to Isolating the Condemnation Sanction," *Yale Law Journal*, 68 (1959). The traditional common law distinction is between "infamous" and "noninfamous" crimes and punishments. Conviction of an "infamous crime" rendered a person liable to such postpunitive civil disabilities as incompetence to be a witness.

ior that are generally undesirable, so that only those with especially strong motivation will be willing to pay the price.[4] In this way deliberate efforts on the part of some Western states to keep roads from urban centers to wilderness areas few in number and poor in quality would be viewed as essentially no different from various parking fines and football penalties. In each case a certain kind of conduct is discouraged without being absolutely prohibited: anyone who desires strongly enough to get to the wilderness (or park overtime, or interfere with a pass) may do so provided he is willing to pay the penalty (price). On this view, penalties are in effect licensing fees, different from other purchased permits in that the price is often paid afterward rather than in advance. Since a similar interpretation of punishments seems implausible, it might be alleged that this is the basis of the distinction between penalties and punishments. However, even though a great number of penalties can no doubt plausibly be treated as retroactive licensing fees, it is hardly possible to view all of them as such. It is certainly not true, for example, of most demotions, firings, and flunkings that they are "prices" paid for some already consumed benefit; and even parking fines are sanctions for rules "meant to be taken seriously as . . . standard[s] of behavior"[5] and thus are more than mere public parking fees.

Rather than look for a characteristic common and peculiar to the penalties on which to ground the distinction between penalties and punishments, we would be better advised, I think, to turn our attention to the examples of punishments. Both penalties and punishments are authoritative

---

[4] That even punishments proper are to be interpreted as taxes on certain kinds of conduct is a view often associated with O. W. Holmes, Jr. For an excellent discussion of Holmes's fluctuations of this question, see Mark De Wolfe Howe, *Justice Holmes, The Proving Years* (Cambridge: *Harvard University Press,* 1963), 74-80. See also Lon Fuller, *The Morality of Law* (New Haven: Yale University Press, 1964), Ch. 2, Part 7, and H.L.A. Hart, *The Concept of Law* (Oxford: Clarendon Press, 1961), 39, for illuminating comparisons and contrasts of punishment and taxation.

[5] H.L.A. Hart, *loc. cit.*

deprivations for failures; but, apart from these common features, penalties have a miscellaneous character, whereas punishments have an important additional characteristic in common. That characteristic, or specific difference, I shall argue, is a certain expressive function: punishment is a conventional device for the expression of attitudes of resentment and indignation, and of judgments of disapproval and reprobation, on the part either of the punishing authority himself or of those "in whose name" the punishment is inflicted. Punishment, in short, has a *symbolic significance* largely missing from other kinds of penalties.

The reprobative symbolism of punishment and its character as "hard treatment," though never separate in reality, must be carefully distinguished for purposes of analysis. Reprobation is itself painful, whether or not it is accompanied by further "hard treatment," and hard treatment, such as fine or imprisonment, because of its conventional symbolism, can itself be reprobatory. Still, we can conceive of ritualistic condemnation unaccompanied by any *further* hard treatment, and of inflictions and deprivations which, because of different symbolic conventions, have no reprobative force. It will be my thesis in this essay that (1) both the "hard treatment" aspect of punishment and its reprobative function must be part of the *definition* of legal punishment, and that (2) each of these aspects raises its own kind of question about the *justification* of legal punishment as a general practice. I shall argue that some of the jobs punishment does, and some of the conceptual problems it raises, cannot be intelligibly described unless (1) is true, and that the incoherence of a familiar form of the retributive theory results from failure to appreciate the force of (2).

I

That the expression of the community's condemnation is an essential ingredient in legal punishment is widely acknowledged by legal writers. Henry M. Hart, for example, gives eloquent emphasis to the point:

What distinguishes a criminal from a civil sanction and all that distinguishes it, it is ventured, is the judgment of community condemnation which accompanies . . . its imposition. As Professor Gardner wrote not long ago, in a distinct but cognate connection:

"The essence of punishment for moral delinquency lies in the criminal conviction itself. One may lose more money on the stock market than in a court-room; a prisoner of war camp may well provide a harsher environment than a state prison; death on the field of battle has the same physical characteristics as death by sentence of law. It is the expression of the community's hatred, fear, or contempt for the convict which alone characterizes physical hardship as punishment."

If this is what a "criminal" penalty is, then we can say readily enough what a "crime" is. . . . It is conduct which, if duly shown to have taken place, will incur a formal and solemn pronouncement of the moral condemnation of the community. . . . Indeed the condemnation plus the added [unpleasant physical] consequences may well be considered, compendiously, as constituting the punishment.[6]

Professor Hart's compendious definition needs qualification in one respect. The moral condemnation and the "unpleasant consequences" that he rightly identifies as essential elements of punishment are not as distinct and separate as he suggests. It does not always happen that the convicted prisoner is first solemnly condemned and then subjected to unpleasant physical treatment. It would be more accurate in many cases to say that the unpleasant treatment itself expresses the condemnation, and that this expressive aspect of his incarceration is precisely the element by reason of which it is properly characterized as punishment and not mere penalty. The administrator who regretfully suspends the license of a conscientious but accident-prone driver can inflict a deprivation without any scolding, express or implied; but the reckless motorist who is sent to prison for six

6 Henry M. Hart, "The Aims of the Criminal Law," *Law and Contemporary Problems*, 23 (1958), II, A, 4.

months is thereby inevitably subject to shame and ignominy
—the very walls of his cell condemn him, and his record becomes a stigma.

To say that the very physical treatment itself expresses
condemnation is to say simply that certain forms of hard
treatment have become the conventional symbols of public
reprobation. This is neither more nor less paradoxical than
to say that certain words have become conventional vehi-
cles in our language for the expression of certain attitudes,
or that champagne is the alcoholic beverage traditionally
used in celebration of great events, or that black is the color
of mourning. Moreover, particular kinds of punishment are
often used to express quite specific attitudes (loosely speaking, this is part of their "meaning"); note the differences, for
example, between beheading a nobleman and hanging a
yeoman, burning a heretic and hanging a traitor, hanging
an enemy soldier and executing him by firing squad.

It is much easier to show that punishment has a symbolic
significance than to state exactly what it is that punishment
expresses. At its best, in civilized and democratic countries,
punishment surely expresses the community's strong *disapproval* of what the criminal did. Indeed, it can be said that
punishment expresses the *judgment* (as distinct from any
emotion) of the community that what the criminal did was
wrong. I think it is fair to say of our community, however,
that punishment generally expresses more than judgments
of disapproval; it is also a symbolic way of getting back at
the criminal, of expressing a kind of vindictive resentment.
To any reader who has in fact spent time in a prison, I ven-
ture to say, even Professor Gardner's strong terms—"hatred, fear, or contempt for the convict"—will not seem too
strong an account of what imprisonment is universally tak-
en to express. Not only does the criminal feel the naked
hostility of his guards and the outside world—that would
be fierce enough—but that hostility is self-righteous as well.
His punishment bears the aspect of legitimized vengefulness. Hence there is much truth in J. F. Stephen's celebrated remark that "The criminal law stands to the passion

of revenge in much the same relation as marriage to the sexual appetite."[7]

If we reserve the less dramatic term "resentment" for the various vengeful attitudes and the term "reprobation" for the stern judgment of disapproval, then perhaps we can characterize *condemnation* (or denunciation) as a kind of fusing of resentment and reprobation. That these two elements are generally to be found in legal punishment was well understood by the authors of the *Report of the Royal Commission on Capital Punishment*:

> Discussion of the principle of *retribution* is apt to be confused because the word is not always used in the same sense. Sometimes it is intended to mean vengeance, sometimes reprobation. In the first sense the idea is that of satisfaction by the State of a wronged individual's desire to be avenged; in the second it is that of the State's *marking its disapproval* of the breaking of its laws by a punishment proportionate to the gravity of the offense.[8]

II

The relation of the expressive function of punishment to its various central purposes is not always easy to trace. Symbolic public condemnation added to deprivation may help or hinder deterrence, reform, and rehabilitation —the evidence is not clear. On the other hand, there are other functions of punishment, often lost sight of in the preoccupation with deterrence and reform, that presuppose the expressive function and would be difficult or impossible without it.

Authoritative disavowal. Consider the standard international practice of demanding that a nation whose agent has unlawfully violated the complaining nation's rights should punish the offending agent. For example, suppose that an airplane of nation *A* fires on an airplane of nation *B* while

[7] *General View of the Criminal Law of England* (London: Macmillan & Co., 1863), 99.
[8] (London, 1953), 17-18. *My italics.*

the latter is flying over international waters. Very likely high authorities in nation *B* will send a note of protest to their counterparts in nation *A* demanding, among other things, that the transgressive pilot be punished. Punishing the pilot is an emphatic, dramatic, and well-understood way of *condemning* and thereby *disavowing* his act. It tells the world that the pilot had no right to do what he did, that he was on his own in doing it, that his government does not condone that sort of thing. It testifies thereby to government *A*'s recognition of the violated rights of government *B* in the affected area and, therefore, to the wrongfulness of the pilot's act. Failure to punish the pilot·tells the world that government *A* does not consider him to have been personally at fault. That in turn is to claim responsibility for the act, which in effect labels that act as an "instrument of deliberate national policy" and hence an act of war. In that case either formal hostilities or humiliating loss of face by one side or the other almost certainly will follow. None of this scenario makes any sense without the clearly understood reprobative symbolism of punishment. In quite parallel ways punishment enables employers to disavow the acts of their employees (though not civil liability for those acts), and fathers the destructive acts of their sons.

Symbolic nonacquiescence: "Speaking in the name of the people." The symbolic function of punishment also explains why even those sophisticated persons who abjure resentment of criminals and look with small favor generally on the penal law are likely to demand that certain kinds of conduct be punished when or if the law lets them go by. In the state of Texas, so-called paramour killings were regarded by the law as not merely mitigated, but completely justifiable.[9] Many humanitarians, I believe, will feel quite

[9] The Texas Penal Code (Art. 1220) until recently stated: "Homicide is justifiable when committed by the husband upon one taken in the act of adultery with the wife, provided the killing takes place before the parties to the act have separated. Such circumstances cannot justify a homicide when it appears that there has been on the part of the husband, any connivance in or assent to the adulterous connection." New Mexico and Utah have similar statutes. For some striking descrip-

spontaneously that a great injustice is done when such killings are left unpunished. The sense of violated justice, moreover, might be distinct and unaccompanied by any frustrated *Schadenfreude* toward the killer, lust for blood or
vengeance, or metaphysical concern lest the universe stay
"out of joint." The demand for punishment in cases of this
sort may instead represent the feeling that paramour killings deserve to be *condemned*, that the law in condoning,
even approving of them, speaks for all citizens in expressing
a wholly inappropriate attitude toward them. For in effect
the law expresses the judgment of the "people of Texas," in
whose name it speaks, that the vindictive satisfaction in the
mind of a cuckolded husband is a thing of greater value
than the very life of his wife's lover. The demand that paramour killings be punished may simply be the demand that
this lopsided value judgment be withdrawn and that the
state *go on record* against paramour killings and the law
testify to the recognition that such killings are wrongful.
Punishment no doubt would also help deter killers. This too
is a desideratum and a closely related one, but it is not to
be identified with reprobation; for deterrence might be
achieved by a dozen other techniques, from simple penalties and forfeitures to exhortation and propaganda; but
effective public denunciation and, through it, symbolic nonacquiescence in the crime seem virtually to require punishment.

This symbolic function of punishment was given great
emphasis by Kant, who, characteristically, proceeded to
exaggerate its importance. Even if a desert island community were to disband, Kant argued, its members should
first execute the last murderer left in its jails, "for otherwise they might all be regarded as participators in the [un-
punished] murder. . . ."[10] This Kantian idea that in failing
to punish wicked acts society endorses them and thus be-

tions of perfectly legal paramour killings in Texas, see John Bain-
bridge, *The Super-Americans* (Garden City: Doubleday, 1961), 238ff.

[10] *The Philosophy of Law*, tr. W. Hastie (Edinburgh: T. & T. Clark,
1887), 198.

comes *particeps criminis* does seem to reflect, however dimly, something embedded in common sense. A similar notion underlies whatever is intelligible in the widespread notion that all citizens share the responsibility for political atrocities. Insofar as there is a coherent argument behind the extravagant distributions of guilt made by existentialists and other literary figures, it can be reconstructed in some such way as this: to whatever extent a political act is done "in one's name," to that extent one is responsible for it; a citizen can avoid responsibility in advance by explicitly disowning the government as his spokesman, or after the fact through open protest, resistance, and so on; otherwise, by "acquiescing" in what is done in one's name, one incurs the responsibility for it. The root notion here is a kind of "power of attorney" a government has for its citizens.

Vindication of the law. Sometimes the state goes on record through its statutes, in a way that might well please a conscientious citizen in whose name it speaks, but then owing to official evasion and unreliable enforcement gives rise to doubts that the law really means what it says. It is murder in Mississippi, as elsewhere, for a white man intentionally to kill a Negro; but if grand juries refuse to issue indictments or if trial juries refuse to convict, and this fact is clearly recognized by most citizens, then it is in a purely formal and empty sense indeed that killings of Negroes by whites are illegal in Mississippi. Yet the law stays on the books, to give ever less convincing lip service to a noble moral judgment. A statute honored mainly in the breach begins to lose its character as law, unless, as we say, it is *vindicated* (emphatically reaffirmed); and clearly the way to do this (indeed the only way) is to punish those who violate it.

Similarly, *punitive damages,* so called, are sometimes awarded the plaintiff in a civil action, as a supplement to compensation for his injuries. What more dramatic way of vindicating his violated right can be imagined than to have a court thus forcibly condemn its violation through the symbolic machinery of punishment?

Absolution of others. When something scandalous has occurred and it is clear that the wrongdoer must be one of a small number of suspects, then the state, by punishing one of these parties, thereby relieves the others of suspicion and informally absolves them of blame. Moreover, quite often the absolution of an accuser hangs as much in the balance at a criminal trial as the inculpation of the accused. A good example of this point can be found in James Gould Cozzens's novel *By Love Possessed.* A young girl, after an evening of illicit sexual activity with her boy friend, is found out by her bullying mother, who then insists that she clear her name by bringing criminal charges against the boy. He used physical force, the girl charges; she freely consented, he replies. If the jury finds him guilty of rape, it will by the same token absolve her from (moral) guilt; and her reputation as well as his rides on the outcome. Could not the state do this job without punishment? Perhaps, but when it speaks by punishing, its message is loud and sure of getting across.

III

A philosophical theory of punishment that, through inadequate definition, leaves out the condemnatory function not only will disappoint the moralist and the traditional moral philosopher; it will seem offensively irrelevant as well to the constitutional lawyer, whose vital concern with punishment is both conceptual, and therefore genuinely philosophical, as well as practically urgent. The distinction between punishment and mere penalties is a familiar one in the criminal law, where theorists have long engaged in what Jerome Hall calls "dubious dogmatics distinguishing 'civil penalties' from punitive sanctions, and 'public wrongs' from crimes."[11] Our courts now regard it as true (by definition) that all criminal statutes are punitive (merely labeling an act a crime does not make it one unless sanctions are

[11] *General Principles of Criminal Law,* 2nd edn. (Indianapolis: The Bobbs-Merrill Co., 1960), 328.

specified); but to the converse question whether all statutes specifying sanctions are *criminal* statutes, the courts are reluctant to give an affirmative reply. There are now a great number of statutes that permit "unpleasant consequences" to be inflicted on persons and yet surely cannot be regarded as criminal statutes—tax bills, for example, are aimed at regulating, not forbidding, certain types of activity. How to classify borderline cases as either "regulative" or "punitive" is not merely an idle conceptual riddle; it very quickly draws the courts into questions of great constitutional import. There are elaborate constitutional safeguards for persons faced with the prospect of punishment; but these do not, or need not, apply when the threatened hard treatment merely "regulates an activity."

The 1960 Supreme Court case of *Flemming* v. *Nestor*[12] is a dramatic (and shocking) example of how a man's fate can depend on whether a government-inflicted deprivation is interpreted as a "regulative" or "punitive" sanction. Nestor had immigrated to the United States from Bulgaria in 1913 and became eligible in 1955 for old-age benefits under the Social Security Act. In 1956, however, he was deported in accordance with the Immigration and Nationality Act for having been a member of the Communist Party from 1933 to 1939. This was a harsh fate for a man who had been in America for forty-three years and who was no longer a Communist; but at least he would have his social security benefits to support him in his exiled old age—or so he thought. Section 202 of the amended Social Security Act, however, "provides for the termination of old-age, survivor, and disability insurance benefits payable to . . . an alien individual who, after September 1, 1954 (the date of enactment of the section) is deported under the Immigration and Nationality Act on any one of certain specified grounds, including past membership in the Communist Party."[13] Accordingly, Nestor was informed that his benefits would cease.

[12] *Flemming* v. *Nestor*, 80 S. Ct. 1367 (1960).
[13] *Ibid.*, 1370.

106

Nestor then brought suit in a district court for a reversal of the administrative decision. The court found in his favor and held Section 202 of the Social Security Act unconstitutional, on the grounds that "termination of [Nestor's] benefits amounts to punishing him without a judicial trial, that [it] constitutes the imposition of punishment by legislative act rendering §202 a bill of attainder; and that the punishment exacted is imposed for past conduct not unlawful when engaged in, thereby violating the constitutional prohibition on *ex post facto* laws."[14] The Secretary of Health, Education, and Welfare, Mr. Flemming, then appealed this decision to the Supreme Court.

It was essential to the argument of the district court that the termination of old-age benefits under Section 202 was in fact punishment, for if it were properly classified as nonpunitive deprivation, then none of the cited constitutional guarantees was relevant. The Constitution, for example, does not forbid all retroactive laws, but only those providing punishment. (Retroactive tax laws may also be harsh and unfair, but they are not unconstitutional.) The question before the Supreme Court, then, was whether the hardship imposed by Section 202 was punishment. Did this not bring the Court face to face with the properly philosophical question "What is punishment?" and is it not clear that, under the usual definition that fails to distinguish punishment from mere penalties, this particular judicial problem could not even arise?

The fate of the appellee Nestor can be recounted briefly. The five-man majority of the Court held that he had not been punished—this despite Mr. Justice Brennan's eloquent characterization of him in a dissenting opinion as "an aging man deprived of the means with which to live after being separated from his family and exiled to live among strangers in a land he quit forty-seven years ago."[15] Mr. Justice Harlan, writing for the majority, argued that the termination of benefits, like the deportation itself, was the exercise

14 *Ibid.*, 1374 (interspersed citations omitted).
15 *Ibid.*, 1385.

of the plenary power of Congress incident to the regulation of an activity.

> Similarly, the setting by a State of qualifications for the practice of medicine, and their modification from time to time, is an incident of the State's power to protect the health and safety of its citizens, and its decision to bar from practice persons who commit or have committed a felony is taken as evidencing an intent to exercise that regulatory power, and not a purpose to add to the punishment of ex-felons.[16]

Mr. Justice Brennan, on the other hand, contended that it is impossible to think of any purpose the provision in question could possibly serve except to "strike" at "aliens deported for conduct displeasing to the lawmakers."[17]

Surely, Justice Brennan seems right in finding in the sanction the expression of Congressional reprobation and, therefore, "punitive intent"; but the sanction itself (in Justice Harlan's words, "the mere denial of a noncontractual governmental benefit"[18]) was not a conventional vehicle for the expression of censure, being wholly outside the apparatus of the criminal law. It therefore lacked the reprobative symbolism essential to punishment generally and was thus, in its hybrid character, able to generate confusion and judicial disagreement. It was as if Congress had "condemned" a certain class of persons privately in stage whispers, rather than by pinning the infamous label of criminal on them and letting that symbol do the condemning in an open and public way. Congress without question "intended" to punish a certain class of aliens and did indeed select sanctions of appropriate severity for that purpose; but the deprivation they chose was not of an appropriate kind to perform the function of public condemnation. A father who "punishes" his son for a displeasing act the father had not thought to forbid in advance, by sneaking up on him from behind and then throwing him bodily across the room against the wall, would be in much the same position as the legislators of the amended Social Security Act, especially

[16] *Ibid.*, 1375-76.   [17] *Ibid.*, 1387.   [18] *Ibid.*, 1376.

if he then denied to the son that his physical assault on him had had any "punitive intent," asserting that it was a mere exercise of his paternal prerogative to rearrange the household furnishings and other objects in his own living room. To act in such a fashion would be to tarnish the paternal authority and infect all later genuine punishments with hollow hypocrisy. The same effect is produced when legislators go outside the criminal law to do the criminal law's job.

In 1961 the New York State legislature passed the so-called Subversive Drivers Act requiring "suspension and revocation of the driver's license of anyone who has been convicted, under the Smith Act, of advocating the overthrow of the Federal government." *The Reporter* magazine[19] quoted the sponsor of the bill as admitting that it was aimed primarily at one person, Communist Benjamin Davis, who had only recently won a court fight to regain his driver's license after his five-year term in prison. *The Reporter* estimated that at most a "few dozen" people would be kept from driving by the new legislation. Was this punishment? Not at all, said the bill's sponsor, Assemblyman Paul Taylor. The legislature was simply exercising its right to regulate automobile traffic in the interest of public safety:

> Driving licenses, Assemblyman Taylor explained . . . are not a "right" but a "valuable privilege." The Smith Act Communists, after all, were convicted of advocating the overthrow of the government by force, violence, or assassination. ("They always leave out the assassination," he remarked. "I like to put it in.") Anyone who was convicted under such an act had to be "a person pretty well dedicated to a certain point of view," the assemblyman continued, and anyone with that particular point of view "can't be concerned about the rights of others." Being concerned about the rights of others, he concluded, "is a prerequisite of being a good driver."[20]

[19] *The Reporter* (May 11, 1961), 14.
[20] *Loc.cit.*

This example shows how transparent can be the effort to mask punitive intent. The Smith Act ex-convicts were treated with such severity and in such circumstances that no nonpunitive legislative purpose could *plausibly* be maintained; yet that *kind* of treatment (quite apart from its severity) lacks the reprobative symbolism essential to clear public denunciation. After all, aged, crippled, and blind persons are also deprived of their licenses, so it is not *necessarily* the case that reprobation attaches to that kind of sanction. And so victims of a cruel law understandably claim that they have been punished, and retroactively at that. Yet, strictly speaking, they have not been *punished*; they have been treated much worse.

IV

The distinction between punishments and mere penalties, and the essentially reprobative function of the former, can also help clarify the controversy among writers on the criminal law about the propriety of so-called strict liability offenses—offenses for the conviction of which there need be no proof of "fault" or "culpability" on the part of the accused. If it can be shown that he committed an act proscribed by statute, then he is guilty irrespective of whether he had any justification or excuse for what he did. Perhaps the most familiar examples come from the traffic laws: leaving a car parked beyond the permitted time in a restricted zone is automatically to violate the law, and penalties will be imposed however good the excuse. Many strict liability statutes do not even require an overt act; these proscribe not certain conduct, but certain *results*. Some make mere unconscious possession of contraband, firearms, or narcotics a crime, others the sale of misbranded articles or impure foods. The liability for so-called public welfare offenses may seem especially severe:

> . . . with rare exceptions, it became definitely established that *mens rea* is not essential in the public welfare offenses, indeed

that even a very high degree of care is irrelevant. Thus a seller of cattle feed was convicted of violating a statute forbidding misrepresentation of the percentage of oil in the product, despite the fact that he had employed a reputable chemist to make the analysis and had even understated the chemist's findings.[21]

The rationale of strict liability in public welfare statutes is that violation of the public interest is more likely to be prevented by unconditional liability than by liability that can be defeated by some kind of excuse; that, even though liability without "fault" is severe, it is one of the known risks incurred by businessmen; and that, besides, the sanctions are *only fines,* hence not really "punitive" in character. On the other hand, strict liability to *imprisonment* (or "punishment proper") "has been held by many to be incompatible with the basic requirements of our Anglo-American, and indeed, any civilized jurisprudence."[22] What accounts for this difference in attitude? In both kinds of case, defendants may have sanctions inflicted upon them even though they are acknowledged to be without fault; and the difference cannot be merely that imprisonment is always and necessarily a greater harm than a fine, for this is not always so. Rather, the reason why strict liability to imprisonment (punishment) is so much more repugnant to our sense of justice than is strict liability to fine (penalty) is simply that imprisonment in modern times has taken on the symbolism of public reprobation. In the words of Justice Brandeis, "It is . . . imprisonment in a penitentiary, which now renders a crime infamous."[23] We are familiar with the practice of penalizing persons for "offenses" they could not help. It happens every day in football games, business firms, traffic courts, and the like. But there is something very odd and offensive in *punishing* people for admittedly

21 Hall, *op.cit.*, 329.
22 Richard A Wasserstrom, "Strict Liability in the Criminal Law," *Stanford Law Review,* 12 (1960), 730.
23 *United States* v. *Moreland*, 258 U.S. 433, 447-448 (1922). Quoted in Hall, *op.cit.*, 327.

faultless conduct; for not only is it arbitrary and cruel to *condemn* someone for something he did (admittedly) without fault, it is also self-defeating and irrational.

Although their abundant proliferation[24] is a relatively recent phenomenon, statutory offenses with nonpunitive sanctions have long been familiar to legal commentators, and long a source of uneasiness to them. This discomfort is "indicated by the persistent search for an appropriate label, such as 'public torts,' 'public welfare offenses,' 'prohibitory laws,' 'prohibited acts,' 'regulatory offenses,' 'police regulations,' 'administrative misdemeanors,' 'quasi-crimes,' or 'civil offenses.' "[25] These represent alternatives to the unacceptable categorization of traffic infractions, inadvertent violations of commercial regulations, and the like, as *crimes*, their perpetrators as *criminals*, and their penalties as *punishments*. The drafters of the new Model Penal Code have defined a class of infractions of penal law forming no part of the substantive criminal law. These they call "violations," and their sanctions "civil penalties."

Section 1.04. Classes of Crimes: Violations

(1) An offense defined by this code or by any other statute of this State, for which a sentence of [death or of] imprisonment is authorized, constitutes a crime. Crimes are classified as felonies, misdemeanors, or petty misdemeanors.

[(2), (3), (4) define felonies, misdemeanors, and petty misdemeanors.]

(5) An offense defined by this Code or by any other statute

[24] "A depth study of Wisconsin statutes in 1956 revealed that of 1113 statutes creating criminal offenses [punishable by fine, imprisonment, or both] which were in force in 1953, no less than 660 used language in the definitions of the offenses which omitted all reference to a mental element, and which therefore, under the canons of construction which have come to govern these matters, left it open to the courts to impose strict liability if they saw fit." Colin Howard, "Not Proven," *Adelaide Law Review*, 1 (1962), 274. The study cited is: Remington, Robinson, and Zick, "Liability Without Fault Criminal Statutes," *Wisconsin Law Review* (1956), 625, 636.

[25] Rollin M. Perkins, *Criminal Law* (Brooklyn: The Foundation Press, 1957), 701-702.

of this State constitutes a violation if it is so designated in this Code or in the law defining the offense or if no other sentence than a fine, or fine and forfeiture or other civil penalty is authorized upon conviction or if it is defined by a statute other than this Code which now provides that the offense shall not constitute a crime. A violation does not constitute a crime and conviction of a violation shall not give rise to any disability or legal disadvantage based on conviction of a criminal offense.[26]

Since violations, unlike crimes, carry no social stigma, it is often argued that there is no serious injustice if, in the interest of quick and effective law enforcement, violators are held unconditionally liable. This line of argument is persuasive when we consider only parking and minor traffic violations, illegal sales of various kinds, and violations of health and safety codes, where the penalties serve as warnings and the fines are light. But the argument loses all cogency when the "civil penalties" are severe—heavy fines, forfeitures of property, removal from office, suspension of a license, withholding of an important "benefit," and the like. The condemnation of the faultless may be the most flagrant injustice, but the good-natured, noncondemnatory infliction of severe hardship on the innocent is little better. It is useful to distinguish violations and civil penalties from crimes and punishments; yet it does not follow that the safeguards of culpability requirements and due process which justice demands for the latter are always irrelevant encumbrances to the former. Two things are morally wrong: (1) to condemn a faultless man while inflicting pain or deprivation on him however slight (unjust punishment); and (2) to inflict unnecessary and severe suffering on a faultless man even in the absence of condemnation (unjust civil penalty). To exact a two-dollar fine from a hapless violator for overtime parking, however, even though he could not possibly have avoided it, is to do neither of these things.

26 American Law Institute, *Model Penal Code, Proposed Official Draft* (Philadelphia, 1962).

V

Public condemnation, whether avowed through the stigmatizing symbolism of punishment or unavowed but clearly discernible (mere "punitive intent"), can greatly magnify the suffering caused by its attendant mode of hard treatment. Samuel Butler keenly appreciated the difference between reprobative hard treatment (punishment) and the same treatment without reprobation:

> . . . we should hate a single flogging given in the way of mere punishment more than the amputation of a limb, if it were kindly and courteously performed from a wish to help us out of our difficulty, and with the full consciousness on the part of the doctor that it was only by an accident of constitution that he was not in the like plight himself. So the Erewhonians take a flogging once a week, and a diet of bread and water for two or three months together, whenever their straightener recommends it.[27]

Even floggings and imposed fastings do not constitute punishments, then, where social conventions are such that they do not express public censure (what Butler called "scouting"); and as therapeutic treatments simply, rather than punishments, they are easier to take.

Yet floggings and fastings do hurt, and far more than is justified by their Erewhonian (therapeutic) objectives. The same is true of our own state mental hospitals where criminal psychopaths are often sent for "rehabilitation": solitary confinement may not hurt *quite* so much when called "the quiet room," or the forced support of heavy fire extinguishers when called "hydrotherapy";[28] but their infliction on patients can be so cruel (whether or not their quasi-medical names mask punitive intent) as to demand justification.

[27] *Erewhon*, new and rev. edn. (London: Grant Richards, 1901), Ch. 10.

[28] These two examples are cited by Francis A. Allen in "Criminal Justice, Legal Values and the Rehabilitative Ideal," *Journal of Criminal Law, Criminology and Police Science*, 50 (1959), 229.

Hard treatment and symbolic condemnation, then, are not only both necessary to an adequate definition of "punishment"; each also poses a special problem for the justification of punishment. The reprobative symbolism of punishment is subject to attack not only as an independent source of suffering but as the vehicle of undeserved responsive attitudes and unfair judgments of blame. One kind of skeptic, granting that penalties are needed if legal rules are to be enforced, and also that society would be impossible without general and predictable obedience to such rules, might nevertheless question the need to add condemnation to the penalizing of violators. Hard treatment of violators, he might grant, is an unhappy necessity, but reprobation of the offender is offensively self-righteous and cruel; adding gratuitous insult to necessary injury can serve no useful purpose. A partial answer to this kind of skeptic has already been given. The condemnatory aspect of punishment does serve a socially useful purpose: it is precisely the element in punishment that makes possible the performance of such symbolic functions as disavowal, nonacquiescence, vindication, and absolution.

Another kind of skeptic might readily concede that the reprobative symbolism of punishment is necessary to, and justified by, these various derivative functions. Indeed, he may even add deterrence to the list, for condemnation is likely to make it clear, where it would not otherwise be so, that a penalty is not a mere price tag. Granting that point, however, this kind of skeptic would have us consider whether the ends that justify public condemnation of criminal conduct might not be achieved equally well by means of less painful symbolic machinery. There was a time, after all, when the gallows and the rack were the leading clear symbols of shame and ignominy. Now we condemn felons to penal servitude as the way of rendering their crimes infamous. Could not the job be done still more economically? Isn't there a way to stigmatize without inflicting any further (pointless) pain to the body, to family, to creative capacity? One can imagine an elaborate public ritual, exploiting the

115

most trustworthy devices of religion and mystery, music and drama, to express in the most solemn way the community's condemnation of a criminal for his dastardly deed. Such a ritual might condemn so very emphatically that there could be no doubt of its genuineness, thus rendering symbolically superfluous any further hard physical treatment. Such a device would preserve the condemnatory function of punishment while dispensing with its usual physical media—incarceration and corporal mistreatment. Perhaps this is only idle fantasy; or perhaps there is more to it. The question is surely open. The only point I wish to make here is one about the nature of the question. The problem of justifying punishment, when it takes this form, may really be that of justifying our particular symbols of infamy.

Whatever the form of skeptical challenge to the institution of punishment, however, there is one traditional answer to it that seems to me to be incoherent. I refer to that version of the retributive theory which mentions neither condemnation nor vengeance but insists instead that the ultimate justifying purpose of punishment is to match off moral gravity and pain, to give each offender exactly that amount of pain the evil of his offense calls for, on the alleged principle of justice that the wicked should suffer pain in exact proportion to their turpitude.

I shall only mention in passing the familiar and potent objections to this view.[29] The innocent presumably deserve *not* to suffer, just as the guilty are supposed to deserve to suffer; yet it is impossible to hurt an evil man without imposing suffering on those who love or depend on him. Deciding the right amount of suffering to inflict in a given case would require an assessment of the character of the offender as manifested throughout his whole life and also his

[29] For more convincing statements of these arguments, see *iter alia*: W. D. Ross, *The Right and the Good* (Oxford: Clarendon Press, 1930), 56-65; J. D. Mabbott, "Punishment," *Mind*, 49 (1939); A. C. Ewing, *The Morality of Punishment* (London: Kegan Paul, Trench, Trubner & Co., 1929), Ch. 1; and F. Dostoevski, *The House of the Dead*, tr. H. Sutherland Edwards (New York: E. P. Dutton, 1912).

total lifelong balance of pleasure and pain—an obvious impossibility. Moreover, justice would probably demand the abandonment of general rules in the interests of individuation of punishment since there will inevitably be inequalities of moral guilt in the commission of the same crime and inequalities of suffering from the same punishment. If not dispensed with, however, general rules must list all crimes in the order of their moral gravity, all punishments in the order of their severity, and the matchings between the two scales. But the moral gravity scale would have to list as well motives and purposes, not simply types of overt acts, for a given crime can be committed in any kind of "mental state," and its "moral gravity" in a given case surely must depend in part on its accompanying motive. Condign punishment, then, would have to match suffering to motive (desire, belief, or whatever), not to dangerousness or to amount of harm done. Hence some petty larcenies would be punished more severely than some murders. It is not likely that we should wish to give power to judges and juries to make such difficult moral judgments. Worse yet, the judgments required are not merely "difficult"; they are in principle impossible to make. It may seem "self-evident" to some moralists that the passionate impulsive killer, for example, deserves less suffering for his wickedness than the scheming deliberate killer; but if the question of comparative *dangerousness* is left out of mind, reasonable men not only can but will disagree in their appraisals of comparative blameworthiness, and there appears to be no rational way of resolving the issue.[30] Certainly, there is no rational way of demonstrating that one criminal deserves exactly twice or three-eighths or twelve-ninths as much suffering as another; yet, according to at least some forms of this theory, the amounts of suffering inflicted for any two crimes should stand in exact proportion to the "amounts" of wickedness in the criminals.

[30] Cf. Jerome Michael and Herbert Wechsler, *Criminal Law and Its Administration* (Chicago: The Foundation Press, 1940), "Note on Deliberation and Character," 170-172.

For all that, however, the pain-fitting-wickedness version of the retributive theory does erect its edifice of moral superstition on a foundation in moral common sense, for justice *does* require that in some (other) sense "the punishment fit the crime." What justice demands is that the *condemnatory aspect* of the punishment suit the crime, that the crime be of a kind that is truly worthy of reprobation. Further, the degree of disapproval expressed by the punishment should "fit" the crime only in the unproblematic sense that the more serious crimes should receive stronger disapproval than the less serious ones, the seriousness of the crime being determined by the amount of harm it generally causes and the degree to which people are disposed to commit it. That is quite another thing than requiring that the "hard treatment" component, considered apart from its symbolic function, should "fit" the moral quality of a specific criminal act, assessed quite independently of its relation to social harm. Given our conventions, of course, condemnation is expressed by hard treatment, and the degree of harshness of the latter expresses the degree of reprobation of the former. Still, this should not blind us to the fact that it is social disapproval and its appropriate expression that should fit the crime, and not hard treatment (pain) as such. Pain should match guilt only insofar as its infliction is the symbolic vehicle of public condemnation.

6

What is the difference between a full-fledged human
action and a mere bodily
movement? Discussion of this
ancient question, long at an

Action and Responsibility

impasse, was revitalized a decade and a half ago by
H.L.A. Hart in a classic article on the subject[1] in which he
argued that the primary function of action sentences is to
ascribe responsibility and that even in nonlegal discourse
such sentences are "defeasible" in the manner of certain
legal claims and judgments. It is now widely agreed, I
think, that Professor Hart's analysis, although it contains insights of permanent importance, still falls considerably
short of the claims its author originally made for it. Yet,
characteristically, there appears to be very little agreement
over which features of the analysis are "insights" and which
"mistakes." I shall, accordingly, attempt to isolate and give
some nourishment to what I take to be the kernel of truth
in Hart's analysis, while avoiding, as best I can, his errors.
I shall begin with that class of action sentences for which
Hart's analysis has the greatest *prima facie* plausibility—
those attributing to their subjects various kinds of substandard performance.

I[2]

If I throw down my cards at the end of a hand of
poker and, with anger in my voice, say to another player

[1] H.L.A. Hart, "The Ascription of Responsibility and Rights," *Proceedings of the Aristotelian Society*, 49 (1948/49), 171-194.

[2] I am grateful to George Pitcher for pointing out some serious errors in an earlier version of this section. I fear there may still be much in it that he disagrees with.

"You kept an ace up your sleeve!" or, more simply, "You cheated!", then surely I am doing more than "describing his bodily movements"; I am *charging* him with an offense, *accusing* him of a wrong. It is at least plausible to interpret utterances of that sort as claims that a person is deserving of censure or punishment for what he did. Charges of deceit, cruelty, and the like no doubt are the most dramatic examples of pronouncements ascribing subpar performance. It would probably be a mistake, however, to consider them to the exclusion of other, no less typical ascriptions of defective behavior. "Condemnatory verbs,"[3] such as "cheat" and "murder," are of course used to impute faulty actions, but they are not the only verbs that serve this function. Such words as "miscalculate" and "stammer" also have faultiness built into their meaning; miscalculating is a faulty way of calculating, and stammering is a defective way of speaking. Yet miscalculators and stammerers are not (necessarily) deserving of censure or punishment. Similarly, we speak of failing tests and muffing lines, of bumbling, botching, breaking, and spoiling—all defective ways of acting, but none necessarily morally defective.

Of the many distinctions that can be drawn between various kinds of faulty-action sentences, perhaps the most interesting philosophically is the distinction between the "defeasible" and "nondefeasible" species. Hart borrowed the term "defeasible" from the law of property, where it is used to refer to an estate or legal interest in land which is "subject to termination or 'defeat' in a number of different contingencies but remains intact if no such contingencies mature."[4] He then extended its meaning to cover all legal claims that are regarded as provisionally established at a certain stage of the litigation process but still vulnerable to defeat, annulment, or revocation at some later stage of the proceedings. Defeasibility, then, if I understand Hart's intentions, is closely associated with the legal notion of a

---

[3] The term is Pitcher's. See his penetrating article "Hart on Action and Responsibility," *The Philosophical Review*, 69 (1960), 226-235.
[4] Hart, *op.cit.*, 175.

prima facie case: "A litigating party is said to have a *prima facie* case when the evidence in his favor is sufficiently strong for his opponent to be called upon to answer it. A *prima facie* case, then, is one which is established by sufficient evidence, and can be overthrown only by rebutting evidence adduced on the other side."[5] If a plaintiff in a civil action fails to state a claim that, if established, would amount to a *prima facie* case, then there is nothing against which the defendant need defend himself and he wins a directed verdict. If the plaintiff does state a claim that, if established, would amount to a *prima facie* case, then there are a variety of defensive postures open to a defendant. He might deny some of the plaintiff's factual allegations, he might argue that the court lacks jurisdiction, or he might make an "affirmative defense," that is, in effect provisionally grant the plaintiff's *prima facie* case but put forward some one or more of a variety of justifications, excuses, or claimed immunities. The burden of proof switches at this point from plaintiff to defendant. And this is just one of several procedural consequences of the distinction between *prima facie* case and affirmative defense. In a grand jury proceeding the *only* question before the court is whether or not there is evidence tending to establish a *prima facie* case against the accused; hence the jury need not even hear the evidence for the defense.

The notion of defeasibility, then, is inextricably tied up with an adversary system of litigation and its complex rules governing the sufficiency and insufficiency of legal claims, presumptive and conclusive evidence, the roles of contending parties, and the burden of proof. Of course, there are no rules of comparable complexity and precision governing our everyday nontechnical use of "faulty-action sentences." At most, therefore, the assertion that these everyday ascriptions are defeasible suggests only that there are revealing analogies between them and legal claims in respect to their presumptiveness and vulnerability. In par-

[5] *Black's Law Dictionary*, 4th edn. (St. Paul: West Publishing Co., 1951), 1353.

ticular, I think, Hart would emphasize the vulnerability of both to defeat by excuses (such as accident or mistake) and justifications (such as forced choice of the lesser evil, special privilege, or consent) but not by such other affirmative defenses as diplomatic immunity, expiration of the period of limitations, and so on. The point is that, given certain rules of courtroom procedure, various types of excuse and justification are among those defenses which can defeat legal claims and charges even when all the other conditions necessary and normally sufficient for their success (the "*prima facie* case") are satisfied. But in everyday life outside of courtrooms there is rarely a conception of "*prima facie* case" at all comparable in definiteness to the legal model (after all, in the law what is to be included in a *prima facie* case is largely determined by administrative convenience and other considerations having no counterparts in private life); hence outside of the law the notion of "necessary and normally sufficient conditions" will be necessarily vague, though not necessarily obscure.

Some ascriptions of "faulty action" are subject to "defeat" or withdrawal, then, if it should turn out that the subject had an excuse or justification for what he did. The very word by which the act is ascribed has, in some instances, this vulnerability to defeat built into its meaning. Consider the verb "cheat," for example. If we find a poker player with an ace up his sleeve, we have established a powerful presumption that he has cheated. Unless he can satisfactorily explain himself, the ascription to him of cheating will be fully warranted by the evidence. But note that part of the evidence is "positive" in nature, consisting of public facts described in positive affirmations, while another part of the evidence consists of "negative" facts about the accused's intentions, beliefs, or abilities (for example, he was not forced or coerced, nor did he slip or fall by accident, nor did he make an honest mistake about the facts or about what was permitted by the rules, and so on) and is therefore usually considered his burden to rebut in an "affirmative defense." The word "cheat" affords an especially clear illustration, for its character as defeasible by excuses seems part of its very meaning, as is shown by the obvious absurdity of such phrases as "unintentional cheating" and "accidental cheating." (Compare "accidental murder" and "unintentional lie.") If the "defeating" excuse is accepted, the fault-imputation *must* be withdrawn; this is what it means for a fault-imputation to be defeasible, and it allows us to show that "cheat," "murder," and "lie" refer to defeasibly faulty actions.

Even when the actor has an excuse that completely defeats the ascription to him of one kind of faulty action (such as murdering or lying), there may nevertheless be another ascription of faulty behavior (such as killing or speaking falsely) that applies to him, excuses notwithstanding. Nondefeasibly faulty actions fall below some standard or other and thus may be regrettable, defective, or untoward, even though the actor cannot rightly be blamed (in a stronger sense) for them.

There are many clear examples of both defeasible and nondefeasible imputations of faulty action. "He broke the window" and "He broke down and cried" are both nondefeasible, whereas their distant relative "He broke faith with his friend" is defeasible. A man who accidentally breaks a window nevertheless breaks the window. We may forgive him because his faulty performance was accidental, but, for all that, we do not withdraw the fault-imputing verb or "defeat" its imputation. He broke down and cried *understandably* perhaps, but the explanation does not cancel the fact of the breakdown. Breaking faith, however, is a fish from another kettle. One cannot break faith unintentionally; for if what one did was done by mistake or accident, it cannot properly be called "breaking faith." We should have to withdraw the charge of faith-breaking altogether once we acknowledged the excuse. Faith-breaking, in short, is defeasible. Other examples of *nondefeasible* charges of faulty performance are: "He drove dangerously," "He dropped the ball" (in a baseball game), "He spoke falsely." But "He drove recklessly," "He fumbled the

123

ball" (in baseball), and "He lied" are all *defeasible*. All of these statements alike are ascriptions of performances that are in some way faulty or defective; but some we would withdraw if the subject had a proper excuse, whereas the others we cannot withdraw so long as we admit that conditions "normally sufficient" for their truth are satisfied.

What is the basis of the distinction between defeasible and nondefeasible ascriptions of faulty performance? Both kinds of ascriptions express blame, at least in the very general sense that they attribute to an agent a performance somehow defective or subpar. The distinctive feature of the defeasible ascriptions is that they express a blame *above and beyond* the mere defectiveness of the ascribed action. Still, as we have seen, it would be much *too* strong to say that all the verbs in the defeasible ascriptions, unlike their more "neutral" counterparts, always express moral condemnation (although it is sometimes plausible to say this of some of them). In what way, then, is their blame "stronger" and "beyond" mere ascription of fault?

There is, I should like to suggest, something quasi-judicial or quasi-official about the defeasible ascriptions, even when uttered outside of institutional contexts, which helps distinguish them from the nondefeasible ones. To lie or cheat, to fail to show due care, to fumble the ball or flub one's lines, is not merely to do something untoward or defective; it is also to be "to blame" for doing it. This in turn means that the doing of the untoward act can be *charged* to one, or *registered* for further notice, or "placed as an entry on one's *record*." Outside of institutional contexts, of course, there are no formal records, but only reputations. Perhaps that is what the notion of a "moral record" comes to. The concept of a record, however, is primarily and originally an institutional concept. Our formal records are found in offices of employment, schools, banks, and police dossiers, and they are full of grades and averages, marks and points, merits, demerits, debits, charges, credits, and registered instances of "fault." These records have a hundred different uses, from determining the value of a baseball player to his team to dictating decisions about whether to trust, hire, fire, reward, or punish someone. Without all these records and their informal analogue (reputation), there would be no point to talk of being "to blame" and no need for the defeasible ascriptions of fault.

To defeat the charge of being to blame by presenting a relevant strong excuse is to demonstrate that an action's faultiness is not properly "registrable" on one of the agent's records, not chargeable to "his account." The reason why a faulty action is sometimes not chargeable to an agent's record even though the action was, under another description, his is that it was performed under such circumstances that to enter it on the relevant record would make it misleading and thus defeat its point or purpose. In a baseball game, for example, a fielder is normally said to have fumbled a ball when he is able to get his glove on it without having to run very far and yet is unable to hold on to the ball once he touches it. If the ball, however, strikes a pebble and takes a bad hop before reaching the fielder's glove, the fielder is not then properly chargeable either with an "error" on his official record or with having "fumbled the ball" on his "unofficial record" or reputation. And the reason for the acceptability of this "strong defense" is found in the very purpose of keeping fielders' records, namely, to allow interested parties to make as accurate as possible an appraisal of the contribution of each player to the success or failure of the team.[6] If we charge fielders with the consequences of fortuitous events, the records will lose their accuracy and fail, accordingly, to achieve their purpose. A similar account, I think, could be given of the rationale of entries on other professional, legal, and even "moral" records.

It might be argued against this sketchy account that *any*

[6] This is very close to the function of "records" in history. Cf. H.L.A. Hart and A. M. Honoré: "History is written not only to satisfy the need for explanation, but also the desire to identify and assess contributions made by historical figures to changes of importance; to triumphs and disasters, and to human happiness or suffering." *Causation in the Law* (Oxford: Clarendon Press, 1959), 59.

125

kind of fault can be put on some sort of record or other, hence "registrability" cannot very well be the characteristic which distinguishes defeasible from nondefeasible faults. But the point I am endeavoring to make is not one about logical conceivability; it is one about practical plausibility. On what sort of record might we register that Jones drove dangerously, if it should turn out that the risk he created by driving ten miles an hour over the speed limit was amply justified by his purpose in getting a critically ill passenger to the hospital? Should we put this down as a fault on his *driving record*? Surely not, if the point of keeping a driving record is to reveal what kind of driver a man is— safe and capable or careless and dangerous. Jones drove dangerously on this occasion, to be sure, but the circumstances were so special that his behavior did nothing to reveal his *predominant tendencies*; hence to register it as a fault would not promote the purpose of the record itself. Smith speaks falsely on a given occasion. On what imaginable record might this have a point as an entry? On his *moral record*? Surely not, unless he spoke with intent to deceive, in which case he *lied*—and that *is* registrable. In general, I should think, a person's faulty act is registrable only if it reveals what sort of person he is in some respect about which others have a practical interest in being informed.

There are at least three different types of "registrable" (defeasible) faults, each exhibiting its own peculiarities. Depending on their purposes, record keepers might register (1) instances of defective skill or ability (for example, "fumbles"), (2) instances of defective or improper care or effort (negligence, laziness), and (3) instances of improper intention (cheating, breaking faith). There are similarities in the uses to which these three distinct types of entries might be put—and also differences. In all three types of cases, to be forewarned is to be forearmed. If there are numerous instances of cheating on a man's record, then we had better not play cards with him, or if we play, we should watch him closely. Similarly, if a man's record shows him to be careless and absentminded, then we should not hire him to be a nightwatchman; and if Butterfinger's fielding average is substantially lower than Orthodigit's, we had better install the latter at third base in the ninth inning with our team ahead in a close game.

On the other hand, corresponding to the three types of faults, there are important differences in the modes of treatment we might inflict on their possessors. We should not punish or censure the fumbler, for example, even if we were in a position to do so, except of course to make him try harder; but then the censure is for defective effort, not defective skill. However else we are to analyze punishment and censure, we must include an element of expressed disapproval, perhaps even hostility and resentment; and these attitudes and judgments, while they might intensify desire and even change intention, could have little effect (except perhaps inhibiting) on skill. Censure apparently works best in fortifying the motivation of otherwise careless, distractible, and lazy people, that is, those with faulty records of the second type. There is now some reason to think that manifest hostility, warnings, and threats work less well in correcting faults of improper intention and, in respect at least to the most severe defects of this sort, are useless or self-defeating. To *express* disapproval, for example, to the man with a powerful grudge against society may simply intensify his hatred and promote, rather than hinder, further hateful and destructive behavior.

If we mean by "blame" any sort of outwardly manifested disapproval of a person for his defective performance, then the relations between blaming and "being to blame" are diverse and complex indeed. The defeasible fault-imputations charge only that a man is *to blame* for his defective performance (and not merely that the performance *was* defective), but not that he is properly subject to any kind of overt blame for it. Whether to blame him or not depends on what use we wish to make of his "record," and this in turn depends upon our prior purposes, the nature of the fault, and the prospects of "utility."

In summary: I have distinguished three different stages in our responses to faulty performance. We can simply note that a given act is Jones's and that it was in some way faulty or defective. At this stage we need not use the language of defeasible fault-ascriptions at all. We might simply say, for instance, that he dropped the ball, departed from the blueprints, spoke falsely, or whatever. At a second stage we might resort to the language of defeasible ascriptions and charge him, for example, with fumbling the ball, botching the job, or lying. Here we not only ascribe to him an action which is somehow defective, we also hold him *to blame* for it. This involves registering the defective performance on the actor's relevant record or, in the absence of a formal record and an institutional context, making it part of his reputation. At a third stage we may put the record or reputation, with the fault duly registered therein, to any one of a great variety of *uses*, including, among other things, overt blame. If we think, on the basis of the record, that overt blame is what the actor deserves, we might say that he is properly subject—or liable—to blame, and then that judgment could be characterized as an *ascription of liability*. But being "to blame" and being subject to further blaming performances are two quite distinct things: the former is usually necessary but not always sufficient for the latter.

We shall stop at the first stage (nondefeasible fault-ascription) if an appropriate defense defeats the charge that the defect is registrable. Or we may stop at the second stage (register that the actor is "to blame" for the fault) where there are no persons granted the right or authority by relevant rules to respond overtly and unfavorably to the actor for his registered fault. Finally, where there are such rules, we may proceed to the third stage and properly judge the actor liable to such responses as censure, demotion, or punishment. In respect to the normal nonfaulty action, however, we do not even get to the first stage.

Utilitarian considerations clearly have no relevance as reasons at the first two stages. It is less clear, but equally true, that they have no relevance at the third stage either—

that is, no relevance to the question of whether liability judgments may be made. A person can properly be said to be liable to blame, censure, or punishment even when in fact no likely good, or much likely harm, would come from responding to him in these ways. To say that he is liable—or properly subject—to these responses is to say that another *may* so respond *if* he wishes; that is, the rules *permit* a response. What is "proper," in other words, is that others should have a certain discretion, not that they should exercise it in a certain way. Whether those with discretion *should* do what they *may* do depends on utilitarian considerations, for surely there is no rational point in acting in a manner that will do more harm than good, if rules grant us the liberty to do otherwise. The actual responsive behavior, then, when it follows a judgment of liability,[7] constitutes still a fourth stage, and it is only at this stage that the principle of utility has relevant application.

II

Can we conclude by accepting this complicated version of Hart's analysis as holding good for faulty-action sentences only? Was Hart simply misled, as some critics[8] have charged, by his own unrepresentative selection of examples, oddly failing to notice the difference between such accusations as "He murdered her" (and "He fumbled the ball"), on the one hand, and such normal, nonaccusing sentences as "He closed the door," on the other? This is a tidy way of disposing of Hart's view, but I suspect that it does less than full justice to his insight. Hart must surely have intended,

[7] More commonly "the record" is used as a ground for direct responsive behavior, and judgments of liability are expressed, if at all, only in justification (showing that one had the right to do what one did) of the responsive action after the fact. A special kind of case is provided by those judgments to the effect that a person is liable to be called upon "to answer" or "to give an accounting" of his conduct. These can occur as early as the second stage, when it remains to be established whether *prima facie* faulty behavior is registrably faulty.

[8] E.g., Pitcher, *op.cit.*, and P. T. Geach, "Ascriptiveness," *The Philosophical Review*, 69 (1960), 221.

and perhaps with good reason, that the notions of ascriptiveness and defeasibility throw some light on the normal cases of action as well as on defective performance. This is the critical possibility that will be explored in the remainder of this essay.

Is there any sense in which normal-action sentences ascribe responsibility? If we consider the matter closely, we shall discover at least five closely related but distinguishable things that might be meant by the phrase "ascription of responsibility."

Straightforward ascriptions of causality. A meteorologist might ascribe today's weather in New England to yesterday's pressure system over the Great Lakes, meaning simply that the latter is the cause of the former. In similar ways we frequently ascribe causality not only to the presence or absence of impersonal events, states, and properties but also to the actions, omissions, properties, and dispositions of human beings. Ascriptions of causality, whether to impersonal or to personal sources, often use the language of responsibility. A low-pressure system over the Great Lakes, we might naturally say, was *responsible* for the storms in New England; and in precisely the same (causal) sense we might say that a man's action was responsible for some subsequent event or state of affairs, imputing no more blame or credit or guilt or liability to the man than we do to the pressure system when we ascribe causality to it. When we assert, then, that Smith is responsible for X, we can mean simply that X is the result of what Smith did or, in equivalent terms, that Smith did something (say, turned the knob) and thereby caused X (the door's opening) to happen.

Gilbert Ryle has argued that we do not speak of persons being responsible for states of affairs unless we are charging them with some sort of offense.[9] There is a point overstated in this claim, but not one which militates against a purely causal sense of "responsible." The point is this: we

[9] Gilbert Ryle, *The Concept of Mind* (New York: Barnes & Noble, 1949), 69.

do not ordinarily raise the question of responsibility for something unless that something has somehow excited our interest; and, as a matter of fact, the states of affairs that excite our interest are very often unhappy ones. But sometimes, unexpectedly, happy circumstances need accounting for too, and sometimes the interest aroused is the desire to understand, not the desire to give credit or blame.

"It makes sense," Ryle argues, "to ask whether a boy was responsible for breaking a window, but not whether he was responsible for finishing his homework in good time."[10] It must be admitted that the latter question *usually* does not "make sense," but it is not difficult to imagine circumstances in which it would be a perfectly natural query. A parent comes home at any early hour and, to his great surprise, discovers Johnny's difficult new math lesson correctly completed and prominently displayed on the dining room table. The parent's interest *may* be purely intellectual: How on earth, he may wonder, did this astonishing event come about? Could Johnny, of all people, be responsible for it? More likely, the parent's interest, at least in part, will be a consequence of his concern to give credit to Johnny, to improve his estimate of him, to have grounds for praising and encouraging him, and so on. But, in this case, he must satisfy himself first that it was indeed Johnny who did (was responsible for) the work and not someone else; and, as we shall see, the language of responsibility is peculiarly well qualified for the raising and settling of such questions.

There are also easily imaginable circumstances in which we might ask of a perfectly whole and unbroken pane of glass who was responsible for it, that is, who caused it to be that way. Obviously, this query would be natural and intelligible if the window in question had been broken for many years and its owner had throughout that time been indifferent or even hostile to the suggestion that he repair it. The point that emerges is that it is *departures from norms* that excite interest in the ways that entitle us to use

[10] Loc. cit.

the language of responsibility. Where there is no departure from a norm, a necessary contextual condition for the intelligible use of such language is violated, and queries about responsibility may seem otiose or melodramatic.

Quite the same point can be made about some purely causal inquiries, even when the word "responsible" is not used. When we ask a question of the form "What caused X to happen?", we expect a simple answer, mentioning a single factor (or small number of factors) that explains why some departure from the normal course of events has occurred. We expect to receive an answer, in such cases, of the form "The cause of X was so-and-so" or else, perfectly equivalently, "So-and-so was *responsible* for X." But if X itself was no departure from the usual, then to ask what caused it, or what was responsible for it, would be as otiose as to ask of the president of the Women's Christian Temperance Union what caused her to be sober today.

Ascriptions of causal agency. In order to characterize the second class of responsibility ascriptions properly, it is necessary to introduce a rough distinction between complex and simple acts. There are, of course, a great number of ways in which actions can be complex, but only one of these concerns us here—that which can be called "causal complexity." An action is "causally complex" if it produces results, intentionally or not, by means of other, relatively simple, constitutive acts. The clearest examples are achievements of certain tasks and goals. To accomplish such a task as moving one's furniture to a warehouse or rescuing a drowning swimmer, one must first take a number of other steps, such as lifting chairs or diving into the water. The complex task in these examples is performed by means of a series of purposively connected "subacts," just as one closes a door *by* pushing and latching it.

A causally simple case of doing, on the other hand, requires no earlier doing as a means. Smiling and frowning are simple actions, and so are raising one's arm and shutting one's eyes. To do any of these things, it is not first

132

necessary to do something else. Nor is it necessary to do something in one's mind as a kind of triggering—to set off a volition or "flex an occult non-muscle."[11] In very special circumstances, of course, these normally simple acts can be complex. I may have to make myself smile, for social purposes, by a kind of interior girding of my tired facial muscles;[12] but normally one smiles spontaneously without having to cause oneself to do so.

Any distinction in terms of simplicity and complexity is, naturally, a matter of degree. Winking and smiling are usually perfectly simple actions; grasping, clutching, throwing, only slightly more complex; baking a cake or building a house, more complex still.

Some relatively complex actions, such as walking, rising, and sitting down, do not involve in their bare descriptions any reference to an external object transformed or manipulated. These can be distinguished from those complex actions usually referred to by transitive verbs, such as "open," "close," "rescue," and "kill," with their objects. I refer here only to the latter by the phrase "causally complex actions." Whereas verbs expressing simple action, then, can be either transitive (raising an arm) or intransitive (smiling), the causally complex action verbs are typically transitive.

Now with respect to causally connected sequences of acts and consequences, our language provides us with numerous alternative ways of talking. J. L. Austin describes one of these options: "a single term descriptive of what he did may be made to cover either a smaller or a larger stretch of events, those excluded by the narrower description being then called 'consequences,' or 'results,' or 'ef-

---

[11] Ryle, *op.cit.*, 74: "To frown intentionally is not to bring about a frown-causing exertion of some occult non-muscle."

[12] Cf. Ralph Waldo Emerson: "There is a mortifying experience . . . I mean 'the foolish face of praise,' the forced smile we put on in company where we do not feel at ease, in answer to conversation which does not interest us. The muscles, not spontaneously moved but moved by a low usurping wilfulness, grow tight about the outline of the face, with the most disagreeable sensation." *Essays, First Series* (Boston: 1895), 56-57.

fects,' or the like of his act."[13] Thus we can say that Peter
opened the door and thereby caused Paul (who was inside)
to be startled, in this way treating Peter's act as the cause
of a subsequent effect; or we can say (simply) "Peter
startled Paul" (by opening the door) and in that way incorporate the consequence into the complex action. If Paul suffered a heart attack and died, we can say that Peter's opening the door caused his death, or that Peter's startling him
caused his death, or simply that Peter killed him (by doing
those things).

This well-known feature of our language, whereby a
man's action can be described almost as narrowly or as
broadly as we please, might fittingly be called the "accordion effect," because an action, like the folding musical instrument, can be squeezed down to a minimum or else
stretched way out. He turned the key, he opened the door,
he startled Paul, he killed Paul—all of these things we
might say that Peter *did* with one identical set of bodily
movements. Because of the accordion effect, we can usually
replace any ascription of causal responsibility to a person
by an ascription of agency or authorship. We can, if we
wish, inflate our conception of an action to include one of
its effects, and more often than not our language obliges us
by providing a relatively complex action word for the purpose. Instead of saying that Peter did *A* (a relatively simple
act) and thereby caused *X* in *Y*, we might say something of
the form "Peter *X*-ed *Y*"; instead of "Peter opened the door
causing Paul to be startled," "Peter startled Paul."

Ascriptions of causal responsibility, then, are often precisely equivalent to ascriptions of the second type, which
I have called ascriptions of causal agency. When this is the
case, whatever difference exists between the two forms of
expression is merely a matter of rhetorical emphasis or
grammatical convenience.[14] Both say something about

13 J. L. Austin, "A Plea for Excuses," *Philosophical Papers* (Oxford:
Clarendon Press, 1961), 149.
14 Cf. John Salmond: "The distinction between an act and its consequences, between doing a thing and causing a thing, is a merely
verbal one." *Jurisprudence*, 11th edn. (London: Sweet & Maxwell,
1957), 402.

causation, the one quite explicitly, the other in the language of agency or authorship.

There are, however, at least two kinds of exceptions to the rule that causal ascriptions to human agency can be translated into ascriptions of causal agency. The first class of exceptions is relatively uninteresting. It may happen, as a purely contingent matter of fact, that there is no single action word in the language that is precisely equivalent to a given causal phrase. In the second, more interesting class of exceptions, transitive verbs of action are available to tempt us, but they cannot be substituted for straightforward causal idioms without distortion of sense. Substitutivity commonly fails in cases of interpersonal causation—where one person, whether by accident or design, causes another person to act. Dr. Ortho, by making certain learned remarks about the musculature of the forearm, may cause Humphrey thoughtfully to wiggle his finger. Even though it would be correct to say that Dr. Ortho's remark caused Humphrey to move his finger, we cannot say that Dr. Ortho *moved* the finger himself. Here is an instance, then, where "causing to move" is not the same as "moving." Hart and Honoré in their impressive work *Causation in the Law*[15] have argued that a fully voluntary act "negatives" causal connection between an earlier causal factor and some upshot. Their theory does not seem to fit the present example, though, for Humphrey's action might well have been unconstrained, undeceived, and very deliberate—that is, "fully voluntary"—and yet, for all that, it would remain true that it was caused by Dr. Ortho's remark. What the example shows, apparently, is not that a voluntary act "negatives" causal connection, but rather that it precludes the extension of causal agency.

Ascriptions of simple agency. Simple actions (or "basic actions," as they are often called) are those that have no causal component. In order to open a door, we must first do something else that will *cause* the door to open; but to

[15] *Op.cit.*, esp. Chs. 2-6. Hart and Honoré's "voluntary intervention thesis" is discussed critically in my "Causing Voluntary Actions," 152-186. below.

move one's finger in the normal way, one simply moves it—no prior causal activity is required. Hence ascriptions of simple agency are ascriptions of agency through and through. One cannot play the accordion with them.

That there are such things as simple acts should be beyond controversy, partly because each person has direct experience of them in his own case and partly because a denial of their existence leads to an infinite regress and attendant conceptual chaos. If, before we could *do* anything, we had to do something else first as a means, then clearly we could never get started. As one writer puts it, "If there are any actions at all, there are basic actions."[16]

Imputations of fault. This motley group, discussed in Part I, have, amidst their many dissimilarities, several important features in common. All of them ascribe agency, simple or (more commonly) causal, for a somehow defective or faulty action. Many of them, but not all, are defeasible. Rather than be qualified in certain ways, these will be withdrawn altogether and replaced with nondefeasible faulty-act ascriptions. If they cannot be so "defeated," however, they are properly entered on a relevant record of the agent's; that is, they are *registrable*. As registered faults, they are *nontransferable*. In the relevant sense of "being to blame," no one is to blame but the agent; hence no one else can "take the blame" (or "shoulder the responsibility") for him.

Ascriptions of liability. These are different in kind from the fault-imputations, even though they are often intertwined or confused with them. The one kind imputes a faulty act, simple or complex, to an agent as its author; the other ascribes, either to the agent or to someone else, liability under a set of rules or customs to some further response for it. Unlike imputations of fault, ascriptions of liability can be transferable, vicarious, or "strict," that is, independent of actual fault. In some situations under some rules, a faultless spectator may effectively say "I'll take the re-

16 Arthur C. Danto, "Basic Actions," *American Philosophical Quarterly*, 2 (1965), 142.

sponsibility for that" or "Charge that to my account," and the liability really does transfer as a result.

There are several morals to be drawn immediately from this fivefold classification. In the first place, all five types of ascription can be made in the language of responsibility. Sometimes "responsibility" *means* causal assignability, sometimes authorship, causal or simple, sometimes fault-imputability or creditability, sometimes liability. Often ascriptions of responsibility blend authorship and liability, these being intimately related in that the most usual (though not the only) reason for holding a person liable for an action (or event) is that he performed (or caused) it. Another thing to notice about the classification is that the first three uses of "responsible," in ascriptions of straight-forward causality, causal agency, and simple agency, apply to the "normal case" of action, where questions of fault, desert of punishment, and the like do not arise. Quite clearly, action sentences *do* ascribe responsibility in these senses.

The classification also suggests what it means to say that a sentence *ascribes* responsibility, in any of the senses of "responsibility." It was very important to Hart in his original article to argue that action sentences are typically "ascriptive" rather than "descriptive." But this is a confusion. Any kind of action sentence can be *used* either descriptively or ascriptively. We describe a person's actions when we have been considering that person and wondering what he did—when the question before our minds is not "Who did it?" but rather "What did *he* do?" When we have occasion to ascribe an action to a person, we have the action, so to speak, in our hands, and we want to know what to do with it, whom to pin it on.

If we wish to know who killed Cock Robin, this must be because we know that *someone* killed Cock Robin, but we do not know *who*. Where complex actions are involved, this sort of curiosity is common, for we can often examine the effects of an action in separation from the action itself and then wonder to whom to ascribe the consequences. A perfectly simple action, however, has no detachable part to examine in leisurely abstraction from the rest. Except for the simple act itself, there is no further "ascriptum" to ascribe. The statement "Jones smiled," when it appears routinely in a novelist's narrative or a newspaper article, simply describes or reports what Jones did at a certain moment. The novelist or journalist has not *assigned* a smile to Jones, as if he had the smile first and then selected Jones to put it on.

Still, rare as they might be, there are occasions for ascribing simple acts. A simple-action sentence is used ascriptively only when a question of personal identity has, for one reason or another, arisen. "Who was that man who smiled?" one might ask, and another might chime in "Oh, did someone smile? Who was it?" Now the stage is set for an ascription. An ascription of simple action is but an identification of the doer of an already known doing.[17]

Some philosophers have argued that it is an "improper way of talking" to speak, after the fact, of a person's being responsible *for his own actions*, that strictly speaking what a person can be held responsible for are the "consequences, results, or upshots of the things he does."[18] This is quite

[17] It is *only* when statements of nonfaulty simple agency are used ascriptively (in the sense explained in the text) that they are ever called "judgments of responsibility." When they are naturally characterized as responsibility judgments, "responsibility" always bears the sense of "proper identifiability." When a simple action has taken place which for some reason interests us in itself, and yet we do not know the author's identity, we may ask "Who did it?" The statement, in those circumstances, that "Mary did it" ascribes *responsibility* for the interesting act only in the sense that it identifies the doer of an already known doing. We may, however, have no interest whatever in the simple act in question except that it was done by the person who (we later learn) is Mary. Thus, having looked right at Mary as she moves her hand to her head, we may turn to a friend and ask "Who is that girl who just raised her hand?" When our friend says that it is Mary who raised her hand, his reply can hardly be described as an ascription of responsibility to Mary for raising a hand. That is because focal interest in these circumstances is on the actor, not the act. We are concerned in this example to learn Mary's identity not because she did an interesting deed; on the contrary, her deed is interesting to us only because it is hers. Hence no question of responsibility *for it* arises.

[18] Pitcher, *op.cit.*, 227.

true if we mean by "responsible" *causally* responsible; for, with rare exceptions, we do not cause our actions, we simply do them. It would be extraordinary, however, if such a widespread idiom as "responsibility for one's actions" always embodied such a crude mistake, and our classification reveals several "proper" uses to which it might be put. First of all, to be responsible for one's own complex actions (for example, closing a door) is properly to have one's simpler actions identified as the cause of an upshot. The knife cuts both ways: if "being responsible for the door's being shut" (by having caused it to close) is a permissible way of speaking, then so is talk of being responsible *for closing* the door, which, in virtue of the accordion effect, is strictly equivalent to it. Secondly, to be responsible for one's simple actions is only to be properly identifiable as their doer. "It was Mary who smiled" ascribes the responsibility *for smiling* to Mary and says nothing whatever about causal upshots. This is especially clear when the simple action is faulty, as, for example, a socially inappropriate smirk or leer. The report that someone had smiled in church, if it were to have received currency in colonial Massachusetts where such simple activity was a crime, would have set the stage for a noncausal responsibility ascription. To say then that it was Mary who did it would be to ascribe responsibility to Mary *for smiling*, not in the sense of doing something to cause the smile to appear, but rather in the sense of being properly identifiable as the doer of the deed.

III

The fivefold classification of responsibility ascriptions thus does tend to support Hart's view that action sentences are ascriptive. It suggests at least that, for all kinds of action sentences, there is some context in which they can be used ascriptively, that is, to identify the "author." On the other hand, it does nothing to support his view that all action sentences ascribe *liability* to formal responses from others or that they are all defeasible in the manner of legal charges and accusations. In this section the classification will be used to restore still more of Hart's view, though perhaps not in the way he intended it to be understood.

We have already noticed one way in which the puzzling term "ascription" can be understood. Ascriptions in this sense have a necessary subjective condition or contextual presupposition. What is not an ascription in one context may well be so in another, depending on the concerns of the speaker. If the question is "What did Jones do?", then the sentence "Jones did *A*" *describes* what Jones did; but if the question is "Who did *A*?", then "Jones did *A*" *ascribes* *A* to Jones. This simple distinction may seem to have very little importance, since ascriptions and descriptions, so understood, may say the same thing about a man with only different emphases provided by our interest. The distinction between ascriptions and descriptions, however, sometimes reverberates with deeper overtones. Instead of a mere matter of emphasis, the distinction is taken to be one of type. P. T. Geach,[19] for example, in criticizing Hart, compares the distinction between descriptive and ascriptive with the better known contrast between descriptive and *pre*scriptive as if they were distinctions of the same order; and K. W. Rankin contrasts "matters of ascription" with "matters of fact."[20] Now whether the sentence "Jones did, *A*" is used to *ascribe* *A* to Jones or to *describe* what Jones did, as we have understood those terms, it surely registers, in either case, a matter of fact. The indicative mood is well suited to express what the sentence does in either use; and ascriptions as well as descriptions can be true or false and are "about" what happened. If ascriptions are to be contrasted, then, with "matters of fact," some new conception of ascriptiveness is involved. The question to be considered now is whether, in this new sense of ascription, there is any reason for treating action sentences as ascriptive.

The stronger notion of ascriptiveness can be explained,

[19] Geach, *op.cit.*, 221.
[20] K. W. Rankin, *Choice and Chance* (Oxford: Basil Blackwell, 1961), 29 and *passim*.

I think, in the following way. There is a familiar common-sense distinction between questions calling for *decisions* and those requiring *discoveries*. I must decide at which restaurant to dine tomorrow, but I must discover the solution of an equation or the population of a town. In the first case, even when all the facts are in, I have a certain amount of discretion; in the latter case, I am bound or committed totally by the facts—I cannot escape the conclusions they dictate. This distinction has been expressed in a great variety of ways: questions of policy versus questions of fact, practical versus theoretical, regulative versus constitutive, and so on. Some philosophers have denied either the existence or the importance of the distinction: Platonists tend to reduce questions of decision to questions of discovery, and pragmatists assimilate the theoretical to the practical. Common sense, however, holds firm to the distinction, even when puzzled about how to explain it or where to draw the line. Philosophers who contrast "ascriptive" with "factual," I suggest, have this distinction in mind. By "ascriptive sentences" they mean (among other things) sentences not *wholly* theoretical or factual, having an irreducibly discretionary aspect.

A second characteristic of ascriptions, closely connected with the first, is what may be called their "contextual relativity." We may have an option of ascribing X to either $A, B,$ or C. To which of these X is properly ascribable may depend on numerous factors other than the relevant characteristics of $A, B,$ and C. Our decision may turn on our own degree of knowledge or ignorance, on our practical purposes, on the type of ascription or the nature of the "context," on our long-range policies, on institutional rules and practices, on "values," and so on. Some of these considerations may conflict and thus call for careful weighing—which is to say that they require not merely decision, but *judgment*. Finally, our well-considered ascriptive judgments may exhibit something like what Hart calls "defeasibility," although outside of legal and quasi-legal contexts talk of "cases" and "claims" and "defenses" may not seem quite at home.

Let us return to the fivefold classification to see what it can tell us now about ascriptiveness construed as irreducibly discretionary, contextually relative, and "something-like-defeasible." The first thing it reveals is that ascriptions of causality, even when they do not involve persons and their actions, commonly exhibit ascriptiveness construed in this fuller way. This is not to suggest that many "causal laws" are decided upon rather than discovered, or that scientists have any discretion at all in discovering and formulating laws of nature. Where scientists and others have some discretion is in a rather different sort of inquiry—when some unexplained happening has occurred, or some interesting or important state of affairs has been discovered, and we must decide to what cause to attribute it. Here, often, even after all of the facts are known, we have some choice, if what we wish to do is to *select* from the welter of causal factors that made some contribution to the event in question one to be denominated *the* cause.[21]

Frequently the selection from among many causal candidates of "the cause" seems so obvious that we may lose sight altogether of the fact that we are selecting, singling out, deciding. But that causal ascriptions are selective becomes clear to anyone who tries to give a *complete* causal explanation of some event in terms of all the conditions severally necessary and jointly sufficient for its occurrence. *All* of these conditions are equally important to the event, a naïve person might argue, in that all were equally necessary to its occurrence. Equally important to the event perhaps, but not equally important to the investigator. The investigator talks of "the cause" in the first place only because he suspects that there is some single event or condition among the many causal contributors to the outcome which it will

---

[21] A great deal has been written in recent years about causal ascriptions. I am probably most indebted to William H. Dray, *Laws and Explanation in History* (London: Oxford Univesity Press, 1957); Douglas Gasking, "Causation and Recipes," *Mind*, 64 (1955); N. R. Hanson, "Causal Chains," *Mind*, 64 (1955); Hart and Honoré, *op.cit.*; and J. L. Mackie, "Responsibility and Language," *Australasian Journal of Philosophy*, 33 (1955).

be of special interest or importance to him or others to identify.

Which "contributor"[22] to an event is to be labeled the cause of that event, then, is always a matter of selection, often an occasion for decision, even for difficult judgment, and is generally "relative" to a variety of contextual considerations. Cataloguing the many forms of causal relativity is a large task, but three might be mentioned here. First, selecting the cause of an event is relative to what is usual or normal in a given context. I. M. Copi bids us ponder the fate of the insurance investigator who reports back to his company that the cause of a mysterious fire in the house of a policyholder was "the presence of oxygen in the air." What the company clearly wanted him to discover was not just any necessary condition, but rather "the incident or action which in the presence of those conditions normally present, made the difference this time."[23] Leaving the insurance investigator to be dealt with by his employers, we can without difficulty think of contexts where his ascription would not have raised an eyebrow. ". . . it is easy to imagine cases," write Hart and Honoré, "where the exclusion of oxygen would be normal, e.g. when some laboratory experiment or delicate manufacturing process depended on its exclusion for safety from fire and hence for success, and in such cases it would be correct to identify the abnormal presence of oxygen as the cause of the fire."[24] What is "the cause," then, depends on what is normal, and what is normal varies with the context.

Another form of causal relativity is relativity to ignorance. Consider how we might explain to a group of workers in a welding shop how an explosion occurred in a nearby

[22] There are circumstances in which "the cause" need not even be a necessary condition. See Hart and Honoré, *op.cit.*, 116-121. Moreover, we do not have complete discretion in selecting, according to our purposes and policies, the cause from the causal conditions, as Hart and Honoré have effectively and thoroughly demonstrated.

[23] I. M. Copi, *Introduction to Logic*, 1st edn. (New York: Macmillan, 1952), 327.

[24] H.L.A. Hart and A. M. Honoré, "Causation in the Law," *Law Quarterly Review*, 72 (1956), Part 1, 75.

warehouse. We might say that the explosion was the result of a spark which, let us suppose, was the last conspicuous event preceding the eruption. But in a welding shop sparks are flying all the time. They are perfectly routine, and hence they cannot explain anything as extraordinary as an explosion. Given the context naturally assumed by the welding shop workers, one must cite as the cause much earlier events, such as the storing of TNT or leaky gasoline drums. The analogy with history, and its own brand of causal relativity, is plain. Historiographers ascribe the causes of wars, revolutions, and other such explosions, and as a rule they write for their own contemporaries. Historiographers of later ages then write of the same events but for a later group of contemporaries with a later set of conceptions of what is routine. As a result, the earlier writer ascribes "the cause" to some political or economic equivalent of the spark, and the later opts for some leaky oil can. One of the functions of an explanation of particular occurrences is to render them intelligible, to induce understanding of them. Intelligibility, however, is always intelligibility *to* someone, and understanding is always *someone*'s understanding, and these are in part functions of what is already known or assumed to be normal or routine.

A third sort of causal relativity is relativity of practical interest. "It is a well known fact," wrote R. B. Perry, "that we describe as the cause of an event that particular condition by which we hope to control it."[25] Accordingly, we tend to select as "the cause" of an event that causal condition which—in Collingwood's felicitous metaphor—has a handle on it which we can grasp and manipulate; and thus even causal generalizations tend to function directively or, as Douglas Gasking puts it, as "recipes" for cooking up desired effects.

The very meaning we assign the word "cause" is likely to vary with our purposes. Those who are concerned to produce something beneficial seek "the cause" of what they

[25] Ralph Barton Perry, *General Theory of Value* (Cambridge: Harvard University Press, 1926), 394.

wish to produce in some new condition which, when conjoined with the conditions usually present, will be *sufficient*
for the desired thing to come into existence. On the other
hand, those whose primary aim is to eliminate something
harmful are for the most part looking for causes in the
sense of *necessary* condition. That is because, in order to
succeed in such a task, one must find some condition in
whose absence the undesirable phenomenon would not occur and then must somehow eliminate *that* condition. Not
just any necessary condition, however, will do as "the
cause"; it must be a necessary condition which technicians
can get at, manipulate, modify, or destroy. Our purposes
here determine what we will accept as "the cause," and
when it is the cause of an illness or a crime wave we are
after, accessibility and manipulability are as important to
our purposes as the "necessity" of the condition. Indeed,
we will accept as the cause of some unhappy state even
some necessary condition which from the point of view of
theory is obvious or trivial, provided only that it *is* necessary and that it is something we can get at.

It would be an oversimplification, however, to identify
"the cause" of an infelicitous condition with *any* manipulable necessary condition, no matter how trivial—an oversimplification not of the processes of nature, but of human
purposes themselves. However much we wish to get rid of
defects and infelicities in our bodies, machines, and societies, we never wish to eliminate them at *any price*. What we
want when we look for "the cause" of unfortunate happen-
ings is an *economical* means of eliminating them, the right
price being determined by our many implicit underlying
purposes.

A boozy pedestrian on a dark and rainy night steps into
the path of a careless speeding motorist and is killed. What
caused this regrettable accident? Since liabilities are at
stake, we can expect the rival attorneys to give conflicting
answers. But more than civil liability is involved. A re-
former argues that the liquor laws are the cause, claiming
that as long as liquor is sold in that region we can count on

so many deaths a year. From traffic engineers, city planners, and educators we can expect still different answers; and in a sense they might all be right, if they named genuine "causal factors." But that is not what their discussion is all about. Should we prevent such accidents by spending a million dollars as the traffic engineer recommends? Or fifty million as the city planner urges? Each would uproot a necessary condition, but at what expense! Perhaps the moralist is on the right track, but do we really wish to penalize thousands of innocent responsible whisky drinkers in order to prevent the deaths of a careless few? In such ways as these are interests and purposes drawn into the context of ascribing causes. They form an implicit part of every causal field determining in part the direction in which we point when we pick "the cause" of an event.

In virtue of their discretionary character and their contextual relativity, causal ascriptions characteristically exhibit a kind of vulnerability logically analogous to the defeasibility of some legal claims and accusations. When a humanly interesting event occurs, it is always possible to mention dozens of factors that have made important causal contributions to its occurrence. Even events that occurred years earlier may so qualify. (Sometimes the straw that breaks the camel's back is in the middle, or even at the bottom, of the pile.) To cite any one of these as "the cause" is always to invite a "rebuttal" from a partisan of one of the other "causal candidates," just as to make an accusation is always to invite a defense; and to show in a proper way that a certain condition did make a contribution or was an indispensable condition is only to make out a presumption of causal importance which holds unless rebutted in one of the many diverse allowable ways.

In general, properly rebuttable causal ascriptions commit the error not of misdescribing, but of representing the less important as the more important. When it is said that the presence of oxygen in the air caused the fire, or that the cause of the stomach ache was the drink of whisky (rather than an unsuspected ulcer), or that the riot was caused by the unprecedented presence of a Negro student in the dormitory, it is less to the point to call these statements false than to call them unwise, misleading, or unfair, in the manner of otherwise accurate accounts that put their emphases in the wrong places. To be sure, but for the oxygen, the drink, the presence of the Negro,[26] there would have been no fire, ache, or riot. However, for the purposes of our more comprehensive understanding and control of such events, other equally necessary causal factors are far more important and deserve to be mentioned first.

Given that causal ascriptions, both those that assign "the cause" to impersonal factors and those that select out human actions, are "ascriptive" in the stronger sense, it follows immediately, in virtue of the accordion effect, that ascriptions of causal agency are so too. If "Jones caused the door to close" is ascriptive, then "Jones closed the door" must be so equally. If "causing a war by an act of assassination" is ascriptive, then the still more complex act of "starting a war" must be so as well. We have found a sense, then, in which one large class of action sentences—those attributing causal agency—are ascriptive and "something-like-defeasible" *even when the activity in question is in no way faulty.*

Ascriptions of simple agency, however, cannot be analyzed in this way, for a simple doing is not the upshot of a prior doing to which it may be ascribed, and *a fortiori* we have no discretion to *decide* whether to *select* a prior doing as "the cause" of the simple doing in question. Whether or not a man smiled is entirely a question of fact whose answer is to be discovered, not "decided" or "selected" presumptively.

[26] For an account of the difficult integration of the University of Georgia, see Calvin Trillin, "An Education in Georgia," *New Yorker*, July 13, 1963: "On the . . . night of the riot, their [the white girls'] behaviour changed drastically. After the first brick and the first coke bottle had crashed into her room, Charlayne [Hunter] went to a partly partitioned office . . . and stayed there during most of what followed. A group of [white] coeds soon formed a circle in front of the office and marched around, each screaming an insult as she got to the door. 'They kept yelling "Does she realize she's causing all this trouble?" ' "

Insofar as the word "smile" is *vague*, of course, there is room for discretion in its application to a borderline case; but the discretion here, which is hardly peculiar to simple-action words, is of a different sort. Whether we call a borderline colored object blue or green, we are likely to say, is a matter of indifference or "a mere question of words." But when we deny that a question of causation is wholly factual, we are not contrasting "question of fact" with "question of language"; nor are we implying that its resolution by a decision is indifferent or arbitrary. We are implying instead that a decision cannot be made without a reference to our own practical purposes and values, which is quite another thing.

Simple-action sentences, then, such as "Jones moved his finger," can be used ascriptively to identify an agent, but they are not ascriptive in the further strong sense that we are left with discretion to accept or reject them even after all the facts are in. Thus, in summary, Hart's critics are right in charging him with overburdening the notion of ascriptiveness, for we have found at least one class of action sentences, the action-simples, which are not ascriptive in the sense that is opposed to "wholly factual." But we have restored a good part of Hart's original theory (considerably reinterpreted) that is often rejected, inasmuch as we have shown that one substantial class of action sentences that do not necessarily impute faults are nevertheless very often ascriptive in a strong sense, and that these sentences, as is revealed by the characteristic ways in which they might be rebutted, are "something-like-defeasible" as well.

IV

How important is this restoration of a part of Hart's original thesis? The answer to that depends in large measure on one's philosophical interests and strategies. For problems of jurisprudence and moral psychology, I should think, the ascriptive and defeasible character of the action sentences of most interest to those disciplines is a matter of great importance indeed. But for "the problem of action" (or of "voluntary action"), construed as a problem of metaphysics, where the concern is to distinguish activity from passivity as very general conceptual categories, the notions of ascriptiveness and defeasibility appear to be of no help whatever. It is no accident that writers in ethics and jurisprudence, when troubled by "the problem of action," typically select as their examples more or less complex, teleologically connected sequences of behavior that cause harm or happiness, success or failure, to self or others. They are likely to ask, for example, what distinguishes a voluntary killing from a mere accidental homicide, or a voluntary from an involuntary signing of a contract, or in general an act freely and deliberately performed from one done in circumstances that gave the agent "no choice." The best answer to *this* question about voluntary action, it seems to me, is the one Hart and Honoré gave in *Causation in the Law*: "In common speech, and in much legal usage, a human action is said not to be voluntary or not fully voluntary if some one or more of a quite varied range of circumstances are present. . . ."[27] These circumstances make a lengthy enumeration. They include, Hart and Honoré inform us,[28] physical compulsion, concussion, shock, dizziness, hypnosis; the motives of self-preservation, preservation of property, safeguarding of other rights, privileges, or interests of self or others; legal or moral obligation; unreflective, instinctive, or automatic movement; mistake, accident, or even negligence. Voluntariness ("actness"?) in this sense is a matter of degree. An action done under a threat of physical violence, for example, comes closer to being fully voluntary than an act done under the threat of death. Further, voluntariness in this sense has no direct and invariant connection with liability. An agent may be held strictly accountable for an action which is considerably "less than fully voluntary" if the act is sufficiently harmful; and where the harm is enormously great (for example, giving military se-

[27] Hart and Honoré, *Causation in the Law*, 38.
[28] *Ibid.*, 134ff.

crets to the enemy), no degree short of complete involuntariness may relieve the agent of liability.[29]

Writers concerned with the metaphysical problem of action typically select as *their* examples such simple movements as raising one's arm or moving one's finger. When they ask what distinguishes a voluntary from an involuntary act, they are inquiring about the difference between an *action* (said with emphasis) and a mere bodily movement—for example, between a wink and a mere eye-twitch. Involuntariness in this sense (lack of muscular control) is only one of the circumstances that can render an act less than fully voluntary in the other sense. That is, some actions which *are* actions through and through, and not automatic twitches or "mere bodily movements," are nevertheless not fully voluntary in the sense discussed earlier because they may be done in response to threats or under moral obligation, and so on. Now whether an action in the sense opposed to mere bodily motion is properly to be ascribed to a person whose arm has moved is not a question that has anything to do with excuses, presumptions, and practical purposes. It has every appearance of being strictly about "the facts," although just what kind of facts it is about is part of the metaphysical perplexity that the question naturally engenders.

On the other hand, whether or not a causally complex act is to be ascribed to a person whose relatively simple act was a causal factor in the production of some upshot depends, as we have seen, on how important a causal contribution it made, as determined by our prior assumptions and practical purposes. It is misleading to attribute "X-ing Y" to a man as his doing when other factors made more important contributions. When the action in question is "faulty," then sometimes the "other conditions" are mitigating *excuses* (the agent's sickness or fatigue), sometimes not—as when between the agent's act and the upshot a dozen unanticipated causal factors intervened. "Burning

[29] Cf. Aristotle, *Nichomachean Ethics*, 1110a 20-1110b, and *ibid.*, 147.

down a forest" cannot be ascribed to a camper whose campfire is suddenly scattered by unprecedented hurricane winds, even though, but for his relatively simple act of making a fire, the forest would never have burned; and to cite the abnormal winds as causally more important factors is not to cite an excuse. Nor does one offer an excuse in pointing out that Jones did not "burn down the forest" because twelve other campfires also burned out of control and any one of them would have been sufficient to consume the whole forest. This consideration does not necessarily relieve Jones of *fault*. What it does is override the presumption that Jones's action is the crucial causal factor in the production of the outcome. But "overriding presumptions of causal importance" and "defeating imputations of personal fault," while of course not one and the same thing, are still sufficiently similar for their comparison to be mutually illuminating; and the discretionary character, contextual relativity, and presumptiveness of the causal ascription, though surely not identical with Hart's "ascriptiveness" and "defeasibility," are strongly analogous to them.

Simple noncausal doings, however, resist these comparisons; and to Wittgenstein's puzzling question "What is left over if I subtract the fact that my arm goes up from the fact that I raise my arm?"[30] the notions of ascriptiveness and defeasibility can provide no answer. Here, as elsewhere in philosophy, analytic techniques help answer the penultimate questions, while the ultimate ones, being incapable of *answer*, must be settled in some other way.

[30] *Philosophical Investigations*, tr. G.E.M. Anscombe (Oxford: Basil Blackwell, 1953), Part 1, §621.

7

*If you would worke any man,
you must either know his nature and fashions and so lead
him, or his ends and so per-
suade him, or his weakness
and disadvantages and so
awe him, or those that have
interest in him and so govern
him.*—FRANCIS BACON, "OF NEGOTIATING"

*It is not in our stars but in ourselves that we are under-
lings.*—SHAKESPEARE'S CASSIUS

I

It is my thesis that there is no conceptual barrier, at
least none imposed by common sense, to our speaking of
the causes of voluntary actions. This is a view in opposition
to that of Professors Hart and Honoré in their remarkable
book *Causation in the Law*.[1] These authors conclude, after
a very careful scrutinizing of common sense and ordinary
language, that "whatever the metaphysics of the matter
may be, a [free and deliberate] human action is never regarded as itself caused."[2] I shall call this thesis of theirs the
first cause principle, for it asserts that every voluntary human action is a new causal start, a kind of prime mover or
uncaused cause.

The first cause principle is one of three closely related

[1] H.L.A. Hart and A. M. Honoré, *Causation in the Law* (Oxford:
Clarendon Press, 1959).

[2] The quoted passage is not from the book, but from the authors'
earlier article "Causation in the Law," *Law Quarterly Review*, 72
(1956), 80.

but logically distinct causal principles which Hart and Honoré, but not I, find deeply embedded in common sense. For purposes of identification it should be distinguished from what I shall call the *voluntary intervention principle*, which Hart and Honoré expressed as follows: *"the free, deliberate and informed act or omission of a human being, intended to produce the consequence which is in fact produced, negatives causal connection."*[3] Thus if an elevator operator improperly leaves an unguarded elevator shaft, and a child falls in, the operator's negligent omission can be adjudged the cause of the child's injury; but if, while the operator is absent, a third party deliberately pushes the child into the shaft, then his act takes the elevator operator off the causal hook, so to speak, severing what would otherwise be a direct causal relation between his omission and the subsequent harm.[4] A fully voluntary act, on this view, is "a barrier and a goal . . . *through* which we do not trace the cause of a later event and something *to* which we do trace the cause through intervening causes of other kinds."[5]

Hart and Honoré offer many persuasive examples that tend to support the voluntary intervention principle. They also concede that there are two large classes of exceptions to it. As far as I can tell, they put forward no more general principle to explain why the exceptions are exceptions; and since I shall be providing still other kinds of counterexamples, it will be necessary for me to explain why the examples that Hart and Honoré cite do seem to support the principle, while the counterexamples seem to tell against it. The exceptions conceded by Hart and Honoré are, first of all, cases where a person persuades, induces, or entices (as opposed to merely advising or facilitating) another to do an act that causes harm and, second, those cases where one person's negligence provides the opportunity for another party's voluntary intervention. In the latter cases, the *provision of the opportunity*—for example, a failure to lock up

[3] *Causation in the Law*, 129.   [4] *Ibid.*, 130.
[5] *Ibid.*, 41.

a house—can be said to be the cause of a subsequent loss, despite the fully voluntary intervention of a burglar.

The third causal principle endorsed by Hart and Honoré to which I shall be taking exception is a kind of limitation on another principle that seems to me perfectly correct. The unobjectionable principle states that causal connection between a wrongful act and a subsequent harm is "negatived" by the intervention of an abnormal or unforeseeable occurrence, a "coincidence," itself also a necessary condition of the harm. Thus although it might be said that a wrongful obstruction of a sidewalk forcing a pedestrian into the street was the cause of his being struck by an automobile, it cannot be said that such an obstruction was the cause of his being struck by a falling airplane; that would be too great a "coincidence." So far so good. But Hart and Honoré do not give the benefit of this principle to abnormal conditions existing at the time the wrongful act commences. This limitation is expressed in what we can call the *stage-setting exclusion principle*, which Hart and Honoré put as follows: "A *state of the person or thing affected* existing at the time of the wrongful act (a 'circumstance' [as opposed to an 'event']), however abnormal, does not negative causal connection."⁶ Common sense, they write, "regards a cause as 'intervening' in the course of events at a given time and the state of affairs then existing as the *'setting of the stage'* before the actor comes on the scene" (my italics). The example that Hart and Honoré use in illustrating this allegedly commonsense principle (which they insist is prior to and independent of legal or moral policies) is so curious that it will save me the trouble of providing my own counterexamples:

Suppose plaintiff is run over through defendant's negligence. If on the way to [the] hospital he is hit by a falling tree, that is a coincidence [negativing causal connection between defendant's earlier negligence and plaintiff's subsequent death]. If, just previously to being run over, he had been hit by a tree

⁶ *Ibid.*, 160-161.

and severely injured, that is a circumstance existing at the time of the running over and will not negative causal connection between the running over and the victim's death, even if the victim would not have died from the running down but for the previous blow from the tree. . . . It is, in a sense, as much a coincidence that the victim had been struck by a tree before he was run over as that he was struck afterwards, but the order in which the two events happen is of crucial importance in determining the consequences of the wrongful act.[7]

Hart and Honoré admit that the stage-setting exclusion principle "may be criticized as irrational"[8] but are nevertheless resolute in imputing it to common sense. Having a rather higher regard for common sense than they do, I shall try to distinguish what it endorses from what it rejects in the application of the principle.

II

First, I shall present four stories, all of which seem to me reasonable counterexamples to the voluntary intervention principle, and the last two (at least) to the first cause principle as well. Since there are also apparently supporting examples for these principles, part of my subsequent task will be to discover the rationale of the division between the cases to which these principles apply and those to which they do not.

Counterexample 1: the foolhardy bank teller. Jones, a depositor in the defendant's bank, was standing in line before the depositor's window when a bank robber entered, drew his gun, and warned "If anyone moves I'll shoot." The teller immediately grabbed something and dived to the floor. The bandit shot at him, and the ricocheting bullet struck Jones, still waiting in line, causing him severe injury. Jones then sued the bank (a more likely defendant than the impecunious bandit), charging that the teller's violation of the

7 *Ibid.*, 161.   8 *Loc.cit.*

bandit's order created an unreasonable risk of harm to the customers and that the teller's thoughtless act was thus the cause of Jones's injury. Let us suppose, for the sake of this example, that the teller's act was "negligent" (that is, unreasonably risky) to the customers and that it was a necessary condition of Jones's injury. Let us suppose also that the bandit entered the bank fully informed of the various kinds of things that might happen and fully prepared to shoot if anyone should call his bluff and that, when he did shoot, he was calm, collected, and fully aware of what he was doing. Now, on these facts, he did not intend to injure Jones since he aimed at the teller; but let us assume that, when he shot at the teller, he was aware of the danger he was creating for others but quite indifferent with regard to the possibility that someone else might be hurt.[9] One might well find, it seems to me, that the teller's negligent act was *the cause* of Jones's injury even though that injury would not have occurred but for the reckless and fully voluntary intervention of the bandit.[10]

Counterexample 2: the ingenious suicide. Mr. Blue, tired of life but too squeamish to kill himself, decides to use a more robust kind of person as an unwitting means. He hears about Manley Firmview, who has often announced to his friends that, if he ever encountered a person who would say so-and-so to him, he would kill the rascal. Mr. Blue

[9] Hart and Honoré hold that an act exhibiting a "reckless disregard of consequences," as well as a voluntary act intending the consequences that do result, negatives causal connection. Cf. *ibid.*, 143-144.

[10] The court in *Noll* v. *Marion*, 347 Pa. 213 (1943)—a case closely similar to the example in the text—held to the contrary that, "while it is possible that the teller might have prevented the injury to plaintiff by remaining standing, he did nothing unlawful in attempting to save himself and his employers' property by making the choice which under the circumstances seemed best to him. . . . The cause of plaintiff's injury was not the teller's violation of the unlawful prohibition to move, but the bandit's shooting." The argument given by the court, however, is primarily directed to the conclusion that the teller was not at fault in what he did (his act was not negligent or unreasonably risky to others), whereas in the hypothetical example in the text we are to assume that the teller's conduct *was* negligent and then raise the question of causation.

156

seeks out Mr. Firmview and says so-and-so to him. Firmview pauses for a moment, calmly considers the consequences, and then shoots the grateful Mr. Blue dead.
Would common sense balk at the claim that Mr. Blue
caused his own death *by means of* Firmview's free and deliberate "intervention?" That he killed himself or literally
committed suicide may be going too far, but that his remarks to Firmview were the cause of his demise could
scarcely be denied.

Counterexample 3: the coldly jealous husband. Mrs.
Green carries on an illicit love affair with Mr. Horner. Mr.
Black, learning of this and fully understanding Mr. Green's
character, informs him of the facts, secretly hoping that he
will kill Horner. True to form, Green investigates, learns the
truth, seriously considers the matter, calmly decides that
Horner deserves to die and that he is the one to kill him,
seeks Horner out, and shoots him dead, to the great delight
of the instigator, Black. On these facts, I submit, the killing
of Horner by Green was a fully voluntary act, and yet common sense, for purposes of its own, might well judge that
the cause of Horner's death was Black's disclosure of the
facts to the cuckolded husband.

Counterexample 4: the cocktail party bore. Imagine
the following cocktail party conversation:

Smith: Oh, no!

Jones: What's the trouble?

Smith: George Grossfellow is here, the worst bore in
the world.

Jones: What does he do?

Smith: He thinks he is a charming conversationalist, but
in fact he has a stock response to almost every
conversational opening, and he repeats the same
self-centered stories over and over again. See for
yourself. Go over and push his button. Casually
mention Senator Leadwater, and I'll bet you ten
dollars he will tell you about the time he met the
great man in a railroad dining car.

Jones then does mention Senator Leadwater in a mixed group containing Grossfellow, and the latter jumps at the chance to tell his boring tale. Smith wins the bet.

One moral of these four stories is that there are many more ways of causing someone to do something than by compelling or forcing him, or persuading and inducing him to do it. One can unintentionally cause him to act by unwisely calling his bluff; or one can "get him to act" by accepting a standing offer, drawing his attention to an inciting situation, or capitalizing on his firmly fixed habits of mind.

III

Much of the confusion shrouding this subject can be removed, I think, by a distinction between two different perspectives from which causal judgments can be made—the productive and the explanatory. From the productive standpoint, a cause is always a doing or a happening. Our most primitive way of making things happen is by direct doing—raising an arm, for example.[11] Rather more sophisticated techniques involve simple manipulations of external objects. By pushing, lifting, bending, and squeezing objects we directly produce changes in them.[12] But direct do-

[11] J. L. Austin thought that this was the original model of causation: " 'Causing,' I suppose, was a notion taken from a man's own experience of doing simple actions, and by primitive man every event was construed in terms of this model: every event has a cause, that is, every event is an action done by somebody—if not by a man, then by a quasi-man, a spirit." "A Plea for Excuses," *Proceedings of the Aristotelian Society*, N.S. 57 (1956/57), 28.

[12] Max Black suggests that forms of direct manipulation of objects provide the most primitive causal models, although such words as "push" and "pull" he calls part of our "pre-causal vocabulary": "As we pass from the homespun language of 'making something happen' to the more sophisticated language of 'cause' and 'effect,' the influence of the paradigm remains powerful. We continue to model descriptions of cases remote from the prototypes on the simpler primitive cases, often by using metaphors literally applicable only to those clear cases. In order to understand clearly what we mean by 'cause and effect' we must labor to understand what we mean by the precausal language in which the more sophisticated vocabulary is embedded." "Making Some-

ing and direct producing are still precausal ways of making things happen, for they do not involve the use of *instruments*. One does not raise an arm, or push or pull an object, by doing something still more elementary as a means; these simple motions and manipulations have a directness missing in full-fledged causal operations.

Instances of indirect producing are the clearest examples of causing things to happen. By manipulating an external object in such a way as to produce direct or primary changes in it, a person often *thereby* produces secondary changes in that or another object. We can say in this case that the manipulator causes the secondary changes *by means of* producing relatively immediate changes, or we can reserve the label "cause" for the primary changes themselves. The root notion in this use of causal language is that of a *means* or *instrumentality*. When a man causes a fire by rubbing sticks together, we can say that the friction (primary change) caused the fire (secondary change) because it was the means by which the fire was produced; and to say that friction causes fire generally comes very close to saying that one could produce an event of the latter sort by producing an event of the former kind.

Causal processes, of course, become much more complicated than simple models like stick-rubbing suggest, and as our means for producing changes become more variegated and complex, our models for understanding causal talk shift and divagate. Many simpler causal operations are mechanical and obvious: changes are initiated by pounding, pushing, or throwing objects. There is no denying that these processes have left a strong mark on our commonsense notion of cause, reflected in the ready priority writers give to the impact of moving objects in their discussions of causation. "At least all of those causal chains initiated by human beings," writes Douglas Gasking, "are initiated by manipu-

thing Happen," in *Determinism and Freedom in the Age of Modern Science*, ed. Sidney Hook (New York: New York University Press, 1958). 20.

lations, that is by matter in motion";[13] and the original "push" given even to many-staged causal processes remains persistently a model of causation in the minds of all of us.

The impact-motion model can easily be overrated, however. It may be true that causal chains initiated by persons typically begin with the moving of material bodies, but the initiating mechanism never has been exclusively that of forcing motion by striking, throwing, pounding, or pushing. Often the primary apparatus is chemical, and the initiating of motion merely the putting into position of the object to be chemically transformed—dropping it into water to be dissolved or into flame to be oxydized. In these cases there is no consciousness in the maker of exerting a force in making something happen; rather, the "making" is simply the bringing together of objects in such a way that they will (surprisingly) change, the actual change-producing mechanism being independent of the maker's direct willing and largely hidden from his eye and his understanding.

Of the various well-known techniques for causing human actions, some involve principles of even greater mystery and refinement. We can, of course, cause people to act by forms of direct bodily manipulation, or we can administer drugs or make sudden startling noises. This kind of causing preserves some analogy to the primitive pushing or forcing model. Hypnotizing and threatening are further removed, and getting people to act by providing them with motives for acting is more special still. It seems arbitrary to deny, however, that we are causing things to be done in these ways simply because our methods bear no resemblance to the crudest productive techniques.

Hart and Honoré overstate their point, then, when they insist on "the guiding analogy with the simple manipulation of things which underlies all causal thought." That the model of causing by means of a moving force does persist

[13] "Causation and Recipes," *Mind*, 64 (1955), 487. The views expressed in the text have been greatly influenced by this ingenious article.

to some degree, however, seems to be indicated by features of ordinary language that Hart and Honoré fasten upon. Sometimes it does seem a bit strained to say that a person caused another to act, even in circumstances where we should wish to cite his actions as the crucial causal factor in the *explanation* of the other's conduct. "Causing a person to act" easily shades into "making him act," and this suggests forcing him to act or leaving him no choice. For that reason, we may in given cases try to avoid saying that someone or something *caused* a person to act and say instead that *the cause of* the second person's action was so-and-so, or that the action was *due to* or a *consequence of* so-and-so. The foolhardy bankteller, for example, may deny that he caused the bank robber to shoot ("He didn't *have* to shoot," he might say) and yet admit that his own sudden motion was *the cause* of the bank robber's action. The distinction between causing and being the cause of, when recognized by ordinary language (of course, it is not always recognized), reflects the difference between the productive and the explanatory standpoints.

It is from the productive standpoint only that common sense embraces the stage-setting exclusion principle. For a person to cause something to happen is always for him to intervene in the natural course of things, directly producing primary changes that result in secondary ones according to a reliable causal recipe. From this standpoint, moreover, the event that causes the effect precedes it very closely in time.

It is otherwise when we approach causal questions from the standpoint of retrospective explanation. What is to be accounted for, from this point of view, is some past event or present state of affairs, and our concern in looking for its cause is to discover why it happened or how it came to be. We *may* phrase our answer in terms of some immediately antecedent event, or of the impact of some moving body, but we *need* not. The cause, we might decide, was an event ten years earlier, or a condition, quality, disposition, action, or omission or, indeed, almost any *kind* of thing at all.

161

Explanations can be long stories or brief citations, and only the latter utilize the notion of "the cause." Cause-citing explanations are always occasioned by the occurrence or discovery of something out of the ordinary, what is objectively a deviation from the normal course of things or else what is subjectively contrary to someone's expectations, hopes, or fears. If the captain is almost always drunk, one might well ask what was the cause of his sobriety today, expecting a brief answer citing some single factor normally present but missing today, or normally missing but present today, but for which the surprising breach of routine would not have occurred. But if the captain is a stalwart citizen who never touches a drop, then the question "What was the cause of his being sober today?" misfires. The first mate, if asked this question by an obviously ingenuous person, might reply, "Oh, the captain is always sober; he doesn't go in for drinking." This would be to offer a short explanation, and a satisfactory one, by rebutting a mistaken presumption of the person asking the question. If the interrogator persists, however, and demands a "fuller explanation" of the captain's sobriety, no simple citation will do. The respondent will now have to tell a long story illustrating what kind of man the captain is and how he came to be that way.

When we explain something by citation, that is, by use of the formula "Its cause was such-and-such," we select out one and only one of its causally relevant conditions as more important than the others. Importance is determined by our prior assumptions, understandings, and purposes; these vary from person to person and from context to context; "the cause," therefore, is a relative thing too. For that reason, a person does not contradict himself if at one time and place he says that "the cause" of X was Y and then in another situation says that "the cause" was Z. Of those factors but for which X would not have occurred, Y might well be the most important for one set of purposes and Z for another; or citation of Y might contribute more to one person's understanding, citation of Z to another's.

An example might make this point clearer. When heavy

industrial smog is trapped over a city, there is often a directly traceable effect on the death rate:

> We know very little about this effect, but we do know that air pollution does the most damage to those who have the least ability to stand any sort of stress—the old, the very young, and the sick. This was indicated in London in 1962, when, during a week-long period of heavy smog, there were four hundred more deaths than might normally have been expected.[14]

Let us imagine that Jones was one of the unlucky four hundred, that but for his severe tuberculosis he would not have died, and also that but for the heavy smog he would have recovered. Eight million other people survived the smog, a physician might reason, and but for his weakened lungs this patient should have too. Therefore, his tuberculosis was the cause of his death. An air pollution control commissioner might put the case otherwise: without the increase in air pollution this patient would have recovered; therefore, the heavy smog was the cause of his death. Of course, there is no real disagreement between the physician and the commissioner. Each has latched on to a causally necessary condition of the event to be explained which is central to his own theoretical interests and most important to his own practical pursuits. Those interests and pursuits do not "contradict" one another, nor need they necessarily conflict in any way.

Often, however, we are not content with this peaceful relativity. Especially when we resort to talk of "the true cause" or "the real cause," we are likely to be less tolerant of different causal citations; and when persons who agree about all the facts continue to opt for different "true causes," their causal language is a very poor disguise for a genuine opposition of purposes or policies. The cause of an ugly riot at a newly integrated Southern school was the court order forcing integration, say the segregationists. No, the true cause was the inflammatory statement of the gover-

[14] Edith Iglauer, "Fifteen Thousand Quarts of Air," *The New Yorker*, March 7, 1964, 58.

nor or perhaps the city's failure to provide adequate police protection or perhaps even the general climate of hatred, reply the Northern liberals. Surely this dispute, naturally framed in causal language, is not simply over what happened, but rather over which necessary condition of what happened is the most important one for purposes of judgment, understanding, prevention, and control.

However plausible it may seem from the productive standpoint, the stage-setting exclusion principle imposes much too severe a restriction on causal inquiries aiming at explanation by citation. Sometimes the missing link in a person's understanding is precisely some feature of the stage setting; and sometimes one of the background conditions of an event is objectively the feature of the situation which is abnormal and without which the consequence to be explained would not have occurred. On still other occasions the causal factor of major professional concern or of focal theoretical interest is part of the setting. Moreover, the stage-setting exclusion principle would often lead to an arbitrary begging of the question when there is genuine disagreement expressed in the statement of opposed causal citations. One might inquire, for example, what caused so many men to be off the job at a factory. One answer might be that the union leaders called a strike. Another might be that the management's refusal to budge from a negative bargaining position was the true cause. This is a familiar and difficult kind of disagreement. If we approach it strictly from the productive standpoint, however, and apply the stage-setting exclusion principle, its resolution is easy. The impasse in negotiations was stage-setting; the union leaders' order to strike was an active intervention on this stage and therefore the cause of the strike. Of course, from one point of view, there is nothing objectionable in saying that the union leaders, by giving their order, caused the strike; that is how strikes are "made to happen." But if we then decide that the unionist is forbidden by "common sense" from citing the management's failure to accede to union demands as "the real cause," we are taking away his tongue. He will now have to say that the management's refusal to bargain was not the cause of the strike but only the most important of all those conditions in the absence of which the strike would not have occurred! Similarly, the Negro children's "intervention" on the stage so carefully set by the segregationists would have to be called the cause of the riot, and the rioters would win their point, as it were, by default.[15]

If we remember that the point of an explanation by causal citation is to induce understanding, we shall be less inclined also to accept the first cause and voluntary intervention principles. We may smile when told that the cause of a grown man's voluntary action was some feature of his infant toilet training, but such a judgment, if based on a correct assessment of the facts, would commit no conceptual solecism. If it is true that but for the manner of his toilet training he would not have acted as he did, we can imagine interests and purposes for which that fact has quite sufficient importance to qualify as "the cause" of his subsequent voluntary behavior. Yet it would be misleading in the extreme (if there were anyone so naïve as to be misled) to suggest that his mother thirty years earlier "made" him act as he did today. "The cause" in this example is not the *in-*

15 Cf. the arguments put forth by Bertrand Russell and others to show that President Kennedy, and not Premier Khrushchev, caused the Cuba crisis of 1962. When Kennedy declared a naval blockade at the time Soviet ships were on their way to Cuba, according to this line of reasoning, he was intervening on a stage part of whose setting was the presence of Soviet rockets in Cuba. His intervention immediately led to the crisis. On this view, I suppose, if war had ensued, it in turn would have been caused by Khrushchev, for the American blockade then would have receded into the causal background against which a Soviet firing on the blockading ships would be the active intervening cause. Thus the stage-setting exclusion principle, in cases like this, turns into a version of the doctrine of the "last clear chance," often applied in law courts. Common sense, I would submit, would not necessarily select the last active intervention, in seeking the cause of the crisis, but rather that act or event that was a radical deviation from routine, which was clearly the Soviet construction of missile bases in Cuba. But see Bertrand Russell, *Unarmed Victory* (New York: Simon and Schuster, 1963), esp. 27-29, 32-65.

strument by which he was "made" to do what he did; rather, it is the *light* by which we come to see and understand his action more clearly.

Similarly, if our goal is understanding, we will not hesitate to trace a puzzling event right back through one, two, or many fully voluntary acts done with the intention of bringing it about, to a much earlier factor, more obscure perhaps, but equally necessary and much more interesting. So some have said that the cause of World War II was the unfair Versailles Treaty; and others have found the cause of the Protestant Reformation in Julius Caesar's failure to conquer the German tribes.

The examples of Hart and Honoré that seem to show that common sense endorses the voluntary intervention principle owe their persuasiveness to the operation of a quite different principle, one endemic in the explanatory standpoint, namely, that a highly abnormal or otherwise especially interesting occurrence, whether a human action or not, negatives causal connection between an earlier act or event and a later upshot. It is certainly correct, for example, that "a diner's death is not said to be caused by, or even a consequence of, the laying of the table from which a murderer seized the fatal knife."[16] But the reason is not that the murderer's act is a "voluntary intervention"; rather, it is that it is the abnormal deviation that distinguishes the whole incident from other dinners where diners are *not* killed. If the murder occurred in a prison dining hall, or a mental hospital, where knives are never set on tables and diners may be expected to get violent, then the laying of the table would be the abnormal event of great explanatory power, and the provision of opportunity "the cause." The pertinent principle here is that *the more expectable human behavior is, whether voluntary or not, the less likely it is to "negative causal connection"*; and when the stakes are high, as in our bank robbery example, consequences will be

---

[16] The words quoted are from Philippa Foot's perceptive review of *Causation in the Law,* in *The Philosophical Review,* 72 (1963), 510. The example is found in Hart and Honoré on 66.

traced right back through a voluntary act providing only that in retrospect it seems "not highly extraordinary"[17] that it intervened.[18]

IV

Among the more familiar examples, from the productive point of view, of causing things to happen are those of *triggering, precipitating,* or *igniting.* The causal instruments employed by these techniques are rather more sophisticated than the elementary tools of the simpler causal models, consisting either of machines (locks, triggers, catches, and springs) or else chemical operations (heating, cooling, mixing reagents). The following elements are generally characteristic of these complex causal processes: (1) In each case there is some point (a threshold) at which a gradual accumulation of small and unnoticed quantitative changes suddenly yields a large and conspicuous transformation. Pressure on a trigger builds up until it unlocks or releases a spring; the temperature of a liquid is gradually lowered until it suddenly yields a solid precipitate; the temperature of an explosive is gradually raised until it ignites. (2) The person who initiates the causal process may have to do a great deal of work first to build the mechanism up to the threshold point, or he may find

[17] This is the phrase used in the *Restatement of the Law of Torts* (Sec. 447). A negligent defendant will be liable for harm, according to the *Restatement,* despite the intervening act of a third person, if "a reasonable man knowing the situation existing when the act of the third person was done would not regard it as highly extraordinary that the person had so acted."

[18] There may be still another explanation for the persuasiveness of some of the examples by which Hart and Honoré support the voluntary intervention principle. In many of them an intentionally wrongful act intervenes between a negligently wrongful act and the harm for which both were necessary conditions. Intentional wrongdoing is usually regarded by moral common sense as more serious than negligence, and it is very difficult to keep separate the questions of moral blameworthiness and causation. This is a point that has not escaped the attention of these authors, however. See their vigorous counterargument, pp. 77f.

the mechanism ready and cocked, needing only the slightest "final push" to go off. (3) The causal mechanism may itself be either a simple machine or an interlocking assemblage of mechanical or chemical parts many of which themselves exploit threshold phenomena. In complex machines there is something like a chain reaction of triggered responses between the operator's initiating movement and its final upshot. (4) There is a great gain in efficiency. The operator does very little work in pushing a button or lighting a fuse; the intervening machinery yields a "stepped-up output," or response out of all proportion to the energy originally expended. (5) Finally, it is characteristic of these systems that, once the process is initiated, through at least one organic phase it is irreversible. Once the rifleman has released the hammer by sufficient pressure on the trigger there is no preventing a bullet from emerging from the barrel and traveling hundreds of feet. The whole physico-chemical stepping-up process is faster by far than the eye or hand of whoever put it in motion.

Now when the initiator has very little to do to put the process in motion—when by merely pushing a button he provides the final straw or the last push—then from the explanatory standpoint his action may be altogether uninteresting. Of course, if we know all about the machine yet wish to know in this instance how an end product came into existence, we may readily be content with a simple citation explanation: the cause was Jones's pushing of the button. But we may *see* Jones push the button and still not understand how the result came about. After all, mere finger pushings are familiar parts of the everyday scene, but rarely are they followed by such extraordinary creative outbursts. In this case we may not settle for any citation explanation. We may need to hear a very long story indeed to acquire a satisfactory understanding of the matter. Or, if we are mechanically sophisticated, we may settle for a citation explanation that mentions some one special feature of *this* machine. The last thing we would settle for, surely, would be the trivial commonplace of the button pushing.

Yet, from the productive standpoint, the operator's pushing of the button is the purest prototype of causing something to happen. The machinery is all stage setting or background against which the newly intervening force of the moving finger sets things going. In short, what clearly causes or makes something happen, from the productive standpoint, may not be worth mentioning when we look for "the cause" from the standpoint of retrospective explanation.

We often use the triggering, precipitating, and igniting metaphors in accounting for human actions, even, I would argue, for fully voluntary ones. A simple remark, a mere gesture, a routine action of all apparent innocence, may bring about an enormously stepped-up response. Triggering metaphors seem especially appropriate in describing these processes, partly because, as P. B. Rice once put it, all living beings come into existence "loaded and cocked"[19] —that is with governing biological propensities—and partly because experience gradually makes its mark on us, building up by little increments to the threshold of big response. Propositions gradually grow more credible to us until suddenly, in a quite ordinary setting, we reach the threshold of belief, as in a flash of insight. Similarly, expensive objects become gradually more tempting until suddenly a disproportionately trivial stimulus triggers a wholesale depletion of our bank account. So also a man struggling with his temper may have it "ignited" by a very small incident or remark.

It happens commonly enough that one person, either knowingly or unintentionally, triggers the action of another. The bank robber was all wound up to shoot, so to speak, at the slightest provocation; the teller, perhaps inadvertently but effectively, provided that slight stimulus. Now when this sort of thing occurs, we may or may not cite the

[19] *On The Knowledge of Good and Evil* (New York: Random House, 1955), 178.

triggering action as "the cause" when we give a retrospective explanation. If it is well known that the second actor had the disposition to act as he did in the circumstances, or that his condition was very near the relevant threshold, then the request for an explanation may ask, given that condition, what made the difference this time, and a satisfactory answer will cite the triggering cause. But the triggering stimulus may seem the "normal" element in the situation to one unacquainted with the dispositions and threshold conditions of the person responding, in which case "the cause" will not be the stimulus, but rather some aspect of the "trigger mechanism." This is another illustration of the relativity essentially residing in the explanatory perspective. But from the productive standpoint the causal issue is much more clear-cut and objective. Triggering another person's action is a very familiar way of "causing things to happen." Mentioning something to a person, for example, may remind him of something else that otherwise would have remained just below the threshold of his attention, and, given his governing habits, he may promptly speak up and recite what he has been reminded of. This is the way the sport in our earlier counterexample caused the bore at the party to tell his oft-told tale.

Now the crucial question arises: if *A*'s action is triggered by *B*'s, and especially if it is caused to happen by *B*'s intentional triggering, how can it possibly be said without qualification to be *A*'s own action, a free, informed, deliberate, that is, "fully voluntary" act? To begin with, I should like to concede that not all acts triggered by other persons can be said to be voluntary. Some triggers are extremely hard to pull, and when the required pressure is great enough, one may have to strain mightily to set things going. When a person's threshold is high and his relevant condition low, a would-be instigator may have to build it up gradually over an extended period of time by coaxing, playing on emotions, "fanning," "putting on the squeeze," before the desired act can be triggered. In circumstances like these, we should be reluctant, of course, to call the triggered act fully voluntary[20]—all the more so when the triggered disposition itself was implanted by the instigator through indoctrination, hypnotic suggestion, or other direct and prolonged manipulative techniques. Further, when the dispositions in question, however acquired, are regarded as diseased or unhealthy, the actions they yield when triggered will not, without severe qualification, be held to be voluntary.

This concession, however, still leaves us a large range of easily triggered, naturally acquired, and psychologically normal dispositions and threshold points. I should like to suggest that the more important to a full and comprehensive understanding of a triggered action the actor's own dispositions and thresholds are, the more likely we are to consider the act truly his, provided that those dispositions and thresholds are not biologically or psychologically abnormal and that they were not imposed on him by manipulation. When the trigger-pull is easy, and only the slightest commonplace sort of stimulus is required to set off an action, then the major part of the explanation of that action will necessarily involve the agent's own complicated self; and the more the triggering diminishes in explanatory significance, the less reluctant we are to regard the act as voluntary.

These points can be illustrated by a story a colleague used to tell to reveal what he took to be the incompatibility of determinism with common sense. Imagine that there are fine invisible wires connected to your body and at-

[20] There are perhaps some exceptions to this generalization. Often triggering is extended *stimulation*. When the stimulated response is not a happy one, we call the stimulation *provocation*; when the response is noble, the stimulation is called *inspiration*. Sometimes it takes a great deal of inspiration to reach the threshold of heroic action or difficult achievement; but in these cases we do not characterize the resultant act as less than voluntary. The point in the text does, however, seem to apply to all "extensively stimulated" bad actions. In this connection it should be noted that triggering is literally *releasing* a lock or catch; and the "lock" or "defenses" of a human being are, after all, a part of him. When it takes a great deal of stimulating for a person to respond, the stimulation is less a releasing than a kind of *overcoming*.

tached to an elaborate machine somewhere in such a way, that, whenever the machine operator pushes a certain button, your left arm rises, and whenever he pushes another, your right arm rises, and so on. Now if you did not know of this arrangement, my friend would argue, you might think that you were raising your arms, and doing all the other things you do, voluntarily. You might be aware of certain purposes, motives, and apparent "volitions" which fostered this illusion, but once you learned the truth, you would abandon the belief forever as an ignorant conceit. At this point someone would always protest that determinism does not imply that there is some *person* deciding at every moment how my body is to move. Well, change the example, then, my friend would reply. Imagine that the invisible wires are hooked up to such things as weathervanes, so that, for example, when the wind comes from the north, you move your left arm, and when it is southerly, your right, and so on. It does not matter *how* we are plugged in to external nature, my friend concluded; insofar as we *are* plugged in, our actions are to that extent not our own, but rather the doings of that, whatever it may be, into which we are plugged.

The reply to this argument, it seems to me, is that it does make a good deal of difference not into *what* we are plugged, but rather *how* we are plugged in. If the determining influences are filtered through our own network of predispositions, expectations, purposes, and values, if our own threshold requirements are carefully observed, if there is no jarring and abrupt change in the course of our natural bent, then it seems to me to do no violence to common sense for us to claim the act as our own, even though its causal initiation be located in the external world. In short, the more like an easy triggering of a natural disposition an external cause is, the less difficulty there is in treating its effect as a voluntary action.

On the other hand, if I were plugged into nature in such a way that the determining influence bypassed my own internal constitution, failing to utilize its latent tendencies, then clearly the resultant act would not be voluntary. If I were a guest at a formal dinner party, and some cosmic button pusher caused me to pass up my favorite dessert and, contrary to all my tastes, inclinations, and scruples, chew hungrily on the discarded cigarette butts in a nearby ashtray, I would surely be taken as the victim of some insane impulse or violent seizure. Triggering another person's actions need be nothing at all like this.

V

Before concluding, I should like to consider briefly a provision of our criminal law for which the causation of voluntary behavior raises serious problems both conceptual and moral, namely, that which allows an accused person, in some circumstances, the defense of "entrapment." When this defense is available to a defendant, he will be acquitted if he can prove that his alleged criminal conduct occurred in response to the "inducement or encouragement" of a police official or his agent.

No one would think of depriving the police of all initiative in trapping criminals. The plainclothes policewoman who mingles with a department store crowd in order to lure purse snatchers, for example, does not tempt honest people to depart from the path of rectitude; she lures the already determined or habitual criminal. Her behavior, perfectly normal and unobtrusive in every other way, attracts precisely one class of persons to whom she provides an opportunity to do what they are already bent on doing. There are some crimes that are almost impossible to detect without such techniques—"bribery, prostitution, and the illegal sale of narcotics, liquor, and firearms seem the most prominent."[21]

At the other extreme are clear examples of police abuses.

[21] "Note on Entrapment," *Harvard Law Review*, 73 (1960), 1338.

If a policeman incites a person to crime either by deceiving him into believing the criminal act is legal or by threatening harm, then the actor's criminal act is involuntary, and without question he may plead the entrapment defense. But between the extremes of passive allurement, on the one hand, and coercion and deception, on the other, are a range of techniques that give rise to many problems. Police agents in plain clothes have caused persons to act criminally by suggesting, inviting, advising, requesting, urging, coaxing, imploring, enticing, and so on. It is difficult to know how to draw the line between the proper and improper employment of such methods.[22]

But the most difficult kind of problem posed by entrapment techniques involves the following kind of case. Suppose that there is such a high degree of "readiness" in a certain person to commit a certain criminal act that only the slightest degree of inducement is required to bring him to the threshold. Perhaps a mere insinuation, an intriguing remark, or an appealing and persuasive tone will do the trick. Since these techniques, unlike insistent requesting, exhorting, seducing, and the like, are commonplace stimuli of gen-

---

[22] The Model Penal Code rule (American Law Institute's final draft, 1962, Sec. 2.13) forbids techniques likely to induce to the performance of a criminal act "persons other than those who *are ready* to commit it" [my italics]. This will hardly yield a workable test of entrapment, however, if the test in turn of a person's readiness is whether it would take a large or small amount of inducement to get him to act. Note the unavoidable analogy to triggering. It is as if we were to say that the test of whether or not a trigger mechanism was in a state of prior readiness is whether or not it took an inordinate amount of pressure to release it; and the test of whether the triggering pressure was "inordinate" is whether it would have been sufficient to trigger even "unready" mechanisms. The Model Penal Code criterion, then, like most legal tests, has only a specious precision. Interpreted as a kind of litmus test, it is imperiled by circularity. It had better be interpreted as a rough guide to the kinds of consideration relevant to the question and the way these considerations (acts of policemen, predispositions of the inducee, predispositions of other people) are interrelated. The test says in effect that the defense of entrapment is not available to those whose prior condition was already *very near* the threshold of criminal action, with "very near" left necessarily vague.

erally small effectiveness, they would almost certainly preclude the entrapment defense. But suppose also that, but for the policeman's use of these techniques, it is highly unlikely that the person incited would ever have committed the criminal act. He may have remained for the rest of his days "ready" to commit the crime—that is, in a condition such that it would not take much to induce him to commit it—and yet never cross that threshold. This is an example of causing a generally law-abiding citizen to commit a crime he would not otherwise have committed while depriving him of his entrapment defense.

Since in cases of this kind the police inducement, however small, is a necessary condition of the criminal act, it seems fair to say that the criminal so induced will be punished for his *predisposition*, that is, his readiness, to commit the crime or, put another way, for his high susceptibility to inducement. The intuition that such punishment is not just is disconcertingly difficult to support with argument. Perhaps much of it is derived from the notion that a legal system promises to punish only acts, and in cases like this the spirit, if not the letter, of that promise is violated. But to circumvent that difficulty, let us discuss the justice of a hypothetical general practice. Imagine a system of law enforcement in which police agents search out people who teeter on the brink of criminality, and who may or may not eventually fall in, and deftly provide them with the final ever-so-slight stimulus to criminal action. Would this be a just or unjust general practice? We are, of course, understandably loath to confer powers on policemen that can be misused, and this might be a quite conclusive reason against the scheme under discussion. But would the scheme be unjust to those persons sought out and trapped? Insofar as they are punished only for their predispositions, are they being treated unfairly?

In support of a system of anticipatory enforcement, one might cite its effectiveness as social prophylaxis. After all, it is socially dangerous to have loaded and cocked weapons lying around, especially those with delicate trigger mechanisms. Why not seek them out and detonate them harmlessly? And if this procedure involves neither coercion nor deception of free and responsible moral agents, how can it be unjust to them?

It might be said that mere predisposition does not constitute sufficient *culpability* for just punishment. But, from the moral point of view, there appears to be no significant difference between the person highly predisposed to crime who is induced to act and the person highly predisposed who never finds his inducer. The locus of moral culpability in each *is* the predisposition, and what distinguishes the two is mere luck; for it is not to the credit of the one that he performed no criminal act if it was only an accident that he was never brought across the criminal threshold. Furthermore, the predisposed criminal is no less guilty for being induced to act by a policeman in a disguise than thousands of others of like disposition who are induced by private persons.

This problem about justice is far too complicated to pursue any further here. The thesis I wish instead to defend is a very modest one: that the problem could not even be formulated without assuming that caused behavior can be fully voluntary. More specifically, the possibility of caused voluntary actions is what gives the moral problem of anticipatory enforcement its difficult and dilemmatic character. Insofar as another party gets a person to do something he might otherwise never have done, we find it unjust to hold that person responsible. The initiative, we say, lay with the other party. On the other hand, insofar as the induced act was freely done by a person who was in a high state of readiness to do it, we find that it was truly his own action, and one for which he is fully responsible. There is no conceptual difficulty, I submit, in this description of an act as caused and voluntary; but that is exactly what, from the moral point of view, causes all the trouble.

176

REJOINDER[23]

One important modification of my view is necessary. Throughout my paper I speak of "the cause" as an interesting or important *necessary* condition simply. I should be better advised to mean by "the cause" of an event generally "a condition which, when conjoined with circumstances normally present, is *sufficient* to bring about events of the type in question" and to mean by the cause of a given event "a condition which, when added to circumstances already present, is *sufficient* for its occurrence." This emendation detrivializes my thesis without diminishing its plausibility, for there is ample support in common sense for the view that some voluntary actions are caused even in this strong sense and, in particular, that they are often caused by the actions, intentional or unintentional, of other people. A much less dramatic example than those in my article might help make this clear. I can get an acquaintance to say "good morning" by putting myself directly in his line of vision, smiling, and saying "good morning" to him. My doing these things is not only a circumstance but for which his voluntary action would not have occurred, it is also a circumstance which, when added to those already present, "made the difference" between his speaking and remaining silent. So much, at least, is conveyed by the phrase "getting him to act," which would not be used if the inciting behavior were not considered a *sufficient* cause.

Mr. Donnellan apparently accepts my main thesis but warns against claiming the truth of certain controversial philosophical doctrines as "the fruit of [my] victory." His

[23] The preceding essay was presented as part of a symposium at the 1964 Oberlin Colloquium in Philosophy. Replies delivered by Professor Keith Donnellan of Cornell and Professor Keith Lehrer of Rochester were subsequently published along with it in the Proceedings of the Colloquium, *Metaphysics and Explanation* (Pittsburgh: University of Pittsburgh Press, 1966), 48-54. This rejoinder, though not delivered orally at Oberlin, appears in the same volume (55-61) and is reprinted here by the kind permission of the publisher.

warning is well heeded. I do not wish to claim that man is but a machine or that human dispositions to act are literally "trigger mechanisms" or that "there are no important differences between the causes of voluntary action and the causes of other events." I strongly regret that my lack of clarity in stating my intentions conveyed such impressions. All I meant to do in the section Mr. Donnellan criticizes was to cite the commonplace that we do often use triggering metaphors in describing some voluntary human actions and to argue for the appropriateness of the metaphors (as metaphors), which still seems to me beyond question. I emphasized certain similarities between the human actions for which these metaphors are appropriate and mechanical contraptions like guns, but I did not intend to suggest that there are "no important differences." F. Scott Fitzgerald is alleged to have insisted once to Ernest Hemingway that there are important differences between the rich and other people, to which Hemingway is supposed to have replied, "Yes, the rich people have more money." Human beings are importantly different from mechanical contraptions, among other ways, in that they have intentions, purposes, values, reasons, and goals; and I have no more desire to underrate the significance of these things than did Hemingway the importance of money. Rather, I thought it goes without saying that human beings have these distinguishing characteristics, just as it goes without saying that rich people have more money, and also that these obviously distinguishing characteristics do not foreclose the presence of less obvious characteristics held in common.

At any rate, because human beings are different in these ways from mere machines, we can ask questions about their behavior of a sort that do not apply to events of other kinds. We can ask, for example, *"Why* did he do that?" meaning "What were his reasons for doing it?" That this is a question appropriate to actions, but not to other events, I readily grant; but it would be incorrect, I believe, to infer from this the converse, that questions of a form readily applicable to mere events are not also applicable to voluntary actions. We can ask, I submit, of anything that has come to be *how it came to pass* that it came to be. Sometimes an adequate answer to a "How did it come about that . . . ?" question is a simple statement of a person's reasons for acting; but sometimes such an explanation fails to resolve perplexity, and one must cite the agent's more remote goals or purposes, or his motives or his habits, policies, or "springs of action," or even a general account of "the sort of person he is." Moreover, although an explanation in terms of reasons for acting does render a voluntary action more intelligible (at least in one dimension), it might be maintained that some actions, at least, do not become wholly comprehensible until one knows, for example, *how it came about that* these reasons "weighed with him,"[24] or that he had these purposes and not purposes of another kind, or that he was this sort of person and not some other type. Satisfactory answers to the latter questions, of course, will not mention further reasons or purposes of the agent but will instead possess a form that assimilates persons and their actions to the rest of nature. In short, even though I must concede to Donnellan that "What were his reasons?" questions cannot be *paraphrased* as "How did it come about that . . . ?" questions, still answers to the latter might supplement or supersede answers to the former, and explanations in terms of reasons might well be subject to a kind of integration with explanations of other kinds.

In one place Donnellan puts his point in terms of the *interest* we have in the connection between a voluntary action and its cited cause. He denies in this passage that such an interest is in a causal mechanism, for which a question in terms of "How does it work?" is appropriate.[25] What he denies with "mechanism" in italics I would affirm with "mechanism" in scare-quotes. After all, there are interests and interests. Is it not *ever* true that our interest in the con-

[24] The phrase is used by Messrs. G. J. Warnock, P. F. Strawson, and J. F. Thomson, in their symposium in *Freedom and the Will*, ed. D. F. Pears (London: St. Martin's Press, 1963).
[25] *Metaphysics and Explanation*, 49.

nection between act and cause is precisely in learning *how* a man's habits or deliberate policies mesh with stimuli of various sorts in yielding certain kinds of voluntary actions? My case for the affirmative must rest on my examples.

Donnellan has another very interesting argument against me. He concedes (1) that a person who causes another's voluntary action may be himself subject to blame for it by a third party but claims (2) that in these instances the principal (second) voluntary actor cannot do the blaming. And yet (3) on my triggering model it is "inexplicable why one should not blame another for triggering his mechanism or taking him over the threshold even though the act is voluntary."[26]

I should like to concentrate my reply to this argument on the second statement and attempt to escape embarrassment by the time-honored tactic of making a number of distinctions. What are some of the more common ways in which one person can cause another to act voluntarily? First, he can provide an opportunity to the other to do what he was already bent on doing. Second, he can, like our fictitious bank teller, call the other's bluff or not heed his warning. Third, he can, like Mr. Black, direct the other's attention to something he might not otherwise have known. Fourth, he can exploit another's carefully studied habits, as in my "good morning" and "party bore" examples. Fifth, he can take advantage of the kind of "conscious habit" that is periodically subject to review, or a full-fledged deliberate *policy* of acting in certain ways in certain kinds of situations, as in my "ingenious suicide" example.

Now it would indeed be absurd for a voluntary actor to blame another for providing him with the opportunity for doing what he already had his heart set on doing. Donnellan asserts, similarly, that "it would be absurd for Mr. Green to blame Mr. Black for causing him to seek out Horner and kill him."[27] This is not quite an example of "providing an opportunity," but it involves a similar principle, and Donnellan may be quite right in his judgment. (I am

26 *Ibid.*, 50.   27 *Ibid.*

not sure he is right, however; I can imagine a heartbroken but unrepentant Mr. Green saying to Black, "Why did you have to tell me anyway? I'd have been better off deceived and unavenged than avenged and undeceived.") In the other three cases, however, I detect no impropriety, moral or conceptual, in the principle actor's "accusing," "blaming," or "holding accountable" the one who caused him to act. There would be an absurdity in this response only if the principal actor, in blaming the other, absolved himself; but I see no reason why, in these cases, he could not hold the other equally responsible with himself for what happened.

Mr. Lehrer complains—with some justice, I think—that, in making my point against Hart and Honoré's voluntary intervention principle, I failed to consider their distinction between explanatory and attributive causal statements. Let me try to remedy that omission here, first by considering how Hart and Honoré's distinction is related to the causal distinctions that play a role in my essay. I used the term *causal citation* to refer to all causal statements of the form "Its cause was such-and-such." Some of these, by citing causal factors that are missing links in a person's understanding, function as explanations; but not all causal explanations are causal citations. An explanation of how a clock runs or how the tides come in, for example, can be what I called a "long-story explanation," and these in turn form a very diverse class indeed.[28] On the other hand, not all causal citations are intended primarily to explain. Prominent among the nonexplanatory causal citations are those made from what I called the "productive standpoint,"

[28] The distinction between causal citations and long-story explanations is illustrated nicely by N. R. Hanson: "A farmer may ask what is causing his crop failure. But he will not, in the same tone of voice, ask what is causing its success. For he realizes that the success of crops depends upon a delicate atmospheric conspiracy of fine weather (but not too fine), warmth in moderation, rain but not flood, etc. Whereas, should his crop show signs of failing, he will hope that an expert will be able to say just what is the cause." "Causal Chains," *Mind*, 64 (1955), 310.

where the concern is to cite the event immediately antecedent to a certain result that was sufficient in the circumstances for its production, whether or not that event contributes any insight to a person seeking understanding.[29] Still other kinds of examples of nonexplanatory causal citations are found in my paper: citations of causal factors easiest to produce, eliminate, or control, or of greatest interest to a given profession, or of central concern for purposes of moral judgment, or enforced compensation, or some other practical interest.

Hart and Honoré's distinction can easily be fit into this scheme. In my terminology, it is a distinction between explanatory causal citations and one very special kind of nonexplanatory causal citation (*not* an exhaustive distinction between explanatory and *all* nonexplanatory citations). Hart and Honoré's "attributive" judgments always cite the actions of *human beings* as "the cause" of some *harm*. Attributive inquiries are often intertwined with, or dependent on, explanatory inquiries, but "searches for explanation are not the source of the lawyer's main perplexities: these arise when, after it is clearly understood how some harm happened, the courts have, because of the form of legal rules,

---

[29] Difficult as this distinction is to characterize in the abstract, it is intuitively clear, as is illustrated by the story of the straw that broke the camel's back. Suppose that Omar's daily routine is to take his camel to ten different stations in the marketplace. At each stop a merchant loads one hundred straws, one at a time, on the camel's back. By the end of the day, then, there are one thousand straws on the camel's back, a weight very near but not quite at the back's breaking point; and Omar then leads the camel to a warehouse to be unloaded. One day, just as the tenth merchant puts the last straw on the load, the camel sags to the ground, his back fractured. A subsequent inquest discloses that early in the day, at the third stop, a mischievous urchin, unnoticed by anyone, slipped one extra straw on the load. Now the question arises: which straw caused the camel's back to break? Both the urchin's straw and the last straw (let us suppose) were necessary conditions of the break, and, depending on what we include in the causal background, both can be regarded as sufficient. From the productive point of view, clearly the last straw was the cause, since *its* arrival at the top of the pile brought the burden above the breaking point. Still Omar does not *understand* why the camel's back broke until he learns of the urchin's straw, and the point of a causal *explanation* is to foster understanding.

to determine whether such harm can be attributed to the defendant's action as its consequence or whether he can properly be said to have caused it. These may be called attributive inquiries."[30] Whether or not a death is to be attributed to tuberculosis or to air pollution is, in this special sense, not an attributive inquiry; but, as the example in my article shows, citation of one or the other as "the cause" need not be explanatory either.

Insofar as I concerned myself with explanatory causal citations in arguing against the voluntary intervention principle, which was intended by Hart and Honoré to apply only to attributive causal statements (in their special sense), I was unfair to them, and Lehrer has a valid point to make against me. The point, however, is hardly as damaging as Lehrer contends, for my counterexamples seem to me to tell just as effectively against the voluntary intervention principle when it is understood to apply only to attributive causal statements. "It is quite clear," Lehrer writes, "that the death of Horner is to be attributed to the husband, Mr. Green, and to no one else. It surely would be a mistake to attribute his death to Mr. Black."[31] This is not at all clear or certain to me. I do not see how the facts of the case would logically foreclose the judgment that the cause of Horner's death was Black's spilling the beans or that the death is to be attributed jointly to Black and Green. The facts leave these possibilities open; our moral standards or legal rules or other practical purposes will determine which logically permissible attributive judgment we make.

"The voluntary intervention principle," Lehrer continues, "does not deny that Black's action might serve as a causal explanation of Horner's death; it only denies that Horner's death may be attributed to Black's action."[32] Explanatory causal citations are relative to the gaps in a person's understanding; but I can imagine two persons who have no such puzzlement—they thoroughly understand exactly how

---

[30] *Causation in the Law*, 22-23.
[31] *Metaphysics and Explanation*, 52-53.
[32] *Ibid.*, 53.

Horner's death came about—and yet one "attributes" it to Black and the other to Green. Here there may be a harmony of understanding and yet a clash of moral judgments or of appraisals of "expectability," or standards of normalcy or the like, leading to opposed attributive judgments.

I must hasten to add that I agree with Hart and Honoré that, after the facts are in, we do not have *complete license* to settle the attributive question in accordance with our moral standards, policies, and purposes, that certain commonsense principles here place effective limits on our discretion. I disagree with them only in my account of what these principles are. I opt for the principle that "the more *expectable* human behavior is, whether voluntary or not, the less likely it is to negative causal connection." They prefer the voluntary intervention principle. The only way the issue can be argued is through examples and counterexamples.

Before leaving this question, I should like to make a stab (it can be no more than that) at locating the source of Lehrer's apparent certainty that the death of Horner is to be attributed to Green and no one else. Our disagreement on this question may be the result of an unnoticed ambiguity. Our language often provides us with alternative but equivalent ways of making causal judgments. We can use the language of causal citation or that of causal agency. Thus we can say either "Jones caused the door to close (by pushing it)" or "Jones closed the door." In many other cases, however, our language does not give us this option. I recently observed two young boys teasing a smaller child by causing him to giggle uncontrollably. Finally, one turned to the other and said (improperly): "We'd better quit or we'll laugh him to death." The boy wanted a transitive verb that could be used interchangeably with "causing another to laugh"; but our language does not carry such a word in stock, there being little demand for it. In still other cases, transitive verbs of action are available to tempt us, but they cannot be substituted for straightforward causal idioms without placing severe strain on sense. Thus the ingenious suicide, in the earlier example, surely caused his own death (the cause of his death was his provocative remark to Manley Firmview); but we cannot express this fact by saying that he *killed* himself without being misleading in the extreme. The killing, Lehrer would quite rightly say, can be attributed to Firmview "and to no one else"; and the same point applies, *a fortiori*, to "shooting" and other more determinate action verbs. Similarly, there might be a point, in some contexts, in saying that the cause of a certain married woman's pregnancy, after many unhappy barren years, was the medication prescribed for her by her obstetrician; but it would raise eyebrows to express this fact by saying that the doctor "got her pregnant," and it would be plain libel to say that he "fathered her child." This was done by the husband and "no one else." Thus the distinction between causing and doing can be of considerable moment.

Perhaps Lehrer would be willing to accept my counterexamples if I made it perfectly plain that I was restricting their application to attributions via causal citations and making no further point about the language of agency.

The argument Lehrer borrows from Locke[33] is a perfectly sound one, and its conclusion is important and insufficiently attended to by philosophers in our time. Its point is that it does not follow from the description of an action as voluntary (unconstrained, informed, and deliberate) that the agent could have done otherwise. If we use the term "avoidable" for the more cumbersome phrase "could have done otherwise," the point can be put pithily: voluntari-

---

[33] I quote from Lehrer, *ibid.*, 53: "In his rather remarkable English prose, Locke once wrote: 'Suppose a man be carried, whilst fast asleep, into a room where is a person he longs to see and speak with; and be there locked fast in, beyond his power to get out: he awakes, and is glad to find himself in so desirable company, which he willingly stays in, i.e. prefers his stay to going away. I ask, is not this stay voluntary? I think nobody will doubt it: and yet, being locked fast in, it is evident he is not at liberty not to stay, he has not freedom to be gone.' I shall refer to the man in this story as 'Mr. Lockedin.' The moral of his story is this: Mr. Lockedin's stay in the room is voluntary even though he could not have done otherwise." The passage from Locke is in *An Essay Concerning Human Understanding*, ed. A. C. Fraser (Oxford: Clarendon Press, 1894), Vol. II, chap. 21, par. 10.

ness does not entail avoidability. Furthermore, the compatibility of voluntariness with causal determination does not entail the compatibility of avoidability with causal determination. But although this is an important point (and one commonly obscured by the leaky-umbrella term "freely"), it hardly counts against anything I have said, for in this essay I defend a thesis about voluntariness only, and one that leaves the further vexatious question about avoidability and determinism entirely open.

I Sua Culpa

It is common enough for philosophers to analyze moral judgments and for philosophers—usually other philosophers—to analyze causal judgments. But statements to the effect that a given harm is some assignable person's fault, having both moral and causal components, import the complexities of judgments of the other two kinds. They are, therefore, especially challenging. Yet they are rarely considered by analytical philosophers. This neglect is to be regretted, because "his fault" judgments (as I shall call them) are important and ubiquitous in ordinary life. Historians employ them to assign blame for wars and depressions; politicians, sportswriters, and litigants use them to assign blame for losses. The disagreements they occasion are among the most common and intensely disputed in all "ethical discourse."

It may seem that most of those who quibble and quarrel about "his fault" are either children or lawyers; and even lawyers, therefore, can seem childish when they are preoccupied with the question. But investigators, editorialists, and executives must assign blame for failures and thereby judge the faults of their fellows. (Indeed, their inquiries and debates are most childish when they do *not* carefully consider fault and instead go scapegoat-hunting.) My assumption in what follows is that the faults that concern nonlawyers, both children and adults, are faults in the same sense of the word as those that concern the lawyer, that the concept of "his fault" is imported into the law from the world of everyday affairs. On the other hand, "proximate cause" (to pick just one of a thousand examples) is a technical term of law invented by lawyers to do a special legal job and subject to continual refashioning in the interests of greater efficiency in the performance of its assigned legal task. To explain this term to a layman is precisely to explain what *lawyers* do with it; if it should ever happen that a child, or a sportswriter, or an historian should use the expression, that fact would be of no relevance to its proper analysis. But to explain the concept of "his fault," we must give an account that explains what both lawyers and laymen do with it and how it is possible for each to understand and to communicate with the other by means of it.

An equivalent way of saying that some result is a man's fault is to say that he is *to blame* for it. Precisely the same thing can also be said in the language of *responsibility*. Of course, to be responsible for something (after the fact) may also mean that one did it, or caused it, or now stands answerable, or accountable, or liable to unfavorable responses from others for it. One can be responsible for a result in all those senses without being to blame for it. One can be held liable for a result either because it is one's fault or for some quite different kind of reason; and one can be to blame for an occurrence and yet escape all liability for it. Still, when one is to blame for a harm, one can properly be said to be "responsible for it *really*"; that is, there is a sense of "responsible for" that simply means "chargeable to one as one's fault." One of the commonest uses of the expression *"morally* responsible for" is for being responsible for something in this sense. (Another is for chargeability to a fault of a distinctively moral kind. Still another is for being *liable* to responses of a distinctively moral kind.)

II

The word "fault" occurs in three distinct idioms. We can say of a man that he *has a fault*, or that he is (or was) *at fault*, or that he is "to blame" for a given harm, which is to say that the harm is (or was) *his fault*. In this essay I shall be directly concerned only with the last of these idioms, except to make some necessary preliminary remarks about the other two.

To have a fault. A fault is a shortcoming, that is, a failure to conform to some norm or standard. Originally, perhaps, the word "fault" gave emphasis to failures through deficiency; but now any sort of failure to "measure up" is a fault, and we find no paradox in "falling short through excess." Not all defective human properties are faults. Evanescent qualities are hardly around long enough to qualify. To be a fault, a defective property must be sufficiently durable, visible, and potent to tell us something interesting about its possessor. A fault can be a durable manifestation almost constantly before the eye; but, more typically, human faults are latencies that manifest themselves only under special circumstances. Flaws of character are tendencies to act or feel in subpar ways, which, as tendencies, are *characteristic* of their possessor, that is, genuinely representative of him. Moreover, faults, like virtues, are commonly understood as comparative notions. An irascible man, for example, is not merely one who can become angry, for on that interpretation we may all be considered irascible. Rather, he is one who is more prone than most to become angry, either in the sense that he becomes angry on occasions when most men would not or in the sense that he gets angrier than most men on those occasions when most men would be angry. Equally commonly, however, we interpret a tendency-fault as a failure to satisfy not merely a statistical norm, but a norm of propriety: an irascible man has a tendency to get angry on occasions when he *ought* not to. And even when the implied norm is a statistical one, the fault predicate does more than describe neutrally. A fault word always expresses derogation.

The concept of fault has a close relation to that of harm, but it would be an overstatement to claim that all human faults create the risk of harm. David Hume was closer to the mark when he divided faults into four categories: those that cause displeasure or harm to self or others. Immediate displeasure, however, is only one of the diverse negative reactions that, quite apart from harmfulness, can be the sign of a fault. I would also include, for example, offense, wounded feelings, disaffection, aversion, disgust, shock, annoyance, and "uneasy sensations"—reactions either of the faulty self or of others. If we use the word "offensiveness" to cover the provoking of this whole class of negative responses, and if we assume that everything that is offensive to self, in this broad sense, is likely also to be offensive to others, we can summarize Hume's view by saying that it is either harmfulness or social offensiveness that makes some characteristics faults. Hume notwithstanding, there are some (though perhaps not many) faults that neither harm nor offend but simply fail to benefit, such as unimaginativeness and various minor intellectual flaws. We can modify Hume's account of the offensive faults further, perhaps in a way Hume would not have welcomed, by adding that it is not the mere *de facto* tendency of a trait to offend that renders it a fault. Normally when we attach the fault label to personal characteristics—that is, when we speak as moralists expressing our own judgments, and not merely as sociologists describing the prevailing sentiments of our communities—we are not simply predicting that the characteristics will offend; we are instead (or also) endorsing offense as an appropriate reaction to them. Most of those faults that do not harm, we think, are traits that naturally, or properly, or understandably offend (in the widest sense of "offend").

Often we speak as if a man's fault can enter into causal relations with various outcomes external to him. These assertions, when sensible, must be taken as elliptical forms of more complex statements. To say that a man's faulty disposition, his carelessness or greed, caused some harm is to say that the man's action or omission that did the causing was of the type that he characteristically does (or would do) in circumstances of the kind that in fact were present, or that the act or omission was of the sort he has a predominant tendency to do in circumstances of that kind. (He may, of course, also have a countertendency to restrain himself by an act of will, or the like.) To cite a man's character flaw as a cause of a harm, in short, is to *ascribe* the cause to an act or omission and then to *classify* that act or omission in a certain way—as characteristic of the actor. (It is just the sort of thing he *would* do, as we say.) It is also, finally, to *judge* the manifested characteristic as substandard and thereby to derogate it.

One can be *at fault* on a given occasion, however, even though one does not act in a characteristic way. Even very careful men sometimes slip up; even the most talented make mistakes; even the very calm sometimes lose their tempers. When these uncharacteristic failures cause harm, it is correct to say that a *faulty aspect* of some act or omission did the causing, but incorrect to ascribe the cause to some faulty characteristic of the actor, for that would be to imply, contrary to the hypothesis, that he is a generally careless, irascible, or inept person. This is the kind of faulty doing (as opposed to "faulty being") that could happen, as we say, to anyone; but in the long run it will be done more often by those who have serious character faults than by those who do not.

"Being at fault," even in one's perfectly voluntary and representative conduct, is in a sense partly a matter of luck. No one has complete control over what circumstances he finds himself in—whether, for example, he lives in times of war or peace, prosperity or depression, under democratic or autocratic government, in sickness or health, and so on. Consequently, a man may, by luck merely, escape those circumstances that would actualize some dreadful latency in him of which he is wholly unaware. It may even be true of *most* of us virtuous persons that we are to some small degree, at least, "lucky" in this sense. (We do not, however, normally refer to the mere absence of very bad luck as "good luck.") Not only can one *have a fault* and "luckily" escape *being at fault* in one's actions (on analogy with the hemophiliac who never in fact gets cut); one can also have a small fault (that is, a disposition very difficult to actualize) and unluckily stumble into those very rare circumstances that can actualize it. (The latter is "bad luck" in a proper sense.) Both of these possibilities—the luckily unactualized and the unluckily actualized latencies—follow from the analysis of faults as dispositions and, if that analysis is correct, should be sufficient at least to temper anyone's self-righteousness about the faulty actions of others.

To be at fault. When a man is "at fault" on a given occasion, the fault characterizes his action itself and not necessarily the actor, except as he was during the performance of the action. There is no necessary relation between this kind of fault and general dispositions of the actor—though, for all we know, every faultily undertaken or executed action *may* exemplify extremely complicated dispositions. When we say that a man is at fault, we usually mean only to refer to occurrent defects of acts or omissions, and only derivatively to the *actor's* flaw as the doer of the defective deed. Such judgments are at best presumptive evidence about the man's general character. An act can be faulty even when not characteristic of the actor, and the actor may be properly "to blame" for it anyway; for if the action is faulty and it is also *his* action (characteristic or not), then he must answer for it. The faultiness of an action always reflects *some* discredit upon its doer, providing the doing is voluntary.

One standard legal classification divides all ways of being at fault into three categories: intentional wrongdoing, recklessness, and negligence. The traditional legal test of intentional doing has been a disjunctive one: there is intentional wrongdoing if either one acts with a wrongful conscious objective or one knowingly produces a forbidden result even incidentally as a kind of side-effect of his effort to achieve his objective. When the occurrence of the forbidden or undesirable side-effect is not certain, but nevertheless there is a known substantial likelihood of its coming about as an incidental byproduct of one's action, its subsequent production cannot be called "intentional" or "knowing" but verges into *recklessness*. What is known in recklessness is the existence of a *risk*. When the actor knowingly runs the risk, when he is willing to gamble with his own interests or the interests of others, then, providing the risk itself is unreasonable, his act is reckless.[1]

One can hardly escape the impression that what is called "negligence" in the law is simply the miscellaneous class of faulty actions that are not intentional (done purposely or knowingly) or reckless; that in this classification of faults, once wrongful intentions and reckless quasi-intentions have been mentioned, "negligence" stands for everything else. This would leave a class of faults, however, that is *too* wide and miscellaneous. Humorlessness (to take just one example) is a kind of fault that is not intentional; yet we would hardly accuse a man of being "negligent" in failing to be amused or to show amusement at what is truly amusing. The point, I think, is that inappropriate failures to be amused are not the sorts of faults likely to cause *harm*. There is no great risk in a blank stare or a suppressed giggle. Negligence is the name of a heterogeneous class of acts and omissions that are unreasonably *dangerous*. Creation of risk is absolutely essential to the concept, and so is fault. But the fault is not merely conjoined coincidentally to the risk; rather, the fault consists in creating the risk, however unintentionally. When one knowingly creates an unreasonable risk to self or others, one is reckless; when one unknowingly but faultily creates such a risk, one is negligent.

There are a large number of ways of "unintentionally but faultily" creating an unreasonable risk. One can consciously weigh the risk but misassess it, either because of hasty or otherwise insufficient scrutiny (rashness), or through willful blindness to the magnitude of the risk, or through the conscientious exercise of inherently bad judgment. Or one can unintentionally create an unreasonable risk by failing altogether to attend either to what one is do-

[1] I intend here no more than what is in the Model Penal Code definition: "A person acts recklessly with respect to a material element of an offense when he consciously disregards a substantial and unjustifiable risk that the material element exists or will result from his conduct. . . . Recklessness involves conscious risk creation."

ing (the manner of execution) or to the very possibility that harmful consequences might ensue. In the former case, best called *carelessness* or *clumsiness* (in execution), one creates a risk precisely in virtue of not paying sufficient attention to what one is doing; in the latter case, which we can call *heedlessness* (in the very undertaking of the action), the risk is already there in the objective circumstances, but unperceived or mindlessly ignored.

There are still other faults that can render a given act or omission, unknown to its doer, unreasonably dangerous. Overly attentive drivers with the strongest scruples and the best intentions can drive as negligently as inattentive drivers and, indeed, a good deal more negligently than experienced drivers of strong and reliable habits who rely on those habits while daydreaming, their car being operated in effect by a kind of psychic "automatic pilot." Timidity, excitability, organic awkwardness, and slow reflexes can create unreasonable risks too, even when accompanied by attentive and conscientious advertence; and so can normal virtues like gallantry when conjoined with inexperience or poor judgment. (Imagine stopping one's car and waving a pretty pedestrian across the street right into the path of a speeding car passing on the right, unseen because momentarily in the "blind spot" of one's rear view mirror.) Almost any defect of conduct, except the likes of humorlessness, can be the *basis* of negligence, that is, the fault in virtue of which a given act or omission becomes, unknown to its actor, unreasonably dangerous. "Negligence" in the present sense is the name of a category of faulty acts. The negligence of any particular act or kind of act in the general category is always a consequential fault, a fault supervenient upon a fault of another kind that leads to an unreasonable risk in the circumstances.

It is worth emphasizing that this analysis applies to *legal negligence* only, which is negligence in a quite special sense. In ordinary nontechnical discourse, the word "negligence" is often a rough synonym for "carelessness" and as such refers to only one of the numerous possible faults that can, in a given set of circumstances, be the faulty basis of negligent conduct in the legal sense.

III

We come now to the main business at hand: the analysis of the concept of "his fault." It should be clear at the outset that, in order for a given harm to be someone's fault, he must have been somehow "at fault" in what he did or omitted to do, and also that there must have been some sort of causal connection between his action or omission and the harm. It is equally obvious that neither of these conditions by itself can be sufficient. Thus a motorist may be at fault in driving with an expired license or in exceeding the speed limit by five miles per hour, but unless his faulty act is a cause of the collision that ensues, the accident can hardly be his fault. Fault without causally determining action, then, is not sufficient. Similarly, causation without fault is not sufficient for the caused harm to be the causer's fault. It is no logical contradiction to say that a person's action caused the harm yet the harm was not his fault.

The triconditional analysis. It is natural at this point to conclude that a harm is "his fault" if and only if (1) he was at fault in acting (or omitting) and (2) his faulty act (or omission) caused the harm. This analysis, however, is incomplete, being still vulnerable to counterexamples of faulty actions causing harm that is nevertheless not the actor's fault. Suppose that *A* is unlicensed to drive an automobile but drives anyway, thereby "being at fault." The appearance of him driving in an (otherwise) faultless manner causes an edgy horse to panic and throw his rider. His faultily undertaken act caused a harm that cannot be imputed to him because the respect in which his act was faulty was causally irrelevant to the production of the harm. (When we come to give a causal explanation of the harm, we will not mention the fact that the driver had no license in his pocket. *That* is not what scared the horse.) This example suggests that a further condition is required

195

to complete the analysis: (3) the aspect of the act that was faulty was also one of the aspects in virtue of which the act was a cause of the harm.

The third condition in the analysis is especially important when the fault in question falls under the general heading of negligence. Robert Keeton in effect devotes most of a book to commentary on a hypothetical example which illustrates this point:

> The defendant, proprietor of a restaurant, placed a large unlabelled can of rat poison beside cans of flour on a shelf near a stove in a restaurant kitchen. The victim, while in the kitchen making a delivery to the restaurant, was killed by an explosion of the poison. Assume that the defendant's handling of the rat poison was negligent because of the risk that someone would be poisoned but that the defendant had no reason to know of the risk that the poison would explode if left in a hot place.[2]

The defendant's action, in Keeton's example, was faulty, and it was also the cause of the victim's death; but, on the analysis I have suggested, the death was nevertheless not his fault. The defendant's conduct was negligent because it created a risk of *poisoning*, but the harm it caused was not within the ambit of *that* risk. The risk of *explosion* was not negligently created. Hence the aspect of the act in virtue of which it was faulty was not the cause of the harm. Keeton puts the point more exactly: the harm was not "a result within the scope of the risks by reason of which the actor is found to be negligent."[3] Keeton's concern is with a theory of liability for negligence, not with an analysis of the nontechnical concept of "his fault"; but, liability aside, the analysis I have given entails that the death, in Keeton's example, was *not* the defendant's fault.

We can refer to this account as "the triconditional analy-

[2] *Legal Cause in the Law of Torts* (Columbus: Ohio State University Press, 1963), 3. The facts in Keeton's fictitious case are closely similar to those in the actual case of *Larrimore* v. *American Nat. Ins. Co.*, 184 Okl. 614 (1939).

[3] *Ibid.*, 10 and *passim*.

sis" and to its three conditions as (in order) "the fault condition," "the causal condition" (that the act was a cause of the harm), and "the causal relevance condition" (that the faulty aspect of the act was its causal link to the harm). I shall conclude that the triconditional analysis goes a long way toward providing a correct account of the commonsense notion of "his fault" and that its three conditions are indeed necessary to such an account even if, in the end, they must be formulated much more carefully and even supplemented by other conditions in an inevitably more complicated analysis. The remainder of this section discusses difficulties for the analysis as it stands which, I think, it can survive (at least after some tinkering, modifying, and disclaiming). One of these difficulties stems from a heterogeneous group of examples of persons who, on our analysis, would be blamed for harms that are clearly not their fault. I try to sidestep these counterexamples by affixing a restriction to the fault condition and making corresponding adjustments in the formulation of the relevance condition. The other difficulties directly concern the causal condition and the relevance condition. Both of these can involve us quickly in some fundamental philosophical problems.

Restrictions on the fault condition. There are some exceptional cases (but readily accessible to the philosophical imagination) in which a person who is clearly not to blame for a given harm nevertheless is the sole person who satisfies the conditions of the tripartite analysis. These cases, therefore, constitute counterexamples to that analysis if it is taken to state not only necessary but sufficient conditions for blame. Nicholas Sturgeon has suggested an especially ingenious case:

> *A* has made a large bet that no infractions of the law will occur at a certain place in a certain period of time; but *B*, at that place and time, opens a pack of cigarettes and fails to destroy the federal tax seal thereby breaking the law. *A*, seeing *B*'s omission, is so frustrated that he suffers a fatal heart attack on the spot. (To simplify matters, we may suppose that no

one has any reason to suppose A is endangering his health by gambling in this way.)[4]

Clearly, A's death is not B's fault. Yet (1) B was at fault in acting contrary to law; (2) his faulty act frustrated A, causing the heart attack; and (3) the aspects of B's act (omission) that were faulty (the illegality of his omission to destroy the tax stamps) were also among the aspects of it in virtue of which there was a causal connection between it and the harm. A similar example is provided by John Taurek:

> C is so programmed (by hypnosis, perhaps C is a clever robot, whatever) that if A lies in answering B's question, C will harm D. B asks A her age and she lies. C harms D. A's action seems to be a causal factor in the production of harm to D, and just in virtue of its faulty aspect. Yet who would hold that D's harm was A's fault?[5]

Perhaps it is possible to add further conditions to the analysis to obviate this kind of counterexample, but a more likely remedy would be to restrict the kinds of faults that can be elements of "his fault" judgments. Sometimes a man can be said to be at fault in acting (or omitting to act) precisely because his action or omission will offend or fail to benefit himself or others, or because it is a violation of faith (even a *harmless* instance of promise-breaking, such as a secret breaking of faith to a person now dead), or simply and precisely because it breaks an authoritative legal rule. Most intentional wrongdoing, on the other hand, and all recklessness and negligence are instances of being at fault for another (perhaps additional) reason—either because "they make a certain kind of harm or injury inevitable, or because they create an unreasonable risk of a certain kind

---

[4] The example is from a very helpful letter sent to me by Professor Sturgeon after I read an earlier version of this paper at Cornell in May 1969.

[5] The example is just one of many in an extremely thorough criticism of an earlier version of this paper made by Professor Taurek, who was my official commentator at the Chapel Hill Colloquium in Philosophy, Oct. 17-19, 1969.

of harm."[6] We can attempt to avoid counterexamples of the sort Sturgeon and Taurek suggested by tampering with the first condition (the fault condition). We can say now (of course, only tentatively and not without misgiving) that, for the purpose of this analysis, the way of being at fault required by the fault condition is to be understood as the harm-threatening way, not the nonbenefiting, offense-threatening, harmless faith-breaking, or law-violating ways. The fault condition then can be reformulated as follows (in words suggested by Sturgeon): a given harm is A's fault only if (1) A was at fault in acting or omitting to act and "the faultiness of his act or omission consisted, at least in part, in the creation of either a certainty or an unreasonable risk of harm. . . ."[7] Now the faulty smoker in Sturgeon's example and the liar in Taurek's example are no longer "at fault" in the requisite way, and the revised analysis no longer pins the blame for coincidental harms on them. To open a cigarette package in an overly fastidious fashion is not to endanger unduly the health of others; nor is lying about one's age (except in very special contexts) to threaten others with harm.

In the light of this new restriction on the fault condition, we can formulate the causal relevance condition in an alternative way, along the lines suggested by Keeton's account of harm caused by negligence. We can now say that the (harm-threatening) "faulty aspect" of an act is a cause of subsequent harm when the risk or certainty of harm in virtue of which the act was at fault was a risk or certainty of "just the sort of harm that was in fact caused,"[8] and not harm of some other sort. The resultant harm, in other words, must be within the scope of the risk (or certainty) in virtue of which the act is properly characterized as faulty. This is more than a mere explication of the original way of putting the third condition. It is a definite modification designed to rule out cases of *coincidence* where the faulty aspect of an act, even when it is of the harm-threatening sort, may be causally linked to a subsequent harm

---

[6] Sturgeon, *op.cit.*   [7] *Ibid.*   [8] *Ibid.*

via such adventitious conditions as standing wagers and programmed robots. Under the revised formulation, the very same considerations involved in the explanation of *why* the act is faulty are also involved, essentially and sufficiently, in the explanation of *how* the harm was caused.

We have not even considered, of course, the crucial question of how reasonable risks are to be distinguished from unreasonable ones; and there are still other problems resulting from the fact that a "sort of harm" (crucial phrase) can be described in either more or less full and determinate ways. These problems, like several other closely related ones, are too complicated to be tackled here.

Fault and cause: dependent and independent determinations. Can we tell whether an act caused a given harm independently of knowing whether the actor was at fault in acting? The answer seems to be that we can determine the causal question independently of the fault question in some cases but not in others. Part of our problem is to explain this variation. Consider first some examples. A blaster takes every reasonable precaution, and yet by a wildly improbable fluke his explosion of dynamite sends a disjarred rock flying through the window of a distant isolated cabin. He was not at fault, but whether he was or not, we are able to say independently that his setting off the blast was the cause of the broken window. Similarly, the motorist in our earlier example, by driving (whether with or without fault is immaterial to this point) along a rarely traveled stretch of country road, caused a nervous horse to bolt. That is, it was his activity as he conducted it then and there, with its attendant noise and dust, that caused the horse to bolt; and we can know this independently of any determination of fault.

Examples provided by J. L. Mackie and William Dray, however, seem to cut the other way. Mackie[9] describes an episode in which a motorcyclist exceeded a speed limit and

[9] "Responsibility and Language," *Australasian Journal of Philosophy*, 33 (1955), 145.

was chased by a policeman, also on a motorcycle, at speeds up to seventy miles per hour. An absentminded pedestrian stepped off a bus into the policeman's path and was killed instantly. The newspapers for the next few days were full of debates over the question of whose conduct was the "real cause" of the death, debates that seemed to center on the question of whose conduct was the least *reasonable* intrusion into the normal course of events. To express an opinion at all on the causal question seemed to be to take a stand, plain and simple, about the *propriety* of pursuits by police in heavily populated areas.

Dray discusses a hypothetical debate between two historians who argue "whether it was Hitler's invasion of Poland or Chamberlain's pledge to defend it which caused the outbreak of the Second World War." The question they *must* be taken to be trying to settle, he avers, is "who was to blame." "The point," he says, "is not that we cannot hold an agent responsible for a certain happening unless his action can be said to have caused it. It is rather that, unless we are prepared to hold the agent responsible for what happened, we cannot say that his action *was* the cause."[10] Mackie comes to a similar conclusion, embracing what he calls a "curious inversion of utilitarianism," namely, that one often cannot tell whether a given harm is a causal consequence of a given act without first deciding whether the actor was *at fault* in acting the way he did.

To clarify the relations between cause and fault, it will be necessary to digress briefly and remind ourselves of certain features of causal judgments as they are made in ordinary life. That one condition is causally necessary or, in a given context, sufficient for the occurrence of a given event is normally a question simply for empirical investigation and the application of a scientific theory. Normally, however, there will be a plurality of distinguishable causal conditions (often called "causal factors") for any given

[10] *Laws and Explanation in History* (London: Oxford University Press, 1957), 100.

event, and the aim of a causal inquiry will be to single out one[11] of these to be denominated "the cause" of the event in question.[12] A judgment that cites one of the numerous eligible causal conditions for an event as "the cause" I call a *causal citation*. The eligibility of an event or state as a causal factor is determined empirically via the application of inductive criteria.[13] On the other hand, the citation of one of the eligible candidates as "the cause" is normally made, as we shall see, via the application of what Dray calls "pragmatic criteria." In Dray's convenient phrase, the inductive inquiry establishes the "importance of a condition to the event," whereas the causal citation indicates its "importance to the inquirer."

The point of a causal citation is to single out one of the certified causal candidates that is especially *interesting* to us, given our various practical purposes and cognitive concerns. These purposes and concerns provide a convenient way of classifying the "contexts of inquiry" in which causal citations are made. The primary division is between explanatory and nonexplanatory contexts. The occasion for an explanatory citation is one in which there is intellectual puzzlement of a quite specific kind. A suprising or unusual

---

[11] In unusual cases, two or three.

[12] The distinction in common sense between a "causal factor" and "the cause" corresponds roughly—very roughly—to the technical legal distinction between "cause in fact" and "proximate cause."

[13] A causal factor is an earlier necessary condition in at least the weaker sense of "necessary condition," *viz.*, a member of a set of jointly sufficient conditions whose presence was necessary to the sufficiency of the set; but it need not be necessary in the stronger sense, *viz.*, a necessary element in every set of conditions that would be jointly sufficient, as oxygen is necessary to every instance of combustion. Not all prior necessary conditions, of course, are genuine causal factors. Analytic connections ("But for his having been born, the accident would not have happened") are ruled out, and so are "incidental connections" (earlier speeding bringing one to a given point just at the moment a tree falls on the road). Unlike necessary conditions connected in a merely incidental way to results, causal factors are "necessary elements in a set of conditions generally connected through intermediate stages with it." See H.L.A. Hart and A. M. Honoré, *Causation in the Law* (Oxford: Clarendon Press, 1959), 114. See also Keeton, *op.cit.*, 62.

event has occurred which is a deviation from what is understood to be the normal course of things. A teetotaler is drunk, or an alcoholic sober; a punctual man is tardy, or a dilatory man early; it rains in the dry season, or it fails to rain in the wet season. Sometimes the breach of routine is disappointing, and we wish to know what went wrong this time. But sometimes the surprise is pleasant or, more commonly, simply stimulating to one's curiosity. We ask what caused the surprising event and expect an explanation that will cite a factor normally present but absent this time, or normally absent but present this time, that made the difference. The occasion for explanation is a breach of routine; the explanatory judgment cites another deviation from routine to correlate with it.

Very often one of the causal conditions for a given upshot is a faulty human action. Human failings tend to be more "interesting" factors than events of other kinds, even for purely explanatory purposes; but it is important to notice that this need not always be the case. Faulty human actions usually do *not* fall within the normal course of events, so that a dereliction of duty, for example, when it is a causally necessary condition for some puzzling breach of routine, being itself a departure from the normal course of things, is a prime candidate for causal citation. But when the faulty conduct of Flavius is constant and unrelieved and known to be such to Titus, it will not relieve Titus's perplexity over how a given unhappy event came about simply to cite Flavius's habitual negligence or customary dereliction of duty as "the cause." What Titus wishes to know is what new intrusive event made the difference *this* time; and it won't help *him* to mention a causal factor that has always been present even on those occasions when no unhappy result ensued.

Not all causal explanations by any means employ causal citations. Especially when we are puzzled about the "normal course of events" itself and wish explanations for standardly recurring regularities (Why do the tides come in? Why do released objects fall? Why do flowers bloom in the spring?), mere brief citations will not do. In such cases we require long stories involving the descriptions of diverse states of affairs and the invocation of various laws of nature. Similarly, not all causal citations are explanatory. Sometimes there is no gap in a person's understanding of how a given interesting event came about, and yet he may seek nevertheless to learn its "real" or "most important" cause. Nonexplanatory citations are those made for some purpose other than the desire simply to put one's curiosity to rest. Most frequently they cite the causal factor that is of a kind that is easiest to manipulate or control. Engineers and other practical men may be concerned to eliminate events of the kind that occasioned the inquiry if they are harmful or to produce more of them if they are beneficial. In either case, when they seek "the cause," they seek the causal factor that has a handle on it (in Collingwood's phrase) that they can get hold of and manipulate. Another of our practical purposes in making causal citations is to *fix the blame*, a purpose which introduces considerations not present when all the leading causal factors are things other than human actions (as they often are in agricultural, medical, or engineering inquiries). Insects, viruses, and mechanical stresses and strains are often "blamed" for harms, but the word "blame" in these uses, of course, has a metaphorical sense.

In summary, causal citations can be divided into those made from explanatory and those made from nonexplanatory standpoints, and the latter group into those made from the "engineering" and those made from the "blaming" standpoints. Explanatory citations single out abnormal interferences with the normal course of events or hitherto unknown missing links in a person's understanding. They are designed simply to remove puzzlement by citing the causal factor that can shed the most light. Hence we can refer to the criterion of selection in explanatory contexts (for short) as *the lantern criterion*. Causal citations made from the "engineering standpoint" are made with a view to facilitating control over future events by citing the most efficiently and economically manipulable causal factor. The criterion for selection in engineering contexts can thus be called (for short) *the handle criterion.* The point of causal citations in purely blaming contexts is simply to pin the label of blame on the appropriate causal factor for further notice and practical use. These judgments cite a causal factor that is a human act or omission "stained" (as an ancient figure of speech would have it) with fault. The criterion in blaming contexts can be called (for short) *the stain criterion.* When we look for "the cause," then, we may be looking for the causal factor that has either a lantern, a handle, or a stain on it.

Purely blaming citations can be interpreted in two different ways. On the first model, to say that a person's act was the cause of the harm is precisely equivalent to saying that he is to blame for the harm, that is, that the harm is his fault. The causal inquiry undertaken from the purely blaming perspective, according to this view, is one and the same as the inquiry into the question of who was to blame or of whose fault it was. On this model, then, causal citation is not a condition for the fixing of blame; it is, rather, precisely the same thing. It is simply a fact of usage, which the examples of Dray and Mackie illustrate, that questions of blame often get posed and answered in wholly causal language. Historians, for example, are said by Dray often to "use expressions like 'was responsible for' [or 'was to blame for'] when they want to put into other words conclusions which they would also be prepared to frame in causal language."[14]

On the second model of interpretation, which is also sometimes *a propos,* the truth of the causal citation "His act was the cause of the harm" is only one of the *conditions* for the judgment that "The harm was his fault." Here we separate cause and fault before bringing them together again in a "his fault" judgment, insisting that the harm was his fault *only if* his action caused it. The causal inquiry, so

[14] Dray, *op.cit.,* 99-100.

205

conceived, is undertaken for the sake of the blame inquiry, but its results are established independently.

Now how do we establish a causal citation on the first model (or, what is the same thing, a "his fault" citation on the second)? Again, we have two alternatives: either we can hold that the person (or his act) was *the cause* of the harm (meaning that he was to blame for it) only if his act was a genuine causal factor in the production of the harm; or we can require that his act be *the cause* of the harm, and not merely a "causal factor." But then we must find a way of avoiding a vitiating circularity. If we mean "the cause" as selected by *the stain criterion*, we have made a full circle; for, on this first model, our *original inquiry* is aimed at citing the cause by a stain criterion, and now we say that the achievement of this goal is a condition of itself. Clearly, if we are going to insist that his act be "the cause" as a condition of its being "the cause for purposes of fixing blame," we have to mean that it must be the cause *as determined by either the lantern or the handle criteria.* A quick examination of cases will show that this is just what we do mean.

When a man sets off a charge of dynamite and the earth shifts, dust rises, and rocks fly, the blasting is conspicuously the cause of these results by the lantern criterion (since it is the abnormal intervention) and equally clearly by the handle criterion (since it is part of the handiest causal recipe for producing results of precisely that kind). We can know, therefore, that the blasting caused the results by these commonsense criteria before we know anything at all about fault. Then we can go on to say, without circularity, that one or another of these causal criteria must be satisfied if those of the results that are harmful are to be charged to the blaster as his fault, but that further conditions of faultiness must also be satisfied.

Should we say that being "the cause" by the other commonsense criteria is *always* a necessary condition of being the cause by the stain criterion? I think this specification would prove to be artificially restrictive, for we sometimes (though perhaps not often) wish to ascribe blame whether or not the blamed action satisfies the lantern and handle criteria, and even in some instances where (allowing for the usual relativity of context) it appears not to. Suppose A, an impressive adult figure, offers a cigarette to B, an impressionable teenager. A is B's original attractive model of a smoker and also one who deliberately seduces him into the habit. Much later, after thirty years of continuous heavy smoking, B begins to suffer from lung cancer. Neither the lantern nor the handle criteria in most contexts are likely to lead one to cite A's earlier act as the cause of B's cancer, for A's act is not conspicuously "the cause" of the harm by these criteria (as the blasting was, in the earlier example). Yet we may wish to say that A's seduction of B was the cause of his eventual cancer for purposes of fixing blame or as a mode of expressing that blame. Such a judgment may not be morally felicitous, but it can be made without committing some sort of conceptual solecism.

The best way of avoiding both circularity and artificial restriction of expression in our account of blame-fixing citations is to require not that the blamed action be citable as "the cause" (by *any* criteria), but only that it be a genuine causal factor, in the circumstances that obtained, and then to add fault and relevance conditions to the analysis. Most of the time, perhaps, being "the cause" by the lantern or handle criteria will also be required; but being a *causal factor merely* will be required always.

The causal relevance condition: is it always necessary? Does the analysis of commonsense "his fault" judgments really require a causal relevance condition? Many people, I suspect, are prepared to make "his fault" judgments in particular cases even when they know that a causal relevance condition has not been satisfied; and many puzzling cases are such as to make even most of us hesitate about the matter. Consider, for example, the case of the calamitous soup-spilling at Lady Mary's formal dinner party. Sir John Stuffgut so liked his first and second bowls of soup that he demanded a third just as Lady Mary was prepared to announce with pride to the hungry and restless guests the arrival of the next course. Sir John's tone was so gruff and peremptory that Lady Mary quite lost her composure. She lifted the heavy tureen with shaking arms and, in attempting to pass it to her intemperate guest, spilled it unceremoniously in the lap of the Reverend Mr. Straightlace. Now both Sir John and Lady Mary were at fault in this episode. Sir John was thoughtless, gluttonous, and, especially, *rude* in demanding another bowl in an unsettling tone of voice. Lady Mary was (perhaps forgivably) negligent in the way she executed her action, and, besides she should have known that the tureen was too heavy for her to lift. Furthermore, both Lady Mary's faulty action and Sir John's faulty action were necessary conditions for the ensuing harm. Assuming that we must fix the blame for what happened, whose fault, should we say, was the harm?

Most of us would be inclined to single out Sir John's rudeness as "the cause" for purposes of blaming, partly because it was the most striking deviation from routine, perhaps, but mainly because, of the causal factors with stains on them, his action was the most deeply stained, which is to say that he was the most at fault. Moreover, his action was a causal factor in the production of the harm precisely in virtue of that aspect which was faulty, namely, its unsettling rudeness, which created an unreasonable risk of upsetting the hostess, the very result that in fact ensued. Thus the causal relevance condition is satisfied in this example.

Suppose, however, that the facts had been somewhat different. Sir John, at just the wrong moment (as before), requested his third bowl, but in a quiet and gentle manner, and in a soft and mellifluous tone of voice, perfectly designed to calm its auditor. Sir John this time was not being rude, though he was still at fault in succumbing to his excessive appetites and indulging them in an unseemly public way to the inconvenience of others. In short, his primary fault in this new example was not rudeness, but plain gluttony; and (as before), but for his act which was at fault, the harm would not have occurred. Likewise (as before) the clumsiness of Lady Mary was a causal factor in the absence of which the harm would not have resulted. This case differs from the earlier one in that the causal relevance condition is not satisfied, for gluttony normally creates a risk to the glutton's own health and comfort, not to the interests of others. Unlike rudeness, it is a primary self-regarding fault. Thus that aspect of Sir John's request for more soup that was faulty was an irrelevant accompaniment of the aspects that contributed to the accident. Hence we could conclude that, although Sir John was *at fault* in what he did, the resulting harm was not *his fault*.[15]

It would be sanguine, however, to expect everybody to agree with this judgment. Mr. Straightlace, for example, might be altogether indisposed to let Sir John escape the blame so easily. He and others might prefer to reject the causal relevance condition out of hand as too restrictive and urge instead that the blame always be placed on the person *most at fault*, whether the fault is causally relevant or not, providing his faulty action was a genuine causal factor. This alternative would enable one to pin the blame on Sir John in both versions of the soup-spilling story. It does not commend itself to the intuitive understanding in a quiet reflective hour, however, and seems to me to have no other merit than that of letting the indignation and vindictiveness occasioned by harm have a respectable outlet in our moral judgments. If we really want to keep Sir John on the hook, *we do not have to say* that the harm was "really his fault" and thereby abuse a useful and reasonably precise concept.

[15] Perhaps a better example to illustrate this condition would be the following: Sir John is not a glutton. He has requested only one bowl of soup, but it is spilled by the hostess. But Sir John is at fault in agreeing to have even one bowl passed his way, since he knows, or ought to know, that this kind of soup always gives him indigestion, insomnia, allergic reactions, and hiccups. It is not only imprudent for him to taste it; it is also inconsiderate to his wife, who is usually kept awake all night by his restlessness. When his wife is kept awake after this party, *that* is his fault; but when the hostess spills the soup (which she should not have had to pass his way in the first place), that is *not* his fault.

Rather, if we are vindictively inclined, we can say that to impose liability on a person to enforced compensation or other harsh treatment for some harm does not always require that the harm be his fault. This would be the moral equivalent of a departure from what is called "the fault principle" in the law of torts. It is an attempt to do justice to our spontaneous feelings, without confusing our concepts, and has the merits at least of openness and honesty.

Disinterested parties might reject causal relevance as a condition for being to blame in a skeptical way, offering as an alternative to it a radical contextual relativism. One might profess genuine bafflement when asked whose fault was the second soup-spilling, on the grounds that the question cannot be answered until it is known for what purpose it is asked. Is the person singled out for blame the one to be punished, forced to make compensation, expected to apologize? What is the point of narrowly pinning blame? We could, after all, simply tell the narrative as accurately as possible and decline to say whose fault, on balance, the harm was, although that evasive tactic might not be open to, say, an insurance investigator. The point, according to this skeptical theory, is that, after all the facts are in, we are still not committed by "the very logic of the everyday concept" to saying anything at all about whose fault it was. The blame-fixing decision is still logically open and will be determined in part by our practical purposes in raising the question. This skeptical theory, however, strikes me as a combined insight and *non sequitur*. The insight is that we are not *forced* to pinpoint blame unless some practical question like liability hinges on it and that it is often the better part of wisdom to decline to do so when one can. But it does not follow from the fact that "his fault" judgments can sometimes be avoided that it is logically open to us to make them in any way we wish when we do make them. I hold, therefore, to the conclusion that, in fixing the blame for harm, we are restricted by our very concepts to the person(s) whose faulty act was a causal factor in the pro-

210

duction of the harm in virtue of its causally relevant faulty aspect.

There often is room for discretion in the making of "his fault" judgments, but it comes at a different place and is subject to strict limitations. The person whose fault the harm is said to be *must* satisfy the conditions of the triconditional analysis (and perhaps others as well); but when more than one person is so qualified, the judgment-maker may sometimes choose between them on "pragmatic grounds," letting some of them off the hook. When this discretion is proper, the three conditions of our analysis must be honored as necessary, but they are no longer taken to be sufficient. Suppose one thousand persons satisfy the three conditions of our analysis in respect to harm X, and they acted independently (not in concert) over a period of many years. To say simply that the harm is (all) *their* fault, or part his, and part his, and part his, and so on, would be to defeat altogether the usual point of a "his fault" judgment, namely, to fix more narrowly, to single out, to focus upon. When fixings of blame become too diffuse, they can no longer perform this function. They might still, of course, be *true*, but just not very useful. It is not exactly false to say of the first soup-spilling example that it was the fault of *both* Lady Mary and Sir John; but "practical purposes" may dictate instead that we ignore minor or expectable faults and confer all the blame on the chief culprit. At any rate, if it is given that we must, for some practical purpose, single out a wrongdoer more narrowly, then we have discretion to choose among those (but only those) who satisfy the necessary conditions of the tripartite analysis.[16]

16 If it is given that a particular "his fault" judgment on a particular occasion must single out one or a small number to be assigned the blame, then the concept of "his fault" can perhaps be understood to limit discretion by providing two additional necessary conditions to the triconditional analysis: (4) there is no other person to whom conditions (1)-(3) apply who was substantially more at fault than the present assignee (s); and (5) there is no other person to whom conditions (1)-(3) apply whose act was a more striking deviation from

Fault and tort liability. Suppose we accept the revised triconditional analysis of "his fault" but jettison the causal relevance condition as a requisite for tort *liability*, so that we can get the likes of Sir John on the hook after all, even though we admit he is not *to blame* for the harm. The prime consequence of dropping the causal relevance condition is to downgrade the role of causation as a ground for liability and to increase the importance of simply being at fault. If causal relevance is not required, it would seem that being at fault is the one centrally important necessary condition for liability, and indeed so important as to render the causal condition itself a mere dispensable formality. To upgrade the fault condition to that extent is most likely to seem reasonable when the fault is disproportionately greater than the harm it occasions. Imagine a heinously faulty act that is a necessary causal condition for a relatively minor harm. Suppose that *A*, a matricidal fiend, in the cruelest way possible sets himself to shoot his mother dead just as *B*, the lady across the street, is fondling a delicate and fragile art object. The sound of the revolver shot startles *B*, causing her to drop the art object which shatters beyond repair. Is its loss *A*'s fault? Let us assume (for the sake of the argument) that the murderous act was at fault in at least two ways: (1) it created a certainty of death or severe injury to the actor's mother (the primary way it was at fault); and (2), in making a loud report, it created an unreasonable risk to (among other things) the art objects of neighbors. Thus, in virtue of (2), *A* is at fault in the manner required for his being to blame for breaking the neighbor's glass vase. His act caused the breaking and did so in virtue of its faulty aspect (2); hence it was his fault. But even if he had (thoughtfully) used a silencer on the gun, and nevertheless the very slight noise caused by his act had startled a supernervous vase-fondling neighbor, causing the drop-

---

routine, or of a kind patently more manipulable, or otherwise a more "direct" or "substantial" cause. In the first soup-spilling example, Lady Mary satisfies conditions (1)-(3), but certainly not condition (4) and possibly not condition (5).

ping and breaking, we might find it proper to charge him for the damage *even though the loss was not his fault.* (The "faulty aspect" of his act—its heinousness—was causally irrelevant to that loss.) It is precisely this kind of case where common sense seems most at home without the causal relevance condition; for no question of "fairness" to the faulty one is likely to trouble us when his fault is so great. Any number of minor harms of which his act was a necessary condition can be charged to his moral bill without disturbing us—at least so long as we remain "spontaneous" and unreflective.

It is another matter, however, when the harm is disproportionately greater than the fault, when a mere slap causes an unsuspected hemophiliac to bleed to death, or a clumsy slip on the sidewalk leads one to bump an "old soldier with an egg shell skull," causing his death. Hart and Honoré suggest that even here commonsense considerations can help justify abandonment, in some cases at least, of the causal relevance condition by mitigating its apparent harshness:

> The apparent unfairness of holding a defendant liable for a loss much greater than he could foresee to some extent disappears when we consider that a defendant is often negligent without suffering punishment or having to pay compensation. I may drive at an excessive speed a hundred times before the one occasion on which my speeding causes harm. The justice of holding me liable, should the harm on that occasion turn out to be extraordinarily grave, must be judged in the light of the hundred other occasions on which, without deserving such luck, I have incurred no liability.[17]

This argument is reminiscent of the Augustinian theory of salvation. We are all sinners; therefore, no one really deserves to be saved. Hence if anyone at all is saved, it can only be through God's supererogatory grace. The others are (relatively) unlucky; but, being undeserving sinners, they can have no just complaint. All of us are negligent, goes the parallel argument; so none of us really deserves to

17 Hart and Honoré, *op.cit.*, 243.

escape liability for great harm. That majority of us who do escape are lucky, but the others who fall into liability in excess of their fault on the occasion have no just complaint, since they have accumulated enough fault on other occasions to redress the disproportion.

If justice truly requires (as the Hart-Honoré argument suggests) that blame and liability be properly apportioned to *all* a person's faults as accumulated in the long run, causal linkage to harm aside, why not go all the way in this direction and drop the "causal factor" condition altogether in the interest of Aristotelian "due proportion" and fairness? To say that we are all negligent is to say that on other occasions, at least, we have all created unreasonable risk of harms, sometimes great harms, of one kind or another, to other persons. Even in circumstances where excessive harm actually results, we may have created other risks of a different kind to other individuals, risks which luckily failed to eventuate in harm. Robert Keeton foresees the consequences for the law of torts of taking all such faults seriously in the assignment of liability for particular harms:

> . . . if it is relevant to take into account defendant's fault with respect to a risk different from any that would include the harm plaintiff has suffered, then would it not also be relevant to take into account his other faults as well? And would it not seem equally relevant to consider plaintiff's shortcomings? Shall we fix legal responsibility by deciding who is the better and who the worse person? An affirmative answer might involve us, and quickly too, in the morality of run-of-the-ranch TV drama, where the good guys always win.[18]

In effect Keeton challenges those who would drop the causal relevance condition to explain why they would maintain any causal condition at all. If the existence of fault of one kind or another, on one occasion or another, is the controlling consideration, why do we not simply tally up

[18] Keeton, *op.cit.*, 21.

merits and demerits and distribute our collective compensation expenses in proportion to each person's moral score? Why not indeed? This is not an unthinkable alternative system. We could, in principle, begin with the notion of a "compensable harm" as one caused by fault. (Other harms could be paid for out of tax funds or voluntary insurance.) Then we could estimate the total cost of compensable harms throughout the country for a one-year period. We would have to acquire funds equal to that amount by assigning demerits throughout the year to persons discovered to be "at fault" in appropriate ways in their conduct. Those who fail to clear their sidewalks of ice and snow within a reasonable period after the finish of a storm would be given so many demerits per square foot of pavement. Those convicted of traffic offenses would be assigned demerits on a graduated scale corresponding to the seriousness (as compounded out of unreasonableness and dangerousness) of their offense. Then, at the end of the year, the total cost of compensable harms would be divided by the total number of assigned demerits to yield the dollar value per demerit, and each person would be fined the dollar equivalent of the sum of his demerits. These fines would all go into a central fund used to compensate all victims of faulty accidents and crimes. Such a system would impose on some persons penalties disproportionately greater than the harm they actually caused; others would pay less than the harm they caused; but as far as is practically possible, everyone would be fined in exact proportion to the unreasonable risks he created (as well as certain and deliberate harms) to others.[19]

[19] This is not quite true of the system as described in the text, for a man's penalty in that system is determined in part by the number of demerits others incur and the total amount of compensable harm caused, both factors over which he has no control. Thus a man who accumulates one hundred demerits in 1970 might pay a smaller fine than he does in 1971 when he accumulates only seventy five. Instead of assigning demerits, therefore, the system would have to impose penalties directly, according to a fixed and invariant retributive scale. These funds could then go into a pool to compensate victims; and if, in a given year, they prove to be insufficient, they could be

The system just described could be called a system of "liability without *contributory* fault," since it bypasses a causation requirement. It is a system of liability based on fault simply, whether or not the fault contributes to harm. It thus differs sharply from the traditional system of liability based in part upon what is called *the fault principle*, which requires that accidental losses be borne by the party whose fault the accident was. This is liability based on "his fault" ascriptions, rather than "at fault" imputations. In contrast, the principle underlying a system of liability based on fault without causation might well be called the *retributive theory of torts*. It surely deserves this name drawn from the criminal law more than the so-called fault principle does, since it bases liability *entirely* upon fault purged of all extraneous and fortuitous elements. To be sure, what is called retributivism in the criminal law[20] is a principle that would base (criminal) liability entirely on *moral* fault,

---

supplemented, say, by tax funds instead of stepped-up fines; for, on a purely retributive theory, there is one "fitting" penalty for a given degree of fault, and that uniquely correct quantum should be independent of the fluctuations of the marketplace.

[20] "Retributivism" has served as the name of a large number of distinct theories of the grounds for justifiable punishment having little in common except that they are all nonutilitarian. The theories referred to in the text are those that hold that a certain degree of pain or deprivation is *deserved* by, or matches, fits, or suits, a certain magnitude of evil, quite apart from consequences. The emphasis is on fitness or proportion; and often the theorist invokes aesthetic analogies. Cf. the definitions of A. C. Ewing in *The Morality of Punishment* (London: Kegan Paul, Trench, Trubner & Co., 1929), 13, and John Rawls, "Two Concepts of Rules," *The Philosophical Review*, 64 (1955), 4-5. G. E. Moore's "theory of organic unities" also suggests this kind of retributivism. But there are many other theories that have borne the retributive label which I do not refer to here—e.g., Hegel's theory of annulment; theories of punishment as putting the universe back in joint, or wiping clean the criminal's slate, or paying a debt to society, or expiating a sin, or expressing social denunciation, or demonstrating to the criminal the logical consequences of the universalization of his maxim, or satisfying the natural instinct for vengeance, or preventing the criminal from prospering while his victim suffers, or restoring a moral equilibrium between the "burdens" of conformity to law as against the "benefits" of disobedience; and even the "logical truism" of A. M. Quinton (*Analysis*, 14 [1954]).

and most retributivists would oppose punishing nonmoral faults, including much negligence, as ardently as they would oppose punishing the wholly faultless. A retributive principle of reparation *could* take this very moralistic form. As we have seen, legal negligence is always supervenient upon a fault of some other kind, sometimes "moral" (callousness, inconsiderateness, self-centeredness), sometimes not (timidity, excitability, awkwardness). A moralistic principle would issue demerits to negligence only when it is supervenient upon a fault judged to be a *moral* failing. In a sense, the more inclusive version of the theory is more "moralistic" still, since it treats even nonmoral failings as essentially deserving of penalty, that is, just *as if* they were moral failings. We can safely avoid these complications here.

One way to understand the retributive theory of torts is to relate it to, or derive it from, a general moral theory that bears the name of retributivism. In treating of this more general theory, it is very important to distinguish a strong from a weak version, for failure to do so has muddled discussions of retributivism in criminal law and would very likely do the same in discussions of principles of tort liability. According to the strong version of the general retributive principle, *all* evil or, more generally still, all *fault* deserves its comeuppance; it is an end in itself, quite apart from other consequences, that all wrongdoers (or faulty doers) be made to suffer some penalty, handicap, or forfeiture as a requital for their wrongdoing. Similarly, it is an end in itself, morally fitting and proper irrespective of other consequences, that the meritorious be rewarded with the means to happiness. Thus the best conceivable world would be that in which the virtuous (or faultless) flourish, the wicked (or, more generally, the faulty) suffer, and those in between perfect virtue and perfect wickedness enjoy happiness or suffer unhappiness in exact proportion to their virtuous and faulty conduct. Both a world in which everyone suffers regardless of moral condition and a world in which everyone flourishes regardless of moral condition

217

would be intrinsically inferior morally to a world in which all and only the good flourish and all and only the bad suffer. If everyone without exception is a miserable sinner, then it is intrinsically better that everybody suffer than that everybody, or even anybody, be happy. There may be intrinsic goods other than the just apportionment of reward and penalty to the virtuous and the faulty respectively; but insofar as a state of affairs deviates from such apportionment, it is intrinsically defective.

Note that this way of putting retributivism makes it apply only to apportionments of a noncomparative kind, where to give to one is not necessarily to take from another and where to take from one is not necessarily to give to another. It is not, therefore, a principle of distributive justice, telling us in the abstract how all pies are to be cut up or how all necessary burdens are to be divided. Indeed, for some situations it would decree that no one get any pie, and in others that no one should suffer any burdens. It is concerned with deserving good or deserving ill, not with deserving one's fair share relative to others. To be sure, the world in which the good suffer and the evil are happy it calls a moral abomination, but not because of the conditions of the parties relative to one another, but rather because the condition of each party is the opposite of what *he* deserves, quite independently of the condition of the others. A world in which every person is equally a sinner and equally very happy would also be a moral abomination, on this view, even though it involves no social inequality.

The weaker version of general retributivism, on the other hand, is essentially a comparative principle, applying to situations in which it is given that someone or other must do without, make a sacrifice, or forfeit his interest. The principle simply asserts the moral priority, *ceteris paribus*, of the innocent party. Put most pithily, it is the principle that *fault forfeits first*, if forfeit there must be. If someone must suffer, it is better, *ceteris paribus*, that it be the faulty than the meritorious. This weaker version of retributivism, which permeates the law, especially the criminal law, has strong

support in common sense. It commonly governs the distribution of that special kind of benefit called "the benefit of
the doubt," so that, where there is doubt, for example,
about the deterrent efficacy of a particular mode of punishment for a certain class of crimes, the benefit of that doubt
is given to potential victims instead of convicted criminals.

I find the weaker version of retributivism much more
plausible intuitively than the stronger, though even it is
limited—for example, by the values of intimacy and friendship. (If I negligently spill your coffee cup at lunch, will you
insist that I pay for a new cup, or will you prefer to demonstrate how much more important my friendship is to you
than the forfeiture of a dime?) The weaker principle allows
us to say, if we wish, though it does not require us to say,
that universal happiness, if it were possible, would be intrinsically better than happiness for the good only, with the
wicked all miserable. (Indeed, what would wickedness
come to if its usually negative effect on the happiness of
others was universally mitigated or nullified?) The weak
principle also permits but does not require us to say that,
even though it is better that the faulty forfeit first where
there is no alternative to *someone's* forfeiting, it is better
still that some other alternative be found.

Now let us return to our tort principles. What is called
the "fault principle" (or, better, the "his fault" principle)
does not derive from, and indeed is not even compatible
with, the strong version of general retributivism. As we
have seen, the causal component of "his fault" ascriptions
introduces a fortuitous element, repugnant to pure retributivism. People who are very much at fault may luckily avoid
causing proportionate harm, and unlucky persons may
cause harm in excess of their minor faults. In the former
case, little or no harm may be a person's fault even though
he is greatly at fault; hence his liability, based on "his
fault," will not be the burden he deserves, and the moral
universe will be out of joint. In the latter case, unhappily
coexistent circumstances may step up the normal magnitude of harm resulting from a minor fault, and again the

219

defendant's liability will not do proper justice to his actual fault.

The tort principle that is called for by strong retributivism is that which I have called "the retributive theory of torts." Being at fault gets its proper comeuppance from this principle, whether or not it leads directly to harm; and the element of luck—except for luck in escaping detection —is largely eliminated. Hence fault suffers its due penalty, and if that is an end in itself, as strong retributivism maintains, then the retributive theory of torts is well recommended indeed. But the lack of intuitive persuasiveness of the general theory, I think, diminishes the plausibility of its offshoot in torts. Weak retributivism, which is generally more plausible, in my opinion, than its strong counterpart, does not uniquely favor either the retributive theory of torts or the "his fault" principle. Except in straightforwardly comparative contexts where the necessity of forfeiture is given, it takes no stand whatever about principles of tort liability. If A and B are involved in an accident causing a loss to B only, which is wholly A's fault, and it is given that either A or B must pay for the loss, no other source of compensation being available, then the weak principle says that A should be made to pay, or rather (put even more weakly in virtue of the *ceteris paribus* clause) it holds that, insofar as the loss was A's fault, that is a good and relevant reason why A should pay and, in the absence of other relevant considerations, a sufficient reason. In short, if someone has got to be hurt in this affair, let it be the wrongdoer (other things being equal). But where there is no necessity that the burden of payment be restricted to the two parties involved, weak retributivism has no application and, indeed, is quite compatible with a whole range of nonfault principles.

One final point remains to be made. If we hold that we are all more or less equally sinners in respect to a certain area of conduct or a certain type of fault—if, for example, we are all as likely, more or less, to be erring defendants as wronged plaintiffs in driving accident suits—then the principle of strong retributivism itself would call for the jettisoning of the "his fault" principle in that area of activity. If fault is distributed equally, the "his fault" principle, in distributing liability *unequally* among a group, will cause a lack of correspondence between fault and penalty. On the assumption of equal distribution of fault, the use of the "his fault" principle would lead to *less* correspondence, *less* exact proportioning of penalty to fault, even than various principles of social insurance that have the effect of spreading the losses as widely as possible among a whole community of persons presumed to be equally faulty. But then these schemes of nonfault liability are supported by strong reasons of their own, principles both of justice and economy,[21] and hardly need this bit of surprising added support from the principle of strong retributivism.

[21] E.g., the *benefit principle* (of commutative justice) that accidental losses should be borne according to the degree to which people benefit from an enterprise or form of activity; the *deep pocket principle* (of distributive justice) that the burden of accidental losses should be borne by those most able to pay in direct proportion to that ability; the *spread-it-out principle* that the cost of accidental losses should be spread as widely as possible "both interpersonally and intertemporally"; the *safety* or *loss-diminution principle* that the method of distributing losses that leads to the smallest net amount of loss to be distributed is the best one.

9

When we state that a person is responsible for some harm, we sometimes mean to ascribe to him *liability* to certain responsive attitudes, judgments, or actions. Some responsive actions require authority; of these some are punitive, and others force compensation of a harmed victim. In the typical case of individual liability to unfavorable responses from others, three preconditions must be satisfied. First, it must be true that the responsible individual did the harmful thing in question, or at least that his action or omission made a substantial causal contribution to it. Second, the causally contributory conduct must have been in some way *faulty*. Finally, if the harmful outcome was truly "his fault," the requisite causal connection must have been directly between the faulty aspect of his conduct and the outcome. It is not sufficient to have caused harm *and* to have been at fault if the fault was irrelevant to the causing. We can use the expression "contributory fault" to refer compendiously to these three conditions. Thus, in the standard case of responsibility for harm, there can be no liability without contributory fault.

Certain familar deviations from the standard case, however, give rise to confusion and misgiving. All primitive legal systems, and our own common law until about the fifteenth century, abound with examples of liability without contributory fault. For three centuries or so these examples were gradually eliminated from the common law, but they have returned in somewhat different form, often via statutes, in the last century, to the great alarm of many critics.

222

Some of this alarm, I think, is justified; but there is little ground for fearing a recrudescence of primitive tribalism. Much legal liability without fault rests on very solid rationales, which are quite another thing than primitive superstition. The cases I have in mind can be discussed under three headings.

Strict liability. What is called "strict liability" in the law is simply any liability for which the contributory fault condition is weakened or absent. This is the most general category; vicarious and collective liability are among its more interesting subspecies. For the most part, contractual liability has always tended to be "strict." Since this is liability that one imposes on oneself voluntarily, there is rarely any doubt expressed about its propriety. And no doubt can be expressed about its utility. Manufacturers brag about their warrantees and unconditional guarantees; and private bargainers quite often find it to their mutual advantage when one promises that, "if anything goes wrong, I'll bear the loss, no matter whose fault it is." In the law of torts, certain classes of persons are put on warning that, if they engage in certain ultra-hazardous activities, then they must be prepared to compensate any innocent parties who may incidentally be harmed, no matter how carefully and faultlessly the activities are carried out. There is always a risk of harm to others when one starts fires even on his own land, or keeps wild animals, or engages in blasting with high explosives. The law, of course, permits such activities, but it assigns the risk in advance to those who engage in them. This may seem to be a hard arrangement, since even if a construction company, for example, takes every reasonable precaution before dynamiting, it nevertheless can be found liable, if through some freakish chance a person at a great distance is injured by a flying rock set in motion by the blast, and can be forced to compensate the injured party for his losses. That the company was faultlessly careful in its operations is no defense. Still, this rule is by no means an arbitrary harassment, and its rigors are easily mitigated. The prospective responsibility imposed on blasters by law applies even to events beyond their control, but, *knowing this in advance* (an all-important consideration), they will be more careful than ever; and, further, they can guard against disastrous expenses by adjusting their prices and figuring compensation fees among their normal business costs.

Strict liability in the criminal law is much less likely to accord with reasonable standards of justice than in contracts and torts; but even penalties and punishments may, in certain circumstances, dispense with the requirement of fault, provided that prior assignments of risks are clear and that some degree of prior control is possible. Perhaps the best known strict liability statutes in the criminal law are those creating "public welfare offenses." Here the rationale for disregarding actual fault is similar, in part, to that supporting strict liability for ultra-hazardous activities in torts. All milk producers, for example, are put on notice by one statute that, if any of their marketed product is found to be adulterated, they will be subject to stiff penalty. The producers have the power and authority to regulate their own facilities, procedures, and employees. The law in effect tells them that, since there is such a paramount public interest in pure foods, they must give the public an unconditional guarantee of the purity of their product. If the guarantee fails, no questions will be asked about fault; the fine will be imposed automatically. Then it will be up to the company to exercise its control by locating and eliminating the fault. If this arrangement seems unfair, the company can be reminded that the risk is well known and is in fact the price producers pay for the privilege of serving the public for their own profit—a price they presumably have been quite willing to pay. Moreover, it really does protect the public by providing incentive to vigilant safety measures; and the penalties, in any case, are only fines. No perfectly innocent persons are sent to prison.

When criminal punishment involving imprisonment is involved, the case for strict liability, of course, is much weaker; but even here, in certain circumstances, the conviction of the "faultless" can sometimes be supported. Among serious crimes for which faultless ignorance ("reasonable mistake") is no excuse, the most celebrated example is the old English offense of taking an unmarried girl, under sixteen, from the possession of her father (for illicit purposes) without his consent. The rationale here, apparently, was that the harm done is so serious, and the opportunity and temptation so great, that any philanderer should be put on warning that, even if he has very good reason to believe his prey to be a thirty-year-old woman, he and he alone assumes the risk that she may be only fifteen—and a serious risk it is! The policy underlying the law was that philandery is a socially undesirable activity which it is the business of the law to discourage, but not the kind of moral offense that can properly (or practically) be prohibited absolutely. Hence young men are permitted to engage in it, but at their own peril. Understanding in advance where the risks lie, they will presumably be far more careful than they might otherwise be. The law here gives young sports a sporting chance. If they gamble and lose, even with the best of odds, they can blame no one but themselves. So interpreted, strict liability seems a relatively libertarian and humane means of social control.

In all the examples of plausibly just strict liability, the liable party must have had some control over his own destiny—some choice whether to take the risk assigned him by the law and some power to diminish the risk by his own care. When liability may be imposed even without such control, however, then it can "fall from the sky," like a plague, and land senselessly on complete strangers. Strict liability, when rational, is never totally unconditional or random.

Vicarious liability. Much, but by no means all, strict liability is also vicarious liability. There can be strict liability when *no one* is at fault, or where the question of contributory fault cannot be settled. There is vicarious liability, on the other hand, when the contributory fault, or some element of it, is properly ascribed to one party (or group of parties), but the liability is ascribed to a different party (or parties). In such cases we say that the latter party is responsible for the harmful consequences of a faulty action or omission of the former party. The person who did or caused the harm is not the one who is called upon to answer for it.

One familiar and surely unobjectionable type of vicarious liability is that which derives from the process of *authorization*. One party, called a "principal," authorizes another party, called the "agent," to act, within a certain range, for him. "He that acteth for another," wrote Hobbes, "is said to bear his person, or act in his name."[1] Acting in another's name is quite another thing than merely acting in his interests (also called "acting for him") or merely substituting for him, as an understudy, for example, replaces an indisposed actor (also called "acting in place of him"). An agent acts "for" or "in place of" his principal in a different sense. The agent is often given the right to act, speak, sign contracts, make appointments, or the like, and these acts are as binding on the principal as if he had done them himself. The relation of authorization, as Hanna Pitkin points out,[2] is lopsided: the rights go to the agent, and the responsibilities to the principal.

The relation of authorization can take two very different forms, depending on the degree of discretion granted to the agent, and there is a continuum of combinations between the extremes. On the one hand, there is the agent who is the mere "mouthpiece" of his principal. He is a "tool" in much the same sense as is a typewriter or telephone: he simply transmits the instructions of his principal. Thus messengers, delegates, spokesmen, typists, and amanuenses are sometimes called agents. Miss Pitkin points out that such persons are often called "mere agents," or (I might add) "bound agents" as opposed to "free agents."[3] The principal acts

[1] *Leviathan*, ed. Michael Oakeshott (Oxford: Basil Blackwell, 1946), Part 1, Ch. 16, 105.
[2] *The Concept of Representation* (Berkeley and Los Angeles: University of California Press, 1967), 19.
[3] *Ibid.*, 122.

through his agent much as he might act through some mechanical medium. On the other hand, an agent may be some sort of expert hired to exercise his professional judgment on behalf of, and in the name of, the principal. He may be given, within some limited area of expertise, complete independence to act as he deems best, binding his principal to all the beneficial or detrimental consequences. This is the role played by trustees and some other investment managers, some lawyers, buyers, and ghost-writers. At the extreme of "free agency" is the Hobbesian sovereign; for each of his subjects has in effect authorized in advance *all* of his "actions and judgments . . . in the same manner, as if they were his own."[4]

It is often said that the very actions of agents themselves, and not merely their normative consequences, are directly ascribable to their principals, through "a kind of fiction";[5] but this, I submit, is a dangerously misleading way of talking. If *A* has *B*'s power of attorney, he may have the right to sign *B*'s signature; and if he signs it on a contract or a check, the pecuniary consequences may be exactly as they would be had *B* himself signed his name. The results are *as if B* had himself acted; but it is nevertheless true that *he* did not act—*A* acted for him. Even the Old Testament, which finds nothing objectionable in the vicarious criminal liability of children for the sins of their fathers, balks at the doctrine of literally transferred agency and causality. In Deuteronomy 24:16, Jeremiah and Ezekiel repeat that, if the fathers had eaten sour grapes, the children's teeth would not be set on edge (though if the fathers had *stolen* the grapes, the children, perhaps, would be punishable).

Another form of vicarious liability derives from the relation between superior and subordinate in hierarchical institutions, of which military organizations are perhaps the clearest model. At the lowest rank persons have no author-

[4] *Leviathan*, Part 2, Ch. 18, 113.
[5] The limits of "fictitious attribution" (the phrase is from Hobbes) are clearly marked out by A. Phillips Griffiths in "How Can One Person Represent Another?", *Proceedings of the Aristotelian Society*, Supp. 34 (1960), 187-224, and by Pitkin, *op.cit.*, 49-54.

ity to command others and are responsible only for their own performances. Officers of the higher ranks have greater authority—that is, the right to command larger numbers of persons and make them "tools"—and correspondingly greater answerability for failures. A superior's failure may be the fault of some of his subordinates, but he must nevertheless answer for it to *his* superiors. Subordinates, on the other hand, are not liable for the foolish or wicked commands of their superiors, since they are not "to reason why" but just to obey. In a way, a military hierarchy, then, can be viewed as a system of unidirectional vicarious liability. Something like it often exists in a less clear-cut form outside of military organizations. A recent press dispatch, for example, reports that there will no longer be automatic promotions of teachers in the Detroit public high schools and that teachers and principals will be held responsible for the academic performance of their students. Thus if students do poorly, their teachers will be "punished," and if they do well, their teachers will be rewarded. This liability is not entirely vicarious, of course, since there is presumably some causal connection between the teacher's performance and the students'; but it can approach pure vicarious liability when classes of students differ widely in ability. Its point, I think, is an interesting one, namely, to bolster the motivation of the *teachers*. (The students presumably do not care enough about the welfare of their teachers to be affected directly by the arrangement). In this respect, it is the very opposite of most forms of vicarious punishment (such as holding hostages, massive reprisals, family liability, blood feuds) whose point is to affect the motivation of the primary wrongdoers, not those who stand to be punished vicariously.

Another form of vicarious liability is the responsibility of employers ("masters") to compensate victims of the negligence or even, in some cases, the deliberate wrongdoing of their employees ("servants"), even when the employee is acting without, or in direct defiance of, the explicit orders of his boss, and the boss committed no negligence in hiring the employee in the first place, or in supervising, instruct-ing, or outfitting him. Here, indeed, "the sins of the servant are visited upon the master." If my dog bites you, the biting is imputed to him, the liability to me.[6] Similarly, if the driver of my delivery truck, while doing his job, puts a dent in your fender or a crease in your skull, the liability to enforced compensation is mine, not his. (*His* liability is to *me*; he is now subject to being fired.) The rationale of this universal but once highly controverted practice is clear enough. If an accident victim has only a truck driver to sue, he may end up paying most of his disastrous medical expenses himself. The employer, having a "deeper pocket," is a more competent compensator; and, moreover, since he has *control* over the selection of employees for dangerous work, the rule will make him more careful in his assignment of tasks. It may be unfair to him to make him pay for an accident that was not his fault, but it would impose an even greater hardship and injustice to put the burden mainly on the shoulders of the equally faultless accident victim. And, again, there are means open to employers of anticipating and redistributing losses caused by their employees' negli-gence.

Still another form of vicarious liability derives from the relation of *suretyship*. A bonding company may insure an employer against the dishonesty of a new employee for a fee that may be paid by either employer or employee. If the employee commits embezzlement and makes his escape, the fault, guilt, agency, and causation all belong to the em-ployee, but the liability to make good the losses is the inno-cent surety's. Similarly, the guarantor of another's debt pays if the other fails; and the poster of bail forfeits, if the bailed prisoner fails to make appearance.

Vicarious liability through authorization, hierarchy, mas-tership, and suretyship can thus be rational, in the sense that they rest on intellectually respectable, if not always convincing, rationales. Most of what has passed as vicarious

[6] W. D. Falk, "Intention, Motive and Responsibility," *Proceedings of the Aristotelian Society*, Supp. 19 (1945), 249.

criminal liability in human history is otherwise. Holmes traced the origin of both civil and criminal liability to certain animistic conceptions common to the Hebrews, Greeks, Romans, and Germans, and apparently to all human cultures at a certain stage in their development. The instrument of harm, whether it were a tool, a weapon, a tree, an ox, a slave, or a child, was regarded as the immediate and "natural" object of vengeance. It was "noxal," that is, accursed, and had to be forfeited to the victim, or his family, to be torn apart and annihilated. Later the principle of composition was adopted, and the owner of the noxal instrument could buy off its victim as an alternative to forfeiture. Nevertheless, in the early centuries of all major legal systems, inanimate objects and animals were "punished"; and the related practices of blood feud, noxal surrender, and substitute sacrifice flourished.

There are more refined forms of vicarious criminal liability for which a more plausible case can be made, although even these "rational" forms are rarely defensible as just. The imposition of punitive vicarious liability arrangements upon a community is always a desperate measure, justifiable at best only in extreme circumstances. I have in mind the taking of hostages by a wartime army of occupation (condemned by The Hague Convention of 1907 but practiced by Germans in two world wars) and stepped-up military reprisals for terrorism or atrocity directed at populations that surely include the innocent as well as the guilty. These cruel practices arouse angry resistance and thus tend to be self-defeating; and, in any case, they are examples of acts of war, rather than rules of a system of criminal law.

Could there be circumstances, in less desperate times, in which authorization, hierarchy, mastership, or suretyship, admittedly plausible bases for noncriminal liabilities, could also be the ground for criminal punishment? Under our present law, a principal will be coresponsible with his agent when the latter commits a criminal act at the former's direction or with his advance knowledge or subsequent ratification. The criminal punishment of superiors for actions done *entirely* on their own by subordinates, however, would be a barbarous regression in normal times. Criminal suretyship is a more difficult matter. I can imagine a voluntary system of suretyship that would permit fathers to arrange in advance to undergo punishment instead of their sons in case the latter committed crimes. Such a system could have some incidental merits among its preponderant disadvantages: deterrence and development of family solidarity. And it makes more sense than certain cosmic systems of criminal law in which the children answer for the sins of their fathers instead of the other way round.

There is an important point about all vicarious punishment: even when it is reasonable to separate liability from fault, it is only the liability that can be passed from one party to another. In particular, *there can be no such thing as vicarious guilt.* Guilt consists in the intentional transgression of a prohibition, "a violation of a specific taboo, boundary, or legal code, by a definite voluntary act."[7] In addition, the notion of guilt has always been essentially connected with the idea of "owing payment." The guilty party must "pay" for his sins, just as a debtor is one who must correct his moral imbalance by repayment. To be guilty is to be out of balance, or unredeemed, stained or impure. The root idea in guilt, then, is to be an appropriate person to make atonement, penance, or self-reproach, in virtue of having intentionally violated a commandment or prohibition. There have been extensions of this idea both through morbid superstition and natural analogy, but flawed intention, transgression, and needed atonement are still its central components.[8]

[7] H. M. Lynd, *On Shame and the Search for Identity* (New York: Science Editions, 1961), 23.

[8] I have been discussing guilt in the sense of one very special way of being *at fault.* Guilt, in this sense, is usually a necessary condition for guilt in a different sense, namely, that of "criminal liability." The model of guilt in the latter sense is the legal condition brought into existence by an authoritatively pronounced verdict in a criminal court. Guilt in this sense is analogous to the state of civil liability also created by authoritative judicial pronouncement as the end product of a civil suit. To be guilty in the sense of criminally liable is to be

Now when an innocent man is punished for what a guilty man has done, he is treated *as if* he were himself guilty. There may be a rational point, and perhaps even justice, in certain circumstances, in doing this. Yet even though criminal liability can transfer or extend vicariously from a guilty to an innocent party, it obviously cannot be literally true that the guilt transfers as well. For guilt to transfer literally, action and intention too must transfer literally. But to say of an innocent man that he bears another's guilt is to say that he had one (innocent) intention and yet another (guilty) one, a claim which upon analysis turns out to be contradictory. I think that theologians and others have found it easy to talk of vicarious guilt only because the concept of guilt has always had the double sense of actual

---

properly subject to the imposition of punitive sanctions, just as to be civilly liable is to be properly subject to legal pressure to make pecuniary compensation for harm. To call a man guilty of a crime is either to report that he has been authoritatively pronounced guilty or else to express one's own quite unofficial opinion that the conditions of criminal liability have in fact been satisfied so that an official verdict of "guilty" is or was called for.

Almost always in criminal law the *conditions* of criminal liability (i.e., of "guilt" in one sense) include the requirement that the defendant intentionally acted (or omitted to act) in a way proscribed (or enjoined) by law (i.e., that he was guilty in the other, "at fault" sense of "guilt"). But there is no conceptual necessity that intentional transgression be a condition of guilt (liability). There is no logical contradiction in the rule that permitted German citizens to be found "guilty" of having a Jewish grandparent, or in the rule that makes even bellhops guilty of "possessing" drugs when they carry a hotel guest's bags to his room, or in rules permitting the punishment of "criminal negligence," or in rules creating "strict liability" in criminal law. In Shirley Jackson's famous short story "The Lottery," the "winner" of an annual lottery is customarily stoned to death by his neighbors. The absurdity of calling the randomly selected sacrificial victim "guilty," I submit, is a moral, not a logical or conceptual, absurdity. The condition of criminal liability in this case is not so much being at fault as being unlucky; but, in the sense of "guilt" under consideration, there is no contradiction in saying that a defendant was faultless but guilty nevertheless, providing he satisfied the conditions for liability specified by some rule. The only limit to the possibility of guilt in this sense is the requirement that there be *some conditions or other* for guilt; but the conditions need not include any kind of fault.

sin, on the one hand, and payment, atonement, redemption, and such, on the other; and of course it is at least logically intelligible for concepts of the latter kind to transfer. In short, liability can transfer, but not agency, causation, or fault (the components of "contributory fault"), and certainly not guilt.

Collective liability. In the remainder of this essay, we shall focus our attention on collective-responsibility arrangements. In principle, these can be justified in four logically distinct ways. Whole groups can be held liable even though not all of their members are at fault, in which case collective responsibility is still another form of liability without contributory fault similar to those discussed above; or, second, a group can be held collectively responsible through the fault, contributory or *noncontributory*, of each member; or, third, through the contributory fault of each and every member; or, finally, through the collective but *nondistributive* fault of the group itself. This section will be concerned only with the first of these forms, the collective liability that is one interesting subspecies of that vicarious liability which in turn is one interesting subspecies of strict liability.

Collective liability, as I shall use the term, is the vicarious liability of an organized group (either a loosely organized, impermanent collection or a corporate institution) for the actions of its constituent members. When the whole group as such is held responsible for the actions of one or some of its members, then, from the point of view of any given "responsible" individual, *his* liability in most cases will be vicarious.

Under certain circumstances, collective liability is a natural and prudent way of arranging the affairs of an organization, which the members might well be expected to undertake themselves, quite voluntarily. This expectation applies only to those organizations (usually small ones) where there is already a high degree of *de facto* solidarity. Collective responsibility not only expresses the solidarity but also strengthens it; thus it is a good thing to whatever extent the preexistent solidarity was a good thing. Where prior solidarity is absent, collective liability arrangements may seek their justification through the desperate prior *need* for solidarity.

When does a group have "solidarity"? Three intertwined conditions, I think, must be satisfied to some degree. There has to be first of all, a large *community of interest* among all the members, not merely a specific overlap of shared specialized interests, of the sort that unite the members of a corporation's board of directors, for example, no matter how strong. A community of interest exists between two parties to the extent that each party's integrated set of interests contains as one of its components the integrated interest-set of the other. Obviously, this will be difficult to arrange in large and diverse groups. A husband, for example, might have as his main interests (whose fulfillment as a harmonious set constitutes his *well-being*) his health, his material possessions, his professional reputation, his professional achievement, *and* the well-being (also defined in terms of an integrated set of interests) of his wife and his children. His interests would thus include or contain the interests of several other people. If those other persons' interests, in a precisely similar way, were to embrace his, then there would be between them a perfect community of interest. Secondly, such "community" is often associated with bonds of sentiment directed toward common objects, or of reciprocal affection between the parties. (R. B. Perry defined "love" as an interest in the interests of someone else). Thirdly, solidarity is ordinarily a function of the degree to which the parties share a common lot, the extent to which their goods and harms are necessarily collective and indivisible. When a father is jailed, his whole family shares the disgrace and the loss of his provisions. There is no hurting one member without hurting them all; and because of the way their interests are related, the successes and satisfactions of one radiate their benefits to the others.

Individuals normally pool their liabilities when they share a common cooperative purpose, and each recognizes in the others complementary abilities of a useful or necessary kind. Thus salesmen combine with administrators to become business partners, pooling their talents and sharing their risks. Joint authorships are often cases of mutual ghost-writing, where each party stands answerable for the joint product of their several labors. Athletic team members must all win or all lose together: victory is not the prize of individual merit alone, nor is defeat linked to "contributory fault." Similarly, in underground conspiracies and desperate dangerous undertakings, the spirit of "all for one and one for all" is not merely a useful device; it is imposed by the very nature of the enterprise. What makes collective liability natural in such cases is that parties who are largely of one mind to begin with are led (or forced) by circumstances to act in concert and share the risk of common failure or the fruits of an indivisible success.

There have been times in the history of civilization when group solidarity was a more common thing, and more easily arranged, than today. In many places, including Northern Europe, the ultimate unit of legal responsibility has been not the individual, but the clan, the kinship group, or the immediate family; and only a couple of centuries ago the English common law still applied to married couples the "fiction of conjugal unity." Only since the passage of Married Women's Acts in the 1840's have married women in America had a legal identity separate, in many kinds of legal situations, from that of their husbands. The world has without a doubt been getting steadily more individualistic in this respect, and it is no wonder. Change is faster, leading at any given time to more continual novelty and consequent greater diversity. Political parties, religious groups, and fraternal associations can no longer count on perfect uniformity and general solidarity across a whole spectrum of attitudes and convictions. And how much harder it is today to be a marriage broker (even with computers) than in other more static ages, when persons were more easily interchangeable and common values could be taken for granted!

De facto solidarity, then, is less easily come by today, even within small family groups. And because it is, there is no longer much point in treating a wife, for example, as part of a single corporate person with her husband. Wives today can own their own property, bargain and trade with their husbands, sign contracts on their own, and sue and be sued in their own names. Still, some of the conditions making for *de facto* solidarity (such as the common lot, and indivisible goods and evils) are necessarily present in every marriage; and when these are reinforced by shared or contained interests and mutual affection, the solidarity that renders joint liabilities reasonable will also be present. When fates are shared, they must be pooled in any case. Where the plural possessive "our" more naturally comes to the lips than the singular "mine," then to enter joint bank accounts and other forms of collective liability is only to certify the given and destroy artificial inconvenience.

There is perhaps no better index to solidarity than vicarious pride and shame. These attitudes occur most frequently in group members on behalf of the larger group, or of some other member(s) of the larger group, of which they are a part. Individuals sometimes feel proud or ashamed of their families, ancestors, countries, or races; and all or most of those who belong to groups may feel pride or shame over the achievements or failures of single members of their groups. Some writers have in effect denied that pride (and presumably shame) can ever be authentically vicarious; and there is no doubt that the appearance of vicariousness can often be explained away. Parental pride in the achievements of a son may be the consequence of a belief that those achievements reflect the influence of the parent, so that it is really pride at "what I have created in my son." This sort of interpretation may be possible in some cases, but it obviously cannot explain the son's filial pride in the achievements of his parents or grandparents. In this connection, H. D. Lewis speaks of "the presumption that we ourselves, having been subject to the same influences, are not without a measure of the qualities for which

others of our group are noted."[9] No doubt many occurrences of filial pride and shame can be traced to this source,
but clearly it cannot account for the immigrant's pride in
the "American way of life" or the war opponent's feeling
ashamed "to wear the same uniform" as those he believes
have committed atrocities. Of course, the latter may be
something different from shame, namely, mortification at
being associated by others with actions of which one disapproves and of which one is totally innocent. Normal embarrassment, like pride at what one has helped others to do
or be and pride over one's qualities presumptively shared
with conspicuously worthy other persons, is a self-centered
attitude; an authentically vicarious feeling, if there can be
such a thing, must be based on the doings or qualities of
others considered entirely on their own account, unrelated
to any doings or qualities of the principal.

H. D. Lewis provides a clue when he speaks of the phenomenon of sympathetic identification: "Our interest in
those with whom we have special ties of affection will enable us to follow their success with a glow of satisfaction as
if it were our own."[10] If this is what authentically vicarious
pride is like, it is a phenomenon of the same order as sympathetic pain or compassion. Indeed, any feeling one person can experience can be experienced vicariously by some
other imaginatively sensitive person. What we want, however, is not so much an account of vicarious or imaginative
sharing alone as an account that will also apply to vicarious
unshared or substitute feeling. Here too sympathy, I think,
is the key. When someone near to me, about whom I care,
makes a fool of himself before others, I can feel embar-
rassed for him, even though he feels no such thing himself.
Yet when some total stranger or some person I despise behaves similarly, my reaction will be indifference or pity or
contempt—reactions that are not vicarious. Compare "I am
proud (or ashamed) because of you" with "I am proud (or
ashamed) for you." The former is like taking partial credit

9 "Collective Responsibility," *Philosophy*, 23 (1948), 7.
10 *Ibid.*, 8.

(or blame); the latter is like congratulating (or condemning) from an internal or sympathetic judgment point. We are inclined to congratulate (or "condemn fraternally") only when we feel some degree of solidarity with the other parties. The solidarity is a necessary condition of the vicarious emotion, which is in turn an index to the solidarity.

I think this account helps explain some puzzling variations. It is natural, for example, that an American Negro should feel solidarity with all other Negroes and speak of what has been done to "the black man" by "the white man" and what the moral relations between "the" black man (all black men) and "the" white man (all white men) ought to be. But I, for one, am quite incapable of feeling the same kind of solidarity with all white men, a motley group of one billion persons who are, in my mind, no more an "organization" than is the entire human race as such. I certainly feel no bonds to seventeenth-century slave traders analogous to those ties of identification an American Negro must naturally feel with the captured slaves. Precisely because of this failure of imagination, I can feel no shame on *their* behalf. Similarly, a European, appalled by American foreign policy, will feel anger or despair, but not vicarious shame unless he has some sentimental attachment to the United States. An American with like views will be ashamed of his country. Indeed, one cannot be intensely ashamed of one's country unless one also loves it.

Collective-responsibility arrangements are most likely to offend our modern sensibilities when the liabilities are to criminal punishment. Yet there was a time when primitive conditions required that the policing function be imposed on local groups themselves through a system of *compulsory universal suretyship*. Among the early Anglo-Saxons, the perfectly trustworthy man was he who did not stray from the village where his many kin resided, for they were his sureties who could guarantee his good conduct. In contrast, the stranger far from his kindred had nothing to restrain him, and since his death would excite no blood feud, he had no legal protection against the assaults of others.[11] With the development of Christian feudalism, the ancient system of kindred liability broke down, for churchmen without kin or local tie began to appear among suspicious villagers, and "as time went on, many men who for one reason or another moved away from their original environments and sought their fortunes elsewhere . . . could not depend on ties of kindred to make them law-worthy and reputable."[12] Hence a new system of compulsory suretyship, based on neighborhood rather than kin was developed. Everyone was *made* "law-worthy and reputable" by being assigned to a neighborhood group every member of which was an insurer of his conduct. If an offender was not produced by his surety group to answer criminal charges, a fine was levied on each member of the group, and sometimes liability to make compensation as well.

Now this may strike us as a barbarous expedient of a primitive people who had no conception of individual justice; but I think that is too severe a judgment. The frank-pledge system was a genuine system of criminal law: there was nothing arbitrary, *ad hoc*, or *ex post facto* about it. It was also a system of compulsory group self-policing in an age when there were no professional police. Moreover, it reinforced a preexisting group solidarity the like of which cannot occur in an era of rapid movement like our own. And most important, the system worked; it prevented violence and became generally accepted as part of the expected natural order of things.

Yet surely there is no going back to this kind of collective responsibility. H. Gomperz concluded an essay by claiming: "that men can be held responsible solely for individual conduct freely willed is certainly wrong; it mistakes a principle characteristic of individualistic ages for an eternal law of

---

[11] L. T. Hobhouse, *Morals in Evolution* (London: Chapman & Hall, 1951), 81.

[12] S. B. Chrimes, *English Constitutional History* (London: Oxford University Press, 1953), 77.

human nature."[13] I agree that the principle of individual responsibility is not an "eternal law"; but Gomperz misleadingly suggests a kind of historical relativism according to which individualistic and collectivistic ages alternate like styles in ladies' skirts. On the contrary, the changes that have come with modern times have dictated quite inevitably that the one principle replace the other, and no "alternation" is remotely foreseeable, unless massive destruction forces the human race to start all over again in tiny isolated farming settlements. Under modern conditions the surety system would not work in the intended way, for the surety groups, being subject to rapid turnover, would lack the necessary cohesion and solidarity to exert much influence or control over their members. It is more difficult now to keep a watchful eye on our neighbors, since we no longer spend the better part of every day working in adjacent fields with them. Moreover, we no longer impose a duty on all citizens to raise the hue and cry upon discovery of a crime, drop their work, arm themselves, and join the hunt, on pain of penalty to their whole surety group. Now we say that detection and pursuit of criminals is the policeman's job. He gets paid for it, not us; and he is much more able to do it well. Besides, we all have other things to do.

But we have paid a price in privacy, which will get steadily stiffer, for the principle of individual criminal responsibility. The technical devices that make modern police work possible are reaching the point where they will make inspection of every person's life and history possible only minutes after a police official desires it. In olden times a man could not wonder for long whether he was his neighbor's keeper, for the voice of authority would instruct him unmistakably that he'd damn well better be. Today we prefer not to become involved in the control of crime, with the result that those who are charged with the control of crime become more and more involved with us.

In summary, collective criminal liability imposed on

[13] "Individual, Collective, and Social Responsibility," *Ethics*, 69 (1943), 342.

groups as a mandatory self-policing device is reasonable only when there is a very high degree of antecedent group solidarity and where efficient professional policing is unfeasible. Furthermore, justice requires that the system be part of the expected background of the group's way of life and that those held vicariously liable have some reasonable degree of *control* over those for whom they are made sureties. It is because these conditions are hardly ever satisfied in modern life, and not because individual liability is an eternal law of reason, that collective criminal responsibility is no longer an acceptable form of social organization.

So much for collective responsibility as a form of *liability without fault*. People often have other models in mind, however, when they speak of "collective responsibility."

Liability with noncontributory fault. Various faults can exist in the absence of any causal linkage to harm, where that absence is only a lucky accident reflecting no credit on the person who is at fault. Where every member of a group shares the same fault, but only one member's fault leads to any harm, and that not because it was more of a fault than that of the others, but only because of independent fortuities, many outsiders will be inclined to ascribe collective liability to the whole group. Other outsiders may deny the propriety of holding even a faulty or guilty person liable for harm that was not "his fault"; but for a group member himself to take this public stand would be an unattractive piece of self-righteousness. It would be more appropriate for him to grieve, and voluntarily make what amends he can, than to insist stubbornly on the noncontributory character of his fault, which was a matter of pure lucky chance.

In this kind of situation we have a handy model for the interpretation of extravagant hyperboles about universal responsibility. One man drinks heavily at a party and then drives home at normal (high) speeds, injuring a pedestrian along the way. The claim that we are all guilty of this crime, interpreted in a certain way, is only a small exaggeration, for it is a very common practice, in which perhaps *most* of us participate, to drive above posted speed limits at night and also to drive in our usual fashion to and from parties at which we drink. Most of us are "guilty" of this practice, although only the motorist actually involved in the accident is guilty of the resultant injury. He is guilty *of* or *for* more than we are, and more harm is his fault; but it does not necessarily follow that he is more guilty or more at fault than the rest of us.

Now there are some character faults that are present to some, though not the same, degree in almost everyone. These flaws sometimes cause enormous amounts of harm. There is some point in saying that all those who share the flaws, even those who have had no opportunity to do mischief by them, are "responsible" when harm results, in the sense that they are morally no better than those whose fault contributed to the harm and are, therefore, properly answerable for the way they are, if only to their own consciences. There is even a point in the exaggeration that ascribes the common fault to everyone without exception, when in fact there are exceptions; for this may serve to indicate that serious and dangerous faults are far more common than is generally believed and may exist in the least suspected places. Since character flaws are dispositions to act or feel in improper ways in circumstances of various kinds, we may never know of a given man that he has the fault in question until circumstances of the appropriate kind arise; and they may never arise.

Can liability of the noncontributorily faulty be morally palatable? Criminal punishment of whole groups of fault-sharers would for a dozen reasons be impracticable. We have no way of confirming statements about what a man with a given character structure would do if the circumstances were different; so if we are determined to avoid punishing the genuinely faultless, we had better wait until the circumstances *are* different. In any case, the larger and more diverse the group of alleged fault-sharers, the less likely it is that they all share—or share to anything like the same degree—the fault in question. If, nevertheless, the fault is properly ascribed distributively to a group of great size, the probability increases that the fault is common also to judge, jury, and prosecutor. Moral uncertainties of this kind are not likely to be present when we have evidence linking the fault of an individual to some harmful upshot. Those luckier ones who share the fault but escape the causal link to harm must, from the point of view of criminal justice, simply be left to profit from their luck. But when we leave political-legal contexts, the case for causation as a necessary condition of liability weakens considerably. The law will neither punish *B* nor force him to compensate *C* for the harm caused by *A*'s fault, when *B* is as prone as *A* to the fault in question; but that is no reason why private individuals should refrain from censuring or snubbing *B* to the same extent as *A*, or why *B* should not hold himself to account.

Contributory group fault: collective and distributive. Sometimes we attribute liability to a whole group because of the contributory fault of each and every member. Group responsibility, so conceived, is simply the sum of all the individual responsibility. Since each individual is corresponsible for the harm in question, no one's responsibility is vicarious. Nevertheless, problems are raised by three kinds of situations: first, where large numbers of people are independently at fault without any concert or communication between them; second, where the harm is caused by a joint undertaking of numerous persons acting cooperatively; and, third, where the harm is to be ascribed to some feature of the common culture consciously endorsed and participated in by every member of the group.

Suppose a man swimming off a public beach that lacks a professional lifeguard shouts for help in a voice audible to a group of one thousand accomplished swimmers lolling on the beach; and yet no one moves to help him, and he is left to drown. The traditional common law imposes no liability, criminal or civil, for the harm in this kind of case. Among the reasons often given are that, if liability were im-

posed on one, it would, in all consistency, have to be imposed on the whole vast group and that, if a duty to rescue
drowning swimmers were imposed on every accomplished
swimmer in a position to help, the results would be confusing and chaotic, with hoards of rescuers getting in each
other's way and no one quite sure he is not violating the
law by not entering the struggle quickly and ardently
enough. On the other hand, so the argument goes, if each
feels a duty to mitigate the dangerous confusion, there
could be an Alphonse-Gaston exchange of courteous omissions on a large and tragic scale. This rationale has always
seemed disingenuous to me. I see no reason why legal
duties should not correspond here with moral ones: each
has a duty to attempt rescue so long as no more than a few
others have already begun their efforts. In short, everyone
should use his eyes and his common sense and cooperate as
best he can. If no one makes any motion at all, it follows
that no one has done his best within the limits imposed by
the situation, and *all* are subject at least to blame. Since all
could have rescued the swimmer, it is true of each of them
that, but for *his* failure to attempt rescue in the circumstances that in fact obtained, the harm would not have occurred. It may be awkward to charge all one thousand persons with criminal responsibility, but the difficulties would
be no greater than those involved in prosecuting a conspiracy of equal size. As for civil liability, the problems are
even less impressive: the plaintiff (widow) should simply
be allowed to choose her own defendants from among the
multitudes who were at fault—those, no doubt, with the
"deepest pockets."

The second kind of case exemplifying group fault dis-
tributable to each member is that where the members are
all privy to a crime or tort as conspirators or accomplices
or joint tortfeasors. In complicated crimes, *complicity* is
ascribed unavoidably to persons whose degree of partici-
pation in the crime is unequal. The common law, therefore,
divides guilty felons into four categories, namely, "perpetrators," "abettors," "inciters" (all three of these are "ac-

complices"), and "criminal protectors," so that one may be guilty of a given crime either as its principal perpetrator (and even perpetration is a matter of degree, abettors counting as "principals in the second degree") or as accessories, that is, inciters or protectors. Thus one can be guilty, as an accessory, even of crimes that one is not competent to perpetrate. A woman, for example, may be found guilty of rape, as an abettor or inciter to the man, who must, of course, be the principal perpetrator of the crime on some other woman.

Suppose C and D plan a bank robbery, present their plan to a respected friend A, receive his encouragement, borrow weapons from B for the purpose, hire E as getaway driver, and then execute the plan. Pursued by the police, they are forced to leave their escape route and take refuge at the farm of E's kindly uncle F. F congratulates them, entertains them hospitably, and sends them on their way with his blessing. F's neighbor G learns of all that has happened, disapproves, but does nothing. Another neighbor, H, learns of it but is bribed into silence. On these facts A, B, C, D, E, and F are all guilty of the bank robbery—C and D as perpetrators, A and B as inciters,[14] E as an abettor, and F as a protector. G is guilty of the misdemeanor called "misprision of felony," and H of the misdemeanor called "compounding a felony." On the other hand, if J, an old acquaintance of C and D, sees them about to enter the bank, notices suspicious bulges in their pockets, surmises that they are up to no good, yet does nothing out of simple reluctance to "get involved," he is not legally guilty. Yet he is certainly subject to blame; and, as moralists, we might decide this marginal case differently than the lawyers and brand him a kind of "moral accessory" before the fact, "morally guilty," though to a lesser degree than the others. We can afford to have stricter standards of culpability than

---

14 "An inciter . . . is one who, with *mens rea*, aids, counsels, commands, procures, or encourages another to commit a crime, or with *mens rea*, supplies him with the weapons, tools, or information needed for his criminal purpose." Rollin M. Perkins, *Criminal Law* (Brooklyn: The Foundation Press, 1957), 558.

the lawyers, since no formal punishment will follow as a result of *our* verdicts and we do not have to worry about procedural complexities.

Part of the problem of determining degrees of responsibility of individuals in joint undertakings, where the responsibility is not vicarious, is assessing the extent of each individual's *contribution* to the undertaking. This involves assessment of various incommensurable dimensions of contribution—degrees of initiative, difficulty or causal crucialness of assigned subtasks, degrees of authority, percentage of derived profit, and so on. Although these matters cannot be settled in any mathematical way, rough and ready answers suggest themselves to common sense, and the legal categories of complicity have proved quite workable. The more difficult problems require estimates of *voluntariness*. Do I carry my own share of "moral guilt" for the Vietnamese abomination as a consequence of my payment of war taxes? Is my position morally analogous to that of *B*, the "inciter" in the bank robbery example? In avoiding protest demonstrations, am I guilty of "cooperating" with evil, perhaps on the model of *J, F, G,* or *H*? The answers to those questions are difficult, I think, not because the (minute) extent of my causal contribution is not easily measurable, but because it is difficult to know how strict should be the standards of voluntariness for cases like this. Since nonpayment of taxes is a crime, the payment of war taxes is less than fully voluntary. To go to prison merely to avoid being associated, however indirectly, with some evil is to adopt the heroic path. The man who "cooperates" with crime under duress is surely in a different position from the man who cooperates, like *H*, as a result of a bribe or, like *J*, out of sloth or cowardice. Yet whether the threat of legal punishment is sufficient duress to excuse "cooperation" with authorities again depends on numerous factors, including the degree of the evil and the probabilities of its alleviation with and without the contemplated resistance. In any case, mere nonresistance does not count as "cooperation" unless various other conditions are fulfilled. Where those conditions are conspicuously unfulfilled, as in Nazi Germany, then nonresistance is entirely involuntary, since its only alternative is pointless self-sacrifice.

The third interesting case of distributive group fault is that which adheres to a group's folkways yet somehow reflects upon every member of the group. Even Dwight Macdonald concedes that there are "folk activities" that a group "takes spontaneously and as a whole . . . which are approved by the popular mores" and which are not merely "things done by sharply differentiated sub-groups."[15] Nazi acts of violence against Jews, Macdonald argued, were not genuine folk activities in this sense. In contrast, the constant and widespread acts of violence "against Negroes throughout the South, culminating in lynchings, may be considered real "people's actions," for which the Southern whites bear collective responsibility [because] the brutality . . . is participated in, actively or with passive sympathy, by the entire white community."[16] The postbellum Southern social system, now beginning to crumble, was contrived outside of political institutions and only winked at by the law. Its brutalities were "instrumentalities for keeping the Negro in his place and maintaining the supraordinate position of the white caste."[17] Does it follow from this charge, however, that "Southern whites [*all* Southern whites] bear collective responsibility?" I assume that ninety-nine percent of them, having been shaped by the prevailing mores, wholeheartedly approved of these brutalities. But what of the remaining tiny fraction? If they are to be held responsible, they must be so vicariously, on the ground of their strong (and hardly avoidable) solidarity with the majority. But suppose a few hated their Southern tradition, despised their neighbors, and did not think of themselves as Southerners at all? Then perhaps Macdonald's point can be saved by excluding these totally alienated souls altogether from the white

15 *Memoirs of a Revolutionist* (New York: Meridian, 1958), 45.

16 *Loc.cit.* (written in 1945).

17 John Dollard, *Caste and Class in a Southern Town*, as quoted *ibid.*, 45.

Southern community to which Macdonald ascribes collective responsibility. But total alienation is not likely to be widely found in a community that leaves its exit doors open; and, in a community with as powerful social enforcement of mores as the traditional Southern one, the alienated resident would be in no happier a position than the Negro. Collective responsibility, therefore, might be ascribed to all those whites who were not outcasts, taking respectability and material comfort as evidence that a given person did not qualify for the exemption.

Contributory group fault: collective but not distributive. There are some harms that are ascribable to group faults but not to the fault of every, or even *any*, individual member. Consider the case of the Jesse James train robbery. One armed man holds up an entire car full of passengers. If the passengers had risen up as one man and rushed at the robber, one or two of them, perhaps, would have been shot; but collectively they would have overwhelmed him, disarmed him, and saved their property. Yet they all meekly submitted. How responsible were they for their own losses? Not very. In a situation like this, only *heroes* could be expected to lead the self-sacrificial charge, so no individual in the group was at fault for not resisting. The whole group, however, had it within its power to resist successfully. Shall we say, then, that the group was collectively but not distributively at fault? Can the responsibility of a group be more than the sum of the responsibility of its members? There is surely a point in affirming so. There was, after all, a flaw in the way the group of passengers was organized (or unorganized) that made the robbery possible. And the train robbery situation is a model for a thousand crises in the history of our corporate lives. No individual person can be blamed for not being a hero or a saint (what a strange "fault" that would be!), but a whole people can be blamed for not producing a hero when the times require it, especially when the failure can be charged to some discernible element in the group's "way of life" that militates against heroism.

One would think that, where group fault is nondistributive, group liability must be so too, lest it fall vicariously on individual members who are faultless. But, for all overt unfavorable responses, group liability is inevitably distributive: what harms the group as a whole necessarily harms its members. Hence if the conditions of justifiable collective liability—group solidarity, prior notice, opportunity for control, and so on—are not satisfied, group liability would seem unjustified.

An exception, however, is suggested by the case where an institutional group persists through changes of membership and faultless members must answer for harms caused, or commitments made, by an earlier generation of members. Commitments made in the name of an organized group may persist even after the composition of the group and its "will" change. When, nevertheless, the group reneges on a promise, the fault may be that of no individual member, yet the liability for breach of contract, falling on the group as a whole, will distribute burdens quite unavoidably on faultless members. Consider the philosophy department which debated whether to pass a graduate student on his preliminary examinations. The main argument against doing so was that passing him would commit the department to the supervision of the student's dissertation, and no one who knew this particular student was willing to read his thesis. The affirmative carried when two members volunteered to direct the dissertation themselves. One year later, however, one of these sponsors died, and the other took employment elsewhere. Thus *no member* was willing to supervise this student, and the department as a whole had to renege on its promise. No member felt personally bound by the promises of his departed colleagues, which had been made to the student in no one's name but the department's. No legal action, of course, was possible; but if the department had been *forc*ed to honor its word, this would have been an excellent example of nondistributive group fault (the departmental reneging) and consequent group liability of a necessarily distributive kind.

There is a different sense of "responsibility," and an important one, in which groups can be responsible collectively and distributively for traits (including faulty traits) in the group structure and history that can be ascribed to no given individual as their cause. Sigmund Freud[18] once raised the question whether individuals are "responsible" for their dreams and then astonishingly answered the question in the affirmative. Freud did not mean, however, that dreams are intentionally *acted out* or *caused* by the dreamer, or that they are, in any sense, the dreamer's *fault*, or that the dreamer is *liable* to censure or punishment or to self-directed remorse or guilt for them. What he did mean was that a person's dreams represent him faithfully in that they reveal in some fundamental way what sort of person he is. Freud was denying that dreams are "the meaningless product of disordered mental activity" or the work of "alien spirits." Rather, they have genuine psychological significance. Hence everyone must "take responsibility" for his dreams and not disown or repudiate them; and this is simply to "own up" to even the unpretty aspects of one's self as truly one's own.

Those who have read such works as Richard Hofstadter's *Paranoid Style in American Politics*[19] can hardly fail to be struck by the similarity between the social historian's revelations about the nation and the psychoanalyst's revelations about the individual. Both dredge up experiences from the past that are held to reveal persisting dispositions, trends, and "styles" of response that might otherwise be unknown to the subject. To deny the reality or significance of the child that still lives in the man, or of the early settlers whose imprint is still upon the nation, is to "deny responsibility" for traits that are truly one's own. When a nation's voices fail to acknowledge its own inherited character, the possibilities of understanding and rational control are just

[18] See *The Collected Papers of Sigmund Freud*, ed. Philip Rieff, BS 189 V, *Therapy and Technique* (New York: Collier Books, 1963), 223-226.
[19] (New York: Alfred A. Knopf, 1965.)

so far diminished, and the consequences for faultless individual citizens (as for the neurotically benighted individual in the other case) can be devastating. But the responsibility I mention here is no kind of agency, causation, fault, or liability; it would less misleadingly, though somewhat awkwardly, be called "representational attributability."

10

That justice consists in treating similar cases in similar ways and dissimilar cases in dissimilar ways is one of the oldest philosophical truisms. Those who are accused of committing serious crimes are all similar in at least *that* respect, and as a consequence

Crime, Clutchability, and Individuated Treatment

they are treated in similar ways—tried, acquitted or convicted, released or punished (usually) by incarceration in a prison. Yet there are many differences between these persons that might well be the basis for dissimilar treatment. The difference that has received most attention recently is that some of them are psychologically normal and others mentally ill; but this, of course, is not the only relevant difference between them, or even necessarily the most prominent or important. Still, it is a useful focus for a moralist's attention since it serves well to highlight a problem: persons who are *both* similar and dissimilar in morally relevant respects should be treated in ways that are both similar and dissimilar, but such treatment would require institutional proliferation of a magnitude to constitute itself a major threat to justice and liberty.

It is not always clear what we are talking about, or whether we are making any sense at all, when we talk about mental illness, and it is even less clear why we should regard mental illness as a bar to moral blame or criminal punishment. Part of this confusion stems from the generic notions of health and sickness themselves; part is peculiar to the notion of mental disease; and part stems from lingering uncertainties about the point of blame and punishment.

I

Central to the concept of disease in general is the idea of the impairment of a vital function, that is, a function of some organ or faculty upon which the important or proper functioning of the whole organism depends.[1] To ascribe a function to a component part of an organic system[2]—a liver or a carburetor—is to say that, in virtue of its morphological structure and its place in the general economy of components, it behaves in a certain way and, further, that the macroscopic functioning of the whole system causally depends upon its behaving in this way. It may seem, then, that ascription of functions to component parts or subsystems is a wholly factual matter consisting of, first, a description of a part's effects and, second, a causal judgment that these effects are necessary conditions for the occurrence of some more comprehensive effects. But the illusion of value-neutrality vanishes when we come to ascribe a function to the organic system itself.[3] We do not turn

---

[1] Disease thus differs from local disorders in that its impairments of part-functions lead to a generalized breakdown of the whole organism. One's body as a whole can continue to function more or less efficiently with a cut finger or a broken arm, but not when it is in high fever, nausea, vertigo, or extreme debility.

[2] Only living organisms are ever called healthy or sick, though complex machines are often enough honored by these terms through courtesy of metaphor. Machines, of course, are different in many ways from living things. For the most part, only the latter are capable of growth and reproduction, for example. But machines and living bodies are perfectly similar in one important respect: both are *organic systems*, that is, complexes composed of component parts related in such a way that the macroscopic functioning of the whole depends on the microscopic functioning of the parts, and to some extent, at least, vice versa.

[3] With a machine or artifact the illusion may persist: the "true function" of a knife or an automobile may be the purpose for which it was designed, or perhaps the task for which it is best suited by its

to the medical profession to learn the function of a man.

It follows that even statements ascribing functions to component organs will not be entirely value-neutral, for the macroscopic functions for which their effects are necessary conditions will contain value specifications in *their* descriptions. Thus Carl Hempel interprets the statement that the heartbeat in vertebrates has the function of circulating the blood to mean that "the heartbeat *has the effect* of circulating the blood, and this ensures the satisfaction of certain conditions (supply of nutriment and removal of waste) that are necessary for the *proper working* of the organism."[4] (In another formulation Hempel refers to conditions "necessary for the system's remaining in adequate, or effective, or proper, working order.")[5] Now there is in fact very little disagreement among us over what constitutes the proper working order of the human *body*. We all would agree that a body with paralyzed limbs was no more in "good working order" than a car with flat tires; and, in general, our culture identifies bodily health with vigor and vitality. But we can imagine a society of mystics or ascetics who find vitality a kind of nervous distraction (much as we regard hyperthyroid activity)—a frustrating barrier to contemplation and mystic experience and a source of material needs that make constant and unreasonable demands for gratification. Such a group might regard bodily vitality as a sickness and certain kinds of vapidity and feebleness as exem-

---

nature. Even a plant or tree might be claimed to have as its "true" or "proper" function the performing of some service for us—yielding fruit or shade. But it becomes quite implausible to interpret judgments about the proper function of an animal—especially a human animal—as pure matters of technological or biological fact.

[4] "The Logic of Functional Analysis," in *Symposium on Sociological Theory*, ed. Llewellyn Gross (New York: Harper & Row, 1959); reprinted in *Purpose in Nature*, ed. John V. Canfield (Englewood Cliffs: Prentice-Hall, 1966). The quote is on page 98 of the latter volume. Italics have been added.

[5] *Ibid.*, 99.

plary health. Our disagreement with these people clearly would not be a purely medical matter.[6]

II

If mental illness shares the generic character of sickness, it must then consist in the disabling impairment of some vital mental function, such as reasoning, remembering, feeling, or imagining. The most conspicuous mental illnesses are those that involve impairment of the cognitive faculties and consequent chronic irrationality of one kind or another. Most forms of "proper functioning" are quite impossible for a person whose memory has totally failed, or who is incapable of drawing inferences or of distinguishing fact from fantasy. There is general agreement among us that the sorts of incapacities directly consequent upon these functional failures constitute "being out of proper working order" and, therefore, being sick.

Much more difficult questions are posed by the mental dysfunctions that are noncognitive. Persons are now commonly called mentally ill when their affective or emotional or volitional faculties are awry, even when there is no attendant cognitive dysfunction. If one's "superego" is a mental faculty, and it fails to instruct or restrain, is its possessor mentally ill? Surely, there is one obvious sense in which no person can function "properly" if he has no conscience. And one might argue that any person who commits batteries,

---

[6] Cf. the following "medical" statement in which a controversial value judgment is hardly disguised at all: "Hormone therapy is based on the theory that the female change of life should be treated as a preventable disease. 'Menopause,' says Dr. Joseph W. Goldzieher . . . 'is one of nature's mistakes.'" *Newsweek*, April 3, 1967, 55.

Steffi Lewis has argued that, if ninety percent of humanity came, through evolution, to be able to digest cellulose, and if, further, this capacity became importantly useful (perhaps through critical shortages of other foods), the remaining ten percent (who are physiologically exactly the same as us, their ancestors) would quite properly be said to be deformed, or sick, or lacking in "basic" human equipment. What is "healthy," then, is relative to our resources, technical capacities, and purposes.

rapes, and murders is not in "good working order" and that certain moral norms, therefore, must be included among the criteria of proper functioning. If failure to act in accordance with the norms of a rational morality is the necessary consequence of some misfunction of mental faculty, such as failure of memory, deformity of conscience, caprice of will, hollowness of affect, perhaps even persistent deviant desires, then such immoral acts are, by definition, "sick." And, indeed, how can any organic system be out of proper working order unless there is some component that is misfiring? If an automobile won't run or runs only with great difficulty, it cannot possibly be that all its parts and component systems are in good working order. By this mode of argument, inclusion of noncognitive faculties among the "components" whose part-failure can cause overall malfunction leads us to the brink of the theory that *all* patently immoral behavior is sick and, therefore, excused.[7] And yet, despite this unwelcome apparent consequence, there is good reason, as I shall try to show, to acknowledge mental illnesses that do not affect reasoning.

[7] One can avoid tumbling into the Erewhonian chasm by denying that a *person* is an organic system, or by denying that moral norms belong among the norms of "proper functioning," or by denying the analogy between the relation that connects at least some of the "noncognitive faculties" and personal functioning, on the one hand, and that which connects organs and bodily functioning, on the other. One way out, however, seems closed by recent developments in psychotherapy. It is no longer open to us to say that sick criminals are those who are treatable by medical means while normal criminals are those not so treatable, for it is no longer clear just what a "medical means" is. As Lady Wootton points out: "We have thus reached the position in which an important branch of medical practice consists simply of talk, even if this is a rather special form of talk. . . . When the medical profession has enlarged its toolbox to make room for words alongside of its traditional bottles, drugs, and forceps—at this stage the definition of medical methods becomes infinitely elastic: and there is no longer any logical reason why the medical treatment of crime should not be interpreted as covering all known methods of dealing with antisocial persons. . . ." *Social Science and Social Pathology* (London: Allen & Unwin, 1959), 243.

III

Let us imagine that there is a small gland whose secretions into the bloodstream help regulate emotional states. When various cells in this gland become cancerous, the character of its secretions is subtly altered, so that a person falls out of emotional equilibrium easily and tends to overreact emotionally to commonplace stimuli. At a certain stage the person is subject to powerful moods of melancholy alternating with consuming inner rages. Soon his consciousness is pervaded by these feelings, and his experience chronically colored by them. Anything done or said to him and anything he can turn his attention to in reverie make him angry. He finds himself, to his own dismay, rehearsing assaults and murders in his imagination. He is subject to paroxysms of resentment and hate. Such a person, we should all agree, is one unhappy fellow.

We should also agree, I think, that he is sick. Because one of his component parts (in this case a physical organ) is not performing its regulative function, it is impossible for the organism as a whole to "function properly." In our imaginary case, there is no other conspicuous impairment of bodily function—no fever, nausea, debility, or pain. If we classify diseases by their causes, this is a physical disease; but if we classify by the type of impairment caused, it is a mental disease, since its symptoms (on the macroscopic level) are primarily emotional. It is the victim's mental life that is disordered.

Let us change the example, so that the symptoms are the same but cannot be accounted for by any physical dysfunction. Now our victim's moods and rages are a mental illness in the strongest sense, namely, the impairment of mental function from no discoverable physical cause. Note that there need not be any cognitive impairment. The victim may still be capable of consecutive reasoning and valid inferences; he may suffer no perceptual aberrations; and although he may enjoy entertaining paranoid fantasies, he does not really believe them.

The chances are good that our unhappy fellow will sooner or later commit a crime of violence. It could come in a sudden explosion of wrath, but that is not the case that interests me. Suppose instead that he broods for days over an affront, considers measures of vengeance, and entertains fantasies in which he inflicts the sharpest agonies on his enemy. Gradually fantasy merges into plan and plan into action. Still he does not *want* to take action; he knows it is wrong and knows it would endanger himself. For many days he constrains himself; but then his angry mood flares up again, and his hateful desire regains its frightening strength. On the day of his crime he could have stopped himself yet again. There was no irresistible compulsion to commit the crime then and there; and if there had been a "policeman at his elbow," he surely would not have done it then and there. But the crime was "in the cards," and it almost certainly would have happened sooner or later.

It is difficult to know exactly what moral judgment to pass on our unhappy criminal. Given that his rational faculties were unaffected by his sick moods and desires, perhaps we should have expected him to be cognizant of his problem and to have made special compensatory efforts to cope with it. On the other hand, the very strength and unprofitable character of the desires themselves may seem to us, in a calm and reflective hour, to have been an unreasonable burden for him to carry (even though they lacked "compulsive force" at the moment of the crime), thereby entitling him to our special consideration. In any case, insofar as we think of the desires themselves as the product of an illness, rather than a natural expression of his character, we must think of him in a way different from that in which we consider other kinds of criminals. If he had not suffered the illness, he would not even have had the desire to commit the crime. In that sense, at least, his motivating desire was sick. But it is not the intrinsic character of the desire that is importantly relevant to our responses to the criminal, but rather the condition that underlies it.

Consider the man with a purely physical illness that sends him to bed with a high fever. Microorganisms have invaded his body, and its temperature has risen to create an inhospitable environment for them. In effect the patient's body has become a battlefield, and the struggle incapacitates him until the tide of battle turns and the heat goes down. The fever in this case *is* the disease, the state of organic incapacity or overall impairment. It can also be taken as a *symptom* of the particular impairments of part-function that underlie the breakdown of the whole organism. If the patient is very thirsty, his craving for water can be taken in turn as a *symptom of the fever*.

Fever is a symptom of underlying subfunctional impairment (such as infection) in a stronger sense of "symptom" than that in which a desire for water is a symptom of fever. In the stronger sense, a symptom is an *infallible indication* (a sufficient condition) of the presence of something else; in the weak sense, a symptom is a mere sign, or clue, or *ground for suspicion*. The mentally ill man's morbid desire to kill is a symptom of his illness in roughly the way the physically ill man's craving for water is a symptom of his fever. One can lust to kill without being ill, just as one can be thirsty without having a fever.[8] On the other hand, the chronically gloomy moods and inner rages are, like the fever, in themselves sickness, that is, states of being in which a person cannot function properly; and, further, they are symptoms (in the strong sense) of some underlying part-functional impairment.

If our suspicions of underlying illness, based on the occurrence of the hateful (or thirsty) desire are confirmed, then what we took to be a sign of possible illness is now

[8] Thus "odd tastes," such as those of the homosexual, the pedophiliac, the bestialist, or the exhibitionist, are not *necessarily* sick desires, even though they are usually consequences of mental illness and always "grounds for suspicion." There is nothing about an odd taste as such which exonerates when it leads to crime. What tends to excuse is a sick condition which may or may not be its cause.

seen to be an actual symptom in still a third sense. The desire is a *necessary consequence* of the pathological condition: given fever, it is necessary that there be dryness, and, given morbid inner rages of the appropriate type, it is necessary that there be murderous desires. A genuinely sick desire, then, is one which is a symptom in this strong third sense. It is the expression of a pathological condition which is not only necessary but even sufficient for its occurrence, a condition in turn which presupposes underlying part-functional impairment.

IV

Our sick criminal has committed a proscribed act and is still a dangerous person. He has this much in common with persons of many other types. But consider also the contrasts! There is the respectable middle-aged bank teller with no previous record who, after having weighed the risks carefully and "rationally," commits embezzlement. His is the type we have in mind when we speak of "gain" as a motive and talk of punishment as a "pricing system" and of the criminal as "paying his debt" and "wiping his moral slate clean." Then there is the fallen sinner—the good man who succumbs to temptation and is susceptible to remorse. Punishment may lead him directly to repentance, since he will feel it to be the proper consequence of his fault. Indeed, it may be the only way to escape the guilt that burdens him. His is the type that led our ancestors to speak of prisons as penitentiaries. The risk-taker and sinner may be one and the same person, or they may be contrasting types. In any case, for rational self-interested men with developed consciences not quite strong enough to constrain them, punishment may provide (1) new self-interested motives to obey the law and (2), after the fact of disobedience, the necessary means of repentance.

Some interested crimes, of course, are not self-interested. Some are done to advance or retard a cause, to help a loved one, or to hurt an enemy, often at great cost to the criminal's own interest. Insofar as these crimes are not self-regarding, it might seem that the usual sorts of price tags put on them by the criminal law are vain and pointless. But this is not so. One may wish to commit a crime solely for another's sake, with no thought of self-advancement, yet refrain out of fear for one's own safety. Nevertheless, the deterrent efficacy of punishment for such crimes as a whole is probably a good deal less than for crimes of gain. Similarly, although it is no doubt common enough for persons to act against their own consciences for benevolent, malevolent, or other nonselfish reasons, still there is probably less genuine repentance for wholly other-regarding crimes than for crimes of gain. The dedicated zealot, the revolutionary, the Robin Hood bandit, the man overcome by love or pity (or hate for that matter) are not as likely to be repentant for their crimes as the ambitious bourgeois embezzler.

For a much larger class of criminals, repentance is a notion with no application whatever. I refer to those psychologically normal individuals who "had the misfortune of adjusting themselves to a weaker part of the community,"[9] the "normal criminal with a criminal superego." Most of these are young and provincial;[10] others are at war with society; some are committed professionals. Punishment per se is not likely to bring any of these to repentance, for none has sinned against his own ideals. Some may weigh risks in deciding when and how to commit crimes, but few weigh the risks of the criminal and noncriminal lives generally. Moreover, excessive prudence may lead to loss of status in criminal subcommunities. Thus methods and tools other than the price tag and the penitentiary seem called for as a response to those in this category: persuasion, reeduca-

[9] Franz Alexander and Hugo Staub, *The Criminal, the Judge, and the Public*, rev. edn. (New York: Collier Books, 1962), 65.

[10] These individuals may be virtually unaware of the moral standards of the larger middle-class community or consciously alienated from that community. They usually adhere faithfully enough to the requirements of their own subculture: they respond with violence to affronts to their manliness, they run in packs, they demonstrate their virtues through acts of reckless bravery or great antisocial impact.

tion, integration into the larger community, provision of a stake in it and a new source of pride. Intimidation "reforms" only the cowardly and dispirited from this group.

Finally, there are those criminals said to suffer from a "psychopathic character disorder," who commit one petty crime after another, are convicted, imprisoned, reassigned to hospitals, released, only to begin the familiar pattern of pointless self-damaging crime again. One could lock the psychopath up for good in solitary confinement, but permanent incarceration would violate his rights; or one could subject him to briefer but equally ferocious treatment. Yet there is no way of terrorizing him. He is incapable of anxiety or any powerful passion. He experiences nothing like inner compulsion; he has no care about the future, about his own good, or about other people's feelings. He is incapable of pangs of conscience; probably because of parental deprivation in childhood,[11] he has no superego at all. This condition can be called "mental illness" with propriety,[12] but it is probably incurable in an adult. Thus the psychopath is not fit to be free, and he is not fit to be tied. Perhaps incorrigibles should be consigned permanently to "places of safety" that are neither hospitals nor prisons but are pleasant and only minimally restrictive. Such places would be no more unpleasant for the psychopath than the outside world; they would be hellish only for the poor attendants and supervisors.

V

Traditionally Western penal systems, no doubt under the direct influence of Christianity, have been designed primarily for the fallen sinner, the moral agent who has succumbed to temptation but is at least potentially capable of remorse. The better self in such persons, as Hegel put

[11] See William and Joan McCord, *The Psychopath* (Princeton: Van Nostrand, 1964), 85-87.

[12] This point is argued convincingly by Hervey Cleckley in his classic *The Mask of Sanity* (St. Louis: C. V. Mosley, 1941).

it, has a right to its punishment and is honored by it. Eventually there was superimposed on this model of *prisoner as penitent* that of *prisoner as debtor*—a properly self-interested individualist who has freely assumed a risk, has lost, and now must pay the price. This superimposition of images has never come into clear focus, but now the situation is more complicated than ever. For still other prisoners are righteous self-sacrificers; others are like prisoners of war in a war that never ends; others must be treated as patients; and the psychopaths must simply be detained as humanely as possible.[13]

The problem for our society is to match the generic mode of treatment to the criminal. It is very likely that *punishment* in a strict sense is not a suitable means of dealing with many types of criminal, perhaps only the penitents and risk-takers. For most of the others, it is pointless or self-defeating. What distinguishes punishment from alternative modes of response is that it is a form of deliberately hard treatment that expresses blame and condemnation. It is a forceful and emphatic way of impressing upon the wrong-doer the public judgment that he has done wrong and that society resents him for it. Punishment is a hard fate for the criminal and also a symbolic way of telling him that he has deserved his hard fate, that he has it coming, that it serves him right. When we punish, as Samuel Butler's visitor to Erewhon put it, "we add contumely to our self-protection," and we rub it in. It is true, of course, that punishment may have extra-punitive effects: *by* punishing we may sometimes reform, deter, cure, intimidate, instruct, or detain. But *in*[14] punishing we (necessarily) condemn and inflict

---

13 Still others are insane in the sense of "totally deranged" and do not know what they are doing; others are children—or are like children—and must be instructed for the first time about what is permitted in the larger community. And the situation is still more complicated because this list of general categories is not exhaustive; the categories are not all mutually exclusive, and each contains a motley of subtypes.

14 Cf. J. L. Austin's distinction between "illocution" and "perlocution" in *How To Do Things With Words* (Cambridge: Harvard University Press, 1962), 94ff.

pain that is meant to be ignominious and shameful.[15] It would be a mistake, however, to infer (as Lady Wootton apparently does)[16] that we must choose *either* punishment *or* preventive treatment and that the choice of punishment can only be made on the grounds that blaming the blameworthy and punishing the wicked are ends in themselves. To draw such a conclusion would be to underestimate grossly the beneficial side effects of punishment for certain types of criminal. For the "fallen sinner," like Dostoevski's Raskolnikov, it may be *the* prescribed course of rehabilitative treatment. It may also be the most effective intimidation for the rational risk-taker. But for the others it is usually vain.

Sound policy would therefore seem to require a wide variety of types of institutions for treating criminals and great administrative flexibility in procedures for selecting among them. But here is the catch. Flexibility presupposes discretion and liberty to experiment. These in turn presuppose freedom from rigid statutory impediments. But such freedom is a form of power over human beings, and relatively unanswerable power at that. Whatever the defects of the traditional system that preserved the linkage between crime and punishment, it at least offered the protections of due process to the criminal from first arrest to final release. If we break that link, do we not also sever the connection between crime and responsible legal procedures? There is already some evidence of the erosion of due process in the plight of those who have been deprived of legally effective means to avoid or eventually to end compulsory therapeutic confinement. The problem posed by justice, then, is: how can we achieve flexibility in our responses to crime without giving up the protection of individual rights long associated with our criminal law?

[15] Lady Wootton adopts this usage in her *Crime and the Criminal Law*, where she distinguishes between "punitive" and "preventive" treatment. It is a useful tautology, I think, that punishment must be punitive. See also my "The Expressive Function of Punishment," in this volume, 95-118.
[16] *Ibid.*, Chs. 2, 3.

Common to some recent attempts to deal with the problem is the idea of what might be called a "clutch line": the criminal trial becomes a mere preliminary hearing to establish whether the state has the right to get a defendant in its clutches. If convicted, the accused is properly under the state's control. He can no longer decide his own fate, and it is up to the authorities to decide what kind of treatment, if any, to impose upon him. Defending the accused's rights through adversary proceedings is held to be an especially important matter before the clutch line is crossed. Hardly any reformers advocate suspension of the requirement that there be a criminal act before there can be criminal liability. Even zealous moralists and psychiatrists have not suggested that courts should have the power to convict people simply on the ground that they have character flaws or neurotic symptoms that make them "dangerous persons." Being a dangerous person has been a crime only in the most oppressive tyrannies. Except when they consider the vexatious question of civil commitment, most writers are still satisfied with the maxim that "every dog is entitled to his first bite." This approach creates risks —one recent dog's first bite was the assassination of a president—but most are content to pay this price for the greater benefits of due process and freedom from arbitrary interference.

Before anyone can properly fall into the state's clutches and forfeit his right to determine his future by his own choice, then, he must do something prohibited by law.[17] Lady Wootton would make this the *only* requirement for conviction, reserving inquiries into the defendant's mental states for a time after the clutch line has been crossed. Presumably, those who committed their "crimes" by accident, or mistake, or under duress, would be released at a subsequent hearing, unless it turned out that they had suspicious symptoms or dangerous tendencies (such as accident-proneness), in which case they would be "sentenced" to

---

[17] Or omit something required by law. I take this to be the legal requirement of *actus reus* (or *corpus delicti*).

an appropriate measure of counseling, therapy, or punishment—whichever would be likely to be most effective.

Professor Hart[18] takes issue with this chilling proposal on the grounds that it would allow persons to fall into the state's clutches even when they had no "fair opportunity" to obey the law and that most of us would be deprived to some extent of the "chance to predict and plan and determine our own future." He concedes that we run some risk of further harm from acquitted offenders but argues that this is preferable to the loss of protection against meddling authorities. Hart does endorse, however, what he calls a modified version of Lady Wootton's proposal. He would require for conviction both a prohibited act (*actus reus*) and most of the "mental conditions" included under the term *mens rea*. He would require the prosecution to prove that the accused acted knowingly or purposely (or recklessly or negligently, as the case may be) in bringing about a certain result. If this is what is meant by *mens rea*, then Hart would make *mens rea* a material element of every crime. But he would stop there. He would not include sanity as one of the elements to be proved by the prosecution, nor would he allow insanity to be an affirmative defense. In short, he agrees with Lady Wootton that no inquiry into the defendant's *mental health* should be permitted before the clutch line is passed. "Not guilty by reason of insanity" would no longer be a possible verdict.

There seem to be at least four reasons for this proposal: (1) the difficulty of evaluating evidence about how capable a person was at some past time of conforming to the law when no external constraints are at issue; (2) the inappropriateness of the courtroom as a forum for deciding questions of medical diagnosis; (3) the great practical difficulty of formulating unconfusing instructions for juries who must be primarily concerned with guilt or innocence and for expert witnesses who prefer their own terminological cate-

18 H.L.A. Hart, *The Morality of the Criminal Law* (Jerusalem: Magnes Press, 1965), Lecture 1; reprinted in *Punishment and Responsibility* (Oxford: Clarendon Press, 1968), Ch. 8.

gories; and (4), perhaps most important, the argument that some mentally ill persons are socially dangerous persons[19] and should not, therefore, be allowed to escape the state's clutches just because they lack the "capacity for guilt," especially since they have already had their "first bite."

The main source of opposition to the proposal is probably the general obsession with blameworthiness. It is widely believed that no one should be pronounced guilty of a crime unless he deserves the odium expressed by that verdict. Mentally ill persons deserve sympathy rather than stigmatization (so the argument goes); therefore, they should not be pronounced guilty. But, in the first place, it is not even true of all sane defendants that guilt implies blameworthiness;[20] and, secondly, to Hart's proposal might be added the recommendation that the entire proceeding prior to crossing the clutch line be reconceived so that all suggestion of disgrace and censure is removed from it. Perhaps the words "guilty" and "innocent" might be expunged altogether, and defendants be found "clutchable as charged" or "unclutchable," on the model of the civil law where they are found "liable" or "not liable" for damages and where no mention is made of guilt. Determining whether the defendant is properly clutchable, then, would require proof beyond a reasonable doubt of all the material elements of the crime. Inquiry into the question of whether he intentionally did an act which is in fact forbidden, and was not compelled or tricked into doing it, would be undertaken for the purpose of establishing not how blameworthy he is, but only whether he had a "fair opportunity" to conform his conduct to the law.

[19] Professor Norvall Morris quite properly took exception to an earlier stronger version of this statement. He pointed out to me that very likely only a small percentage of socially dangerous people are mentally ill, and that even a smaller percentage of mentally ill people are socially dangerous. The overlap between the two classes has been grossly exaggerated.

[20] Some "guilty" persons—patriots, civil protesters, men of rocklike integrity—make the law look bad, rather than vice versa. The stigma of "criminal" looks good to them, like a badge of honor.

The primary weakness of Hart's proposal consists in its failure to recognize that a defendant's mental health may have some bearing on the question of *mens rea*, so that it may be impossible to exclude the former while considering the latter. The defense may well introduce evidence of cognitive derangement to cast doubt on the prosecution's proof that the defendant knew what he was doing when he committed the crime. Since the prosecution's failure to prove every element of the crime beyond a reasonable doubt results in acquittal in the sense of outright release, evidence of derangement could turn dangerous madmen loose on the community. But there is a way out for Hart. Mental illness *without cognitive impairment*, I believe, would not tend to overturn evidence of *mens rea*; only "insanity" in a strict and narrow sense (say, as determined by the McNaghten Rules) would do that. And if the defense established that degree of derangement, it would by the same token have established the need for detainment for medical treatment. Thus any evidence of mental disorder strong enough to overturn guilt will be strong enough to establish proper clutchability.[21] Hence no evidence of mental illness could be sufficient to defeat clutchability— the conclusion Hart embraces.

VI

The real problems for the Hart-Wootton proposal come after the clutch line has been crossed. Procedures must be devised to make possible the assignment of clutch-

[21] Since the Criminal Lunatics Act of 1800, acquittal on the ground of insanity both in England and in most American jurisdictions has not meant outright release, but rather commitment in a nonpenal institution. Thus the effect of the insanity defense in our present system has not been to defeat clutchability. Joseph Goldstein and Jay Katz comment: "Like defense of self, the defense of insanity, if successfully pleaded, results in 'acquittal.' But unlike the acquittal of self-defense which means liberty, the acquittal of the insanity defense means deprivation of liberty for an indefinite term in a 'mental institution'. . . . Thus the insanity defense is not a defense, it is a device for triggering indeterminate restraint." "Abolish the Insanity Defense—Why Not," *Yale Law Journal*, 72 (1963), 858, 868.

ables to appropriately individualized modes of treatment and also the effective protection at every stage of their right not to be mistreated. Clutchability must involve at least temporary forfeiture of not only the right to liberty of movement but also the right to privacy. If the system is to have any chance of working, the clutchable will be subjected to tests, interviews, and measurements. Many of the inquiries that were banned at the first trial now become centrally important: inquiries into his motives in committing the crime, his ulterior objectives, and his emotional states, his cognitive capacities, his affective dispositions; his praise- or blameworthy traits of character, his attitudes and beliefs. He should be examined by sociologists and moralists as well as psychologists, and little respect should be shown for the line between severe "character disorder" and mental illness; for the totally depraved and incorrigibly vicious man of deeply rooted, lifelong bad habits of feeling and action is a not implausible nominee for mental illness himself, if we mean by illness the incapacity to "function properly" based on some failure of part-function. A vicious character, as Aristotle saw, can be very much like a fever making it difficult for its possessor to be in "proper control of himself"; and, as Bishop Butler saw, meanness and malevolence can themselves be states of pure misery.

I should think that such inquiries, if unimpeded, could yield evidence of high reliability, even in our present backward state of social scientific knowledge, that the convicted clutchable is either a clear case of one or another of the main categories of criminal—gambling consumer, fallen sinner, class enemy, mentally disturbed, or whatever—or else a marginal case, or otherwise one not easily classifiable. This evidence then would be presented at another hearing to a committee of post-clutch-line judges, perhaps composed of jurists, sociologists, psychologists, and lay jurymen in equal numbers, with the prisoner's lawyer present to challenge parts of it if he wishes, but not necessarily in accordance with the strict assignments of presumptions and burdens and other procedures characteristic of the adversary system. The prisoner himself would be interrogated by the committee; and, finally, a decision would be reached either to release him outright as no longer dangerous or to condemn him to penal servitude for a time-period with a fixed upper limit, or fine him, or parole him under supervision, or assign him to a mental hospital, or rehabilitory work camp, or some comfortable but permanent "place of safety." Wherever he goes, if the committee does its work well, he will find others of his own type; he may in the course of his career move from one kind of institution to another, but no institution will mix functions indiscriminately,[22] for the different kinds of required treatment can get in the way of one another; and what is good for one kind of clutchable may be poison for another.

But now how are we to protect the prisoner from falling permanently under the arbitrary power of some doctor or administrator who regards him as too dangerous ever to be released, whatever his own opinion of the matter may be? Obviously, we must keep as much protection of due process at every stage as is possible. Too much power over the fate of other human beings is as dangerous to the public security and to individual justice as crime itself and must everywhere be made to be responsible. If outside friends are not available to look after the prisoner's interests and press his claims, the state should have officers of its own to perform precisely this service. These officers should come from some administratively autonomous agency, like the Inspector General's Office in the Army. They should actively investigate the condition of every prisoner at regular intervals, and, like the Scandinavian ombundsman, they should be available continuously to receive complaints. Moreover, there should be elaborate procedures for *appeals* of decisions, not only court decisions but also those of assignment committees, or penal or therapeutic authorities. There

---

[22] The sketch here differs from the one offered by Lady Wootton, who would (in her words) "obscure the present rigid distinction between the penal and the medical institution" and send all clutchables to a kind of neutral "place of safety." *Crime and the Criminal Law*, 79.

should be mandatory reviews at regular intervals, and disagreements should be adjudicated by specialist, mixed-specialist, and nonspecialist juries.

The social cost of these checks and balances would no doubt be very high. The system of individuated treatment with protected rights would make us a more litigious society than ever, with hospital rooms and training camps and detainment centers turned into little courtrooms, and fates of persons decided more directly and more often by greater numbers of free citizens. This would in a sense make all of us more responsible generally for what happens to our social misfits, since all of us would have more occasion to participate in the decisionmaking that determines their fates. Constant litigation can become a burden and a bore, but that is the price we shall have to pay if we are to have effective social control and protected human liberty too.

11

Professor Dershowitz has very effectively put psychiatry in its proper place.[1] As far as the law and public policy are concerned, a psychiatrist is an expert on the diagnosis and treatment of mental illness. His testimony becomes relevant to questions of responsibility only when mental illness itself is relevant to such questions, and that is only when it deprives a person of the capacity to conform his conduct to the requirements of law. Mental illness should not itself be an independent ground of exculpation, but only a sign that one of the traditional standard grounds—compulsion, ignorance of fact, or excusable ignorance of law—may apply. Mental illness, then, while often relevant to questions of responsibility, is no more significant—and significant in no different way—than other sources of compulsion and misapprehension.

What Is So Special about Mental Illness?

Now although I am almost completely convinced that this is the correct account of the matter, I am nevertheless going to air my few lingering doubts as if they were potent objections, just to see what will happen to them. I shall suggest, then, in what follows, that mental illness has an independent significance for questions of responsibility not fully accounted for by reference to its power to deprive one of the capacity to be law-abiding.

[1] Alan M. Dershowitz, "The Psychiatrist's Power in Civil Commitment: A Knife that Cuts Both Ways." An abridged version of this talk was published in *Psychology Today*, 2/9 (Feb. 1969), 43-47.

I

At the outset we must distinguish two questions about the relation of mental illness to criminal punishment. (There are two parallel questions about the bearing of mental illness on civil commitment.)

(1) How are mentally sick persons to be distinguished from normal persons?

(2) When should we accept mental illness as an excuse? The first appears to be a medical question that requires the expertise of the psychiatrist to answer; the second appears to be an essentially controversial question of public policy that cannot be answered by referring to the special expertise of any particular group.

Some psychiatrists may wish to deny this rigid separation between the two questions. They might hold it self-evident that sick people are not to be treated as responsible people; hence the criteria of illness are themselves criteria of nonresponsibility. But, obviously, this won't do. First of all, the fact of illness itself, even greatly incapacitating illness, does not automatically lead us to withhold ascription of responsibility, or else we would treat *physical* illness as an automatic excuse. But in fact we would not change our judgments of Bonnie and Clyde one jot if we discovered that they both had had 103-degree fevers during one of their bank robberies, or of Al Capone if we learned that he had ordered one of his gangland assassinations while suffering from an advanced case of chicken pox. Secondly, there are various crimes that can be committed by persons suffering from mental illnesses that can have no relevant bearing on their motivation. We may take exhibitionism to be an excuse for indecent exposure, or pedophilia for child molestation, but neither would be a plausible defense to the charge of income-tax evasion or price-fixing conspiracy. These examples show, I think, that the mere fact of mental illness, no more than the mere fact of physical illness, automatically excuses. We need some further criterion, then, for distinguishing cases of mental illness that

273

do excuse from those that do not, and this further question is not an exclusively psychiatric one. What we want to know is this: what is it about mental illness that makes it an excuse when it is an excuse?

So much, I think, is clear. But now there are two types of moves open to us. The first is preferred by most legal writers, and it is the one about which I intend to raise some doubts. According to this view, there is nothing very special about mental disease as such. Mental illness is only one of numerous possible causes of *incapacity*, and it is incapacity —or, more precisely, the incapability to conform to law— that is incompatible with responsibility. Ultimately, there is only one kind of consideration that should lead us to exempt a person from responsibility for his wrongful deeds, and that is that he *couldn't help it*. Sometimes a mental illness compels a man to do wrong, or at least makes it unreasonably difficult for him to abstain, and in these cases we say that, because he was ill, he couldn't help what he did and, therefore, is not to be held responsible for his deviant conduct. But in other cases, as we have seen, mental illness no more compels a given wrongful act than the chicken pox does, or may be totally irrelevant to the explanation of the wrongdoing, in that the wrongdoer would have done his wrong even if he had been perfectly healthy. What counts, then, for questions of responsibility is whether the accused could have helped himself, not whether he was mentally well or ill.

Aristotle put much the same point in somewhat different but equally familiar language. A man is responsible, said Aristotle, for all and only those of his actions that were voluntary; to whatever extent we think a given action less than voluntary, to that extent we are inclined to exempt the actor from responsibility for it. There are, according to Aristotle, two primary ways in which an action can fail to be voluntary: it can be the result of *compulsion*, or it can be done in *ignorance*. Thus if a hurricane wind blows you twenty yards across a street, you cannot be said to have crossed the street voluntarily, since you were compelled to do it and given no choice at all in the matter. And if you put arsenic in your wife's coffee honestly but mistakenly believing it to be sugar, you cannot be said to have poisoned her voluntarily, since you acted in genuine ignorance of what you were doing.

Now if we take just a few slight liberties with Aristotle, we can interpret most of the traditionally recognized legal excuses in terms of his categories. Acting under duress or necessity, or in self-defense, or defense of others, or defense of property, and so on, can all be treated as cases of acting under compulsion, whereas ignorance or mistake of fact, ignorance or mistake of law, and perhaps even what used to be called "moral idiocy" or ignorance of the "difference between right and wrong" can all be treated as cases of acting in responsibility-cancelling ignorance. On the view I am considering (a view which has gained much favor among lawyers, and to which Professor Dershowitz, I feel sure, is friendly), the mental illness of an actor is not still a third way in which his actions might fail to be voluntary; rather, it is a factor which may or may not compel him to act in certain ways, or which may or may not delude, or mislead, or misinform him in ways that would lead him to act in ignorance. Indeed, on this view, mental illness ought not even to be an independent category of exculpation on a level with, say, self-defense or mistake of fact. Self-defense and relevant blameless mistakes of fact always excuse, whereas mental illness excuses only when it compels or deludes. We now know of the existence of inner compulsions unsuspected by Aristotle: obsessive ideas, hysterical reactions, neurotic compulsion, phobias, and addictions. Other mental illnesses characteristically produce delusions and hallucinations. But not all neurotic and psychotic disorders by any means produce compulsive or delusionary symptoms, and even those that do are not always sufficient to explain the criminal conduct of the person suffering from them.

The nineteenth-century judges who formulated the famous McNaghten Rules were presumably quite sympathetic with the view I have been describing, that there really is nothing very special about mental illness. These rules are not at all concerned with neurotically compulsive behavior—a category which simply was not before their minds at the time. Rather, they were concerned with those dramatic and conspicuous disorders that involve what we call today "paranoid delusions" and "psychotic hallucinations." The interesting thing about the rules is that they treat these aberrations precisely the same as any other innocent "mistakes of fact"; in effect the main point of this part of the McNaghten Rules is to acknowledge that mistakes of fact resulting from "disease of the mind" really are genuine and innocent and, therefore, have the same exculpatory force as more commonplace errors and false beliefs. The rules state that, "when a man acts under an insane delusion, then he is excused only when it is the case that *if* the facts were as he supposed them his act would be innocent. . . ." Thus if a man suffers the insane delusion that a passerby on the street is an enemy agent about to launch a mortal attack on him and kills him in what he thinks is "self-defense," he is excused, since if the facts were as he falsely supposed them to be, his act would have been innocent. But if (in James Vorenberg's example) he shoots his wife because, in his insane delusion, he thinks her hair has turned gray, he will be convicted, since even if her hair had turned gray, that would not have been an allowable defense. Note that the mental disease that leads to the insane delusion in these instances is given no special significance except insofar as it mediates the application of another kind of defense that can be used by mentally healthy as well as mentally ill defendants.

The McNaghten Rules do, however, make one important concession to the peculiarity of mental illness. Mentally normal persons, for the most part, are not permitted to plead *ignorance of the law* as a defense, especially for crimes that are "malum *in se.*" No normal person, for example, can plead in the state of Arizona that "he didn't know that murder is prohibited in Arizona." *That* kind of ignorance could hardly ever occur in a normal person, and even if it did, it would be negligent rather than innocent ignorance. (One should at least take the trouble to find out whether a state prohibits murder before killing someone in that state!) If a person, however, is so grossly ignorant of what is permitted that he would murder even (as the saying goes) with "a policeman at his elbow," then if his ignorance is attributable to a diseased mind and therefore innocent, he is excused. One can conceive (just barely) of such a case. Imagine a man standing on a street corner chatting with a policeman. A third person saunters up, calmly shoots and kills the man, turns to the astonished policeman and says "Good morning, officer," and starts to walk away. When the policeman apprehends him, then *he* is the astonished one. "Why, what have I done wrong?" he asks in genuine puzzlement.

In accepting this kind of ignorance when it stems from disease as an excuse, the McNaghten Rules do not really make *much* of a concession to the uniqueness of mental illness. Ignorance of law does not excuse in the normal case because the law imposes a duty on all normal persons to find out what is prohibited at their own peril. When a statute has been duly promulgated, every normal person is presumed to know about it. If any given normal person fails to be informed, his ignorance is the consequence of his own negligence, and he is to blame for it. But when the ignorance is the consequence of illness, it is involuntary or faultless ignorance and may therefore be accepted as an excuse. Again, it is not the mental illness as such which excuses, but rather the ignorance which is its indirect by-product. The ultimate rationale of the exculpation is that the actor "couldn't help it." We hardly need the separate insanity defense at all if we accept the propositions that mentally ill people may be subject to internal compulsions, that mental illness can cause innocent ignorance, and that both compulsion and innocent ignorance are themselves excuses.

Suppose a mentally ill defendant is acquitted on the ground that his illness has rendered his unlawful conduct involuntary in one of these traditional ways. He may still be a menace to himself or others, even though he is perfectly innocent of any crime. Hence the state reserves to itself or to others the right to initiate civil commitment proceedings. Now whether it follows acquittal or is quite independent of any prior criminal proceedings, civil commitment can have one or both of two different purposes, and for each of these purposes the mere fact of mental illness is not a sufficient condition. The two purposes are (1) forcible detention of a dangerous person to prevent him from committing a crime and (2) compulsory therapeutic confinement of a mentally ill person "for his own good." For the purpose of preventive detention, mental illness is neither a necessary nor a sufficient condition: not necessary because mentally normal persons too can be very dangerous in certain circumstances,[2] and not sufficient because some mentally ill people, unhappy or withdrawn as they may be, are still quite harmless. Hence psychiatric testimony that a person is mentally ill is hardly sufficient to justify detaining him without a further showing of dangerousness. What is needed are very high standards of due process at detention hearings analogous to those governing criminal trials and, as Professor Dershowitz points out, clear and precise legal definitions of "harmfulness" and "danger."

The other possible purpose of civil commitment—com-

[2] Consider Professor Dershowitz's example of Dallas Williams, "who at age thirty-nine had spent half his life in jail for seven convictions of assault with a deadly weapon and one conviction of manslaughter. Just before his scheduled release from jail, the government petitioned for his civil commitment. Two psychiatrists testified that although 'at the present time [he] shows no evidence of active mental illness . . . he is potentially dangerous to others and if released is likely to repeat his patterns of criminal behavior, and might commit homicide.' The judge, in denying the government's petition and ordering Williams' release, observed that: 'the courts have no legal basis for ordering confinement on mere apprehension of future unlawful acts. They must wait until another crime is committed or the person is found insane.' Within months of his release, Williams lived up to the prediction of the psychiatrists and shot two men to death in an unprovoked attack." *Ibid.*, 44.

278

pulsory therapy—does of course require mental illness as a necessary condition, and here psychiatric testimony is crucial. But if civil liberty has any appeal to us and if state paternalism is repugnant, we can hardly regard the simple fact of mental illness as sufficient warrant for imposing therapeutic confinement on a person against his will. To force a person to submit to our benevolence is a fearsome and ugly kind of tyranny. The traditional doctrine of *Parens Patriae* to which Professor Dershowitz refers, however, authorizes such coercion only in very special and, I think, unobjectionable circumstances. Some mental illnesses so affect the cognitive processes that a victim is unable to make inferences or decisions—a severe disablement indeed. According to the *Parens Patriae* doctrine, the state has the duty to exercise its "sovereign power of guardianship" over these intellectually defective and disordered persons who are unable to realize their needs on their own. But even on occasions where this doctrine applies, the state presumes to "decide for a man as . . . he would decide for himself if he were of sound mind."[3] By no means all mentally ill persons, however, suffer from defects of reason. Many or most of them suffer from emotional or volitional disorders that leave their cognitive faculties quite unimpaired. To impose compulsory therapy on such persons would be as objectionably paternalistic as imposing involuntary cures for warts or headaches or tooth decay.

To summarize the view I have been considering: a mere finding of mental illness is not itself a sufficient ground for exempting a person from responsibility for a given action; nor is it a sufficient ground for finding him not to be a responsible or competent person generally, with the loss of civil rights such a finding necessarily entails. At most, in criminal proceedings mental illness may be evidence that one of the traditional grounds for moral exculpation—compulsion or ignorance—applies to the case at hand, and in civil commitment hearings it may be evidence of danger-

---

[3] Note on "Civil Restraint, Mental Illness, and the Right to Treatment," *Yale Law Journal*, 77/1 (1967), 87.

ousness or of cognitive impairment. But it has no independent moral or legal significance in itself either as an excuse or as a ground for commitment.

II

I fully accept this account of the relation of mental illness to civil commitment. Preventive detention of a person who has committed no crime is a desperate move that should be made only when a person's continued liberty would constitute a clear and present danger of substantial harm to others. We should require proof of a very great danger indeed before resorting to such measures if only because people are inclined generally to overestimate threats to safety and to underestimate the social value of individual liberty. Mere evidence of mental illness by itself does not provide such proof. Nor does it by itself provide proof of that mental derangement or incompetence to grant or withhold consent that is required if compulsory therapeutic confinement is to be justified. But, for all of that, I have a lingering doubt that the above account does full justice to the moral significance of mental illness as it bears on blame and punishment. I shall devote the remainder of my remarks to a statement of that doubt.

Let me turn immediately to the kind of case that troubles me. I have in mind cases of criminal conduct which appear to be both voluntary (by the usual Aristotelian tests) and sick. Let me give some examples and then contrast them with normal voluntary criminal acts.

First consider a nonviolent child molester. He is sexually attracted to five- and six-year-old boys and girls. His rational faculties are perfectly normal. He knows that sexual contacts with children are forbidden by the criminal law, and he takes no unnecessary risks of detection. For the most part, he manages to do without sex altogether. When he does molest a child he characteristically feels guilt, if not remorse, afterward. He has no understanding of his own motivation and often regrets that his tastes are so odd.

Next in our rogues' gallery is a repetitive exhibitionist. He has been arrested numerous times for exposing his genitalia in public. He does this not to solicit or threaten, but simply to derive satisfaction from the act itself: exposure for exposure's sake. For some reason he cannot understand, he finds such exposure immensely gratifying. Still, he knows that it is offensive to others, that it is in a way publicly humiliating, that it is prohibited by law, and that the chances of being caught and punished are always very great. These things trouble him much, and they often, but not always, lead him to restrain himself when the impulse to self-exposure arises.

My third example is drawn from a landmark case in the criminal law, one of the first in which kleptomania was accepted as an excuse: *State* v. *McCullough*, 114 Iowa 532 (1901). The defendant, a high school student, was charged with stealing a school book worth seventy-five cents. It was discovered that stolen property in his 'possession included "14 silverine watches, 2 old brass watches, 2 old clocks, 24 razors, 21 pairs of cuff buttons, 15 watch chains, 6 pistols, 7 combs, 34 jack knives, 9 bicycle wrenches, 4 padlocks, 7 pair of clippers, 3 bicycle saddles, 1 box of old keys, 4 pairs of scissors, 5 pocket mirrors, 6 mouth organs, rulers, bolts, calipers, oil cans, washers, punches, pulleys, spoons, penholders, ramrods, violin strings, etc." ["etc."!]. One can barely imagine the great price in anxiety this boy must have paid for his vast accumulation of worthless junk.

Finally, consider a well-off man who shoplifts only one kind of item, women's brassieres. He could easily afford to pay for these items and, indeed, often does when there is no other way of getting them, or when he is in danger of being caught. He does not enjoy stealing them and suffers great anxiety in worrying about being found out. Yet his storerooms are overflowing with brassieres. He burgles homes only to steal them; he assaults women only to rip off their brassieres and flee. And if you ask him for an explanation of his bizarre conduct, he will confess himself as puzzled by it as any observer.

Now, for contrast, consider some typical voluntary normal crimes. A respectable middle-aged bank teller, after weighing the risks carefully, embezzles bank funds and runs off to Mexico with his expensive lady friend. A homeowner in desperate need of cash sets his own house on fire to defraud an insurance company. A teenager steals a parked car and drives to a nearby city for a thrill. An angry man consumed with jealousy, or indignation, or vengefulness, or spite, commits criminal battery on a person he hates. A revolutionary throws a bomb at the king's carriage during an insurrection. These criminals act from a great variety of unmysterious motives—avarice, gain, lust, hate, ideological zeal; they are all rationally capable of calculating risks; they all act voluntarily.

How do the "sick" criminals in my earlier list differ from these normal ones? We might be tempted to answer that the pedophiliac, the exhibitionist, the kleptomaniac, and the fetishist are all "compulsives" and that their criminal conduct is therefore not entirely voluntary after all; but I believe it is important to understand that this answer is unsatisfactory. There is no *a priori* reason why the desires, impulses, and motives that lead a person to do bizarre things need necessarily be more powerful or compulsive than the desires that lead normal men to do perfectly ordinary things. It is by no means self-evident, for example, that the sex drives of a pedophiliac, an exhibitionist, or a homosexual must always be stronger than the sexual desires normal men and women may feel for one another.

There is much obscurity in the notion of the "strength of a desire," but I think several points are clear and relevant to our purposes. The first is that, strictly speaking, no impulse is "irresistible." For every case of giving in to a desire, I would argue, it will be true that, if the person had tried harder, he would have resisted it successfully. The psychological situation is never—or hardly ever—like that of the man who hangs from a windowsill by his fingernails until the sheer physical force of gravity rips his nails off and sends him plummeting to the ground, or like that of the man who dives from a sinking ship in the middle of the ocean and swims until he is exhausted and then drowns. Human endurance puts a severe limit on how long one can stay afloat in an ocean; but there is no comparable limit to our ability to resist temptation. Nevertheless, it does make sense to say that some desires are stronger than others and that some have an intensity and power that are felt as overwhelming. Some desires, in fact, may be so difficult to resist for a given person in a given state at a given time that it would be unreasonable to expect him to resist. A dieting man with a strong sweet tooth may find it difficult to resist eating an ice cream sundae for dessert; but a man who has not eaten for a week will have a much harder time still resisting the desire to eat a loaf of bread, which just happens to belong to his neighbor. Any person in a weakened condition, whether the cause be hunger or depression, fatigue or gripping emotion, will be less able to resist any given antisocial impulse than a person in a normal condition. But, again, there is no reason to suppose that bizarre appetites and odd tastes are always connected with a "weakened condition," so that they are necessarily more difficult to resist than ordinary desires. And thus there is no reason to suppose that so-called sick desires must always be compulsive or unreasonably difficult to resist.

It might seem to follow that there is *no* morally significant difference between normal and mentally ill offenders, that the one class is just as responsible as the other, provided only that their criminal actions are voluntary in the usual sense. But if this is the proper conclusion, then I am at a loss to see what difference there can be between mental illness and plain wickedness. As an ordinary citizen, before I begin to get confused by philosophy, I sometimes permit myself to feel anger and outrage at normal criminals, whereas I cannot help feeling some pity (mixed, perhaps, with repugnance) toward those whose conduct appears bizarre and unnatural. But unless I can find some morally telling difference between the two classes of criminals, then these natural attitudes must be radically reshaped, so that the fetish thief, for example, be thought as wicked as the professional burglar.

There do seem to be some striking differences between the two classes, however, and perhaps some of these can rescue my prephilosophical attitudes. Most of them have to do not with the criminal's intentions, but with his underlying motivation—the basis of the appeal in his immediate goals or objectives. The first such difference is that the sick criminal's motives appear quite *unintelligible* to us. We sometimes express our puzzlement by saying that his crimes have no apparent motive at all. We cannot see any better than the criminal himself "what he gets out of it," and it overburdens our imaginative faculties to put ourselves in his shoes. We understand the avaricious, irascible, or jealous man's motives all too well, and we resent him for them. But where crimes resist explanation in terms of ordinary motives, we hardly know what to resent. Here the old maxim "to understand all is to forgive all" seems to be turned on its ear. It is closer to the truth to say of mentally ill wrongdoers that to forgive is to despair of understanding.

Yet mere unintelligibility of motive is not likely to advance our search for the moral significance of mental illness very far, especially if we take the criterion of unintelligibility in turn to be the frustration of our "imaginative capacities" to put ourselves in the criminal's shoes and understand what he gets out of his crimes. This test of imaginability is far too elastic and variable. On the one hand, it seems too loose, since it permits the classification as unintelligible (or even sick) of *any* particular passion or taste, provided only that it is sufficiently different from those of the person making the judgment. Some nonsmokers cannot understand what smokers get out of their noxious habit, and males can hardly understand what it is like to enjoy bearing children. On the other hand, once we begin tightening up the test of imaginability, there is likely to be no stopping place short of the point at which *all* motives become intelligible to anyone with a moderately good imagination and sense of analogy. The important thing is not that the sick criminal's motives may seem unintelligible, but rather that they are unintelligible in a certain respect or for a certain reason.

We get closer to the heart of the matter, I think, if we say that the mentally ill criminal's motives are unintelligible because they are irrational—not just unreasonable, but *irrational*. All voluntary wrongdoing, of course, is unreasonable. It is always unreasonable conduct to promote one's own good at another's expense, to be cruel, deceitful, or unfair. But in a proper sense of "rational," made familiar by economists and lawyers, wrongdoing, though unreasonable, can be perfectly rational. A wrongdoer might well calculate his own interests, and gains and risks thereto, and decide to advance them at another's expense, without making a single intellectual mistake. A rational motive, in the present sense, is simply a *self-interested* motive, or perhaps an intelligently self-interested one. The motives of mentally ill criminals are not usually very self-interested. The Supreme Court of Iowa, in overturning the conviction of young McCullough, held that the question for the jury should have been: did the accused steal because of a mental disease driving him by "an insane and irresistible impulse" to steal, or did he commit said acts "through excessive greed or avarice?" The Court's alternatives are not exhaustive. Very likely McCullough's impulses were neither irresistible nor "greedy and avaricious." Greed and avarice are forms of selfishness, excessive desires for material goods and riches for oneself. As motives they are preeminently self-interested and "rational." McCullough's sick desires, however, were not for his own good, material or otherwise. He stole objects that could do him no good at all and assumed irrational risks in the process. The desire to steal and hoard these useless trinkets was a genuine enough desire, and it was *his* desire; but it does not follow that it was a desire to promote his own good.

This point too, however, can be overstated. It may well be true that none of the mentally ill crimes we are considering is done from a self-interested motive, but this feature hardly distinguishes them (yet) from a wide variety of voluntary crimes of great blameworthiness committed by perfectly normal criminals. By no means all voluntary crimes by normal criminals are done from the motive of gain. Some are done to advance or retard a cause, to help a loved one, or to hurt an enemy, often at great cost to the criminal's self-interest. What distinguishes the sick crimes we have been considering is not that they are unself-interested, but rather that they are *not interested at all*. They do not further *any* of the actor's interests, self *or* other-regarding, benevolent or malevolent. The fetishist's shoplifting is not rational and self-serving; he attains no economic objective by it. But neither does it hurt anyone he hates nor help anyone he loves; it neither gains him good will and prestige, nor satisfies his conscience, nor fulfills his ideals. It is, in short, not interested behavior.

But even this distinction does not quite get to the very core of the matter. The fetishist's behavior not only fails to be interested; it fails even to appear interested to him. To be sure, it is designed to fulfill the desire which is its immediate motive; but fulfillment of desire is not necessarily the same thing as abiding satisfaction. He may be gratified or relieved for an instant, but this kind of fulfillment of desire leaves only the taste of ashes in one's mouth. The important point is that his behavior tends to be *contrary to interest*, as *senseless* almost as the repetitive beating of one's head against an unyielding stone wall. Bishop Butler was one of the first to point out how profoundly misleading it is to call such behavior "self-indulgent" simply because it appears voluntary, fulfills the actor's own desire, and leads to an instant's satisfaction before a torrent of guilt and anxiety. One might as well call the thirsty marooned sailor "self-indulgent" when he drinks deeply of the sea water that will surely dry him out further, as he well knows.

I believe there is a tendency in human nature, quite opposite to the one I have already mentioned, to consider the senselessness of a crime a kind of moral aggravation. That a cruel crime seemed pointless or senseless, a source of no gain to anyone, makes the harm it caused seem in the most absolute sense *unnecessary*, and that rubs salt in our psychic wounds. The harm was *all for nothing*, we lament, as if an intelligible motive would make our wounds any less injurious or the wounder less blameable. What happens, I think, is that the senselessness of a crime, particularly when it seems contrary to the criminal's interest, is profoundly frustrating. We are naturally disposed to be angry at the selfishly cruel, the ruthlessly self-aggrandizing man; but that anger is frustrated when we learn that the criminal, for no reason *he* could understand, was hurting *himself* as well as his victim. That is simply not the way properly self-respecting wicked persons are supposed to behave! But then we become angry at him precisely because we cannot be angry in the usual ways. We blame him now for our own frustration—not only for the harm he has caused, but for his not getting anything out of it. Indignation will always out.

Still, in a calmer reflective moment, punishment of the pitiably odd is likely to seem a kind of "pouring it on." Indeed, we might well say of such people what the more forgiving Epictetus said of all wrongdoers, that they are sufficiently punished simply to be the sorts of persons they are. Their crimes are obviously profitless to themselves and serve no apparent other-regarding interest, either malevolent or benevolent. Thus if the point of punishment is to take the profit out of crime, it is superfluous to impose it upon them.

Not only are the motives of some mentally ill but noncompulsive wrongdoers *senseless*, they are senseless in the special way that permits us to speak of them as *incoherent*. Their motives do not fit together and make a coherent whole because one kind of desire, conspicuous as a sore thumb, keeps getting in the way. These desires serve ill the rest of their important interests, including their overriding interest in personal integration and internal harmony. They "gum up the works," as we would say of machinery, and

287

throw the person out of "proper working order." The reason they do is that, insofar as these desires are fulfilled, barriers are put in the paths of the others. They are inconsistent with the others in that it is impossible for all to be jointly satisfied, even though it is possible that the others could, in principle, be satisfied together. Moreover, the "senseless" desires, because they do not cohere, are likely to seem alien, not fully expressive of their owner's essential character.[4] When a person acts to satisfy them, it is as if he were acting on somebody else's desires. And, indeed, the alien desires may have a distinct kind of unifying character of their own, as if a new person were grafted on to the old one.

The final and perhaps most important feature common to the examples of voluntary crimes by mentally ill persons is the actor's *lack of insight into his own motives*. The normal person, in rehearsing the possibilities open to him, finds some prospects appealing and others repugnant, and he usually (but not always) knows what it is about a given prospect that makes it appealing or repugnant. If robbing a bank appeals to him, the reason may be that the excitement, the romance, or (far more likely) the money attracts him; and if having more money appeals to him, he usually knows *why* it does too. Normal persons, to be sure, can be mistaken. A criminal may think it is the adventure that is attracting him, instead of the money, or vice versa. It is easy enough to be confused about these things. Often enough we can test our understanding of our own motives by experimental methods. I may think that prospect X, which has characteristics a, b, and c, appeals to me solely because of a; but then, to my surprise, prospect Y, which has characteristics a and b, but not c, *repels* me. Hence I conclude that it was not simply the a-ness of X after all that attracted me. Moreover, even a person who is a model of mental health will be often ignorant or mistaken about the *ultimate* basis of appeal in the things that appeal to him.

[4] Hence the point of the ancient metaphor of "possession."

The mentally ill person, however, will be radically and fundamentally benighted about the source of the appeal in his immediate objectives, and the truth will be hid from his view by an internal iron curtain. He may think that he is constructed in such a way that little children arouse him sexually, and that is the end of the matter, hardly suspecting that it is the playful, exploratory, irresponsible, and nonthreatening character of his recollected childhood experiences that moves him; or he may think that "exposure for exposure's sake" is what appeals to him in the idea of public undress, whereas really what appeals to him is the public "affirmation of masculinity, a cry of 'Look, here is proof I am a man.' "[5] The true basis of appeal in the criminal's motivation may be, or become, obvious to an outsider, but his illness keeps him blind to it, often, I think, because this blindness is a necessary condition of the appeal itself. At any rate, his lack of self-awareness is no merely contingent thing, like the ignorance that can be charged to absentmindedness, unperceptiveness, objective ambiguities, or the garden varieties of self-deception. The ignorance is the necessary consequence, perhaps even a constituent, of the mental illness, which, taken as a collection of interconnected symptoms, is an alien condition involuntarily suffered.

III

We come back to our original question, then, in a new guise: why should the incoherent and self-concealed character of the mentally ill man's motives be a ground for special consideration when he has voluntarily committed a crime? Perhaps we should enlarge our conception of *compulsion* so that senseless, misunderstood motives automatically count as compulsive. If Jones's chronic desire to do something harmful is as powerful as, but no more powerful than, normal people's desires to do socially acceptable

5 Paul H. Gebhard et al., *Report on Sex Offenders* (New York: Harper & Row, and Paul B. Hoeber, 1965), 399.

things, then we might think of Jones's desire as a kind of unfair burden. It is no harder for him to restrain on individual occasions, but he must be restraining it *always*; one slip and he is undone. He is really quite unlucky to have this greater burden and danger. The ordinary person is excused when he is made to do what he does not want to do; but the mentally ill man, the argument might go, is excused because of the compulsive weight of his profitless *wants* themselves.

There may be some justice in this argument, but there is little logic. When we begin to tamper this profoundly with the concept of compulsion, it is likely to come completely apart. If men can be said to be compelled by their own quite resistible desires, then what is there left to contrast compulsion with?

A more plausible move is to enlarge our conception of what it is to act "in ignorance"—the other category in the Aristotelian formula. The kleptomaniac and the fetishist have no conception of what it is that impels them to their bizarre actions. As we have seen, their conduct may well seem as puzzling to themselves as to any observer. So there is a sense in which they do not know, or realize, what it is they are really doing, and perhaps we should make this ignorance a ground for exculpation; but if we do, we shall be in danger of providing a defense for almost all criminals, normal and ill alike. The bank robber, who is deceived into thinking that it is the adventure that appeals to him when it really is the money, has this excuse available to him, as well as the bully who thinks he inflicts beatings in self-defense when it really is the sight of blood that appeals to him. Lack of insight by itself, then, can hardly be a workable extension of the ignorance defense in courts of law.

It is plain, I think, why the penal law requires rather strict interpretations of compulsion and ignorance. One of its major aims is to deter wrongdoers by providing them with a motive, namely, fear of punishment, which they would not otherwise have for refraining from crime. In close cases involving competent calculators, this new motive might be sufficient to tip the motivational scales toward self-restraint. Mentally ill but rationally competent offenders of the sort I have been discussing, provided only that they *can* restrain themselves, are eminently suited for responsibility because the fear of punishment might make some difference in their behavior. But if they truly cannot help what they do, then the fear of punishment is totally useless and might as well not be induced in them in the first place.

Thus, from the point of view of what punishment can achieve for others, it is a perfectly appropriate mode of treatment for rationally competent, noncompulsive, mentally ill persons. But from the point of view of what can be achieved for the offender himself, I still think it is altogether inappropriate. Some of the aims of an enlightened criminal law, after all, do concern the offender himself. Sometimes punishment is supposed to "reform" him by intimidation. This no doubt works once in a while for normally prudent and self-interested offenders. For others, greater claims still are made for punishment, which is expected to achieve not merely effective intimidation but also moral regeneration of the offender. But if we treat the mentally ill criminal in precisely the same way as we treat the normal one, we can only bring him to the point of hopeless despair. The prisoner, still devoid of insight into his own motives, will naturally come to wonder how his so-called illness differs from plain wickedness. His bizarre desires will be taken as simply "given," as evil impulses with no point and no reward, simply "there," an integral and irreducible part of himself; and there is no one more pitiably incorrigible than the man convinced of his own intrinsic wickedness and simply resigned to it.

I agree with Professor Dershowitz that it is outrageous to impose compulsory therapeutic treatment on an unwilling, mentally competent subject. I submit, however, that punishment imposed on the mentally ill, even though it might produce a small social gain in deterrence, is an equally odious measure. I admit that, insofar as the sick offender has voluntarily committed a crime he could have avoided, the state has a perfect right to deprive him of his liberty for a limited period; but, instead of using that time to have him break up rocks with the convicted embezzlers and burglars, we should be making every sympathetic effort to enable him to understand himself, in the hope that self-revelation will permit him to become a responsible citizen.[6] There is no easy way to avoid the problems that come from the institutional mixture of compulsion and therapy.[7] I am afraid I must leave them for my legal and psychiatric friends. My aim in this paper has been the very limited one of showing that mental illness, even without compulsion and general cognitive impairment, is a good deal more pertinent to our moral concerns than the mumps or chicken pox.

[6] I.e., he is clutchable, but not necessarily punishable.

[7] But see my "Crime, Clutchability, and Individuated Treatment," in this volume, 252-271, for some suggestions.

INDEX

DEMCO